It is difficult to imagine living and studying at Cambridge in the late sixteenth and early seventeenth centuries, dominated as it was by the rigorous supralapsarian Calvinism of William Perkins. These must have been heady days indeed, and a generation of Puritan preachers imbibed it and preached it with equal enthusiasm. With the publication of Perkins's complete works almost complete, updated for the first time since their original seventeenth-century prose, interest in him is bound to increase in the coming days. And so it begins with Andrew Ballitch's analysis of Perkins's preaching and interpretive method. If we can but capture Perkins's zeal for expounding Scripture—his commitment to sola Scriptura—then the church in our time is heading for reformation. Ballitch's study is very fine indeed, a page turner if ever there was one. I will return to it often.

—**Derek W. H. Thomas**, senior minister,
First Presbyterian Church, Columbia, SC;
Chancellor's Professor, Reformed Theological Seminary;
teaching fellow, Ligonier Ministries

Scholars increasingly recognize the work of Reformed and Puritan divines as exegetes of the Holy Scriptures. In this well-researched, clearly written study, Ballitch gives us a front-row seat to observe William Perkins in both his principles and practice of expositing God's word for life application. Given the prominence of Perkins as a preacher and theologian in the Reformed experiential tradition, Ballitch's work will benefit not only students of history but also Reformed experiential preachers and theologians today.

—**Joel R. Beeke**, president,
Puritan Reformed Theological Seminary, Grand Rapids

William Perkins has long been recognized as the leading first light of the English Puritan movement. His polemical and theological treatises along with his pastoral aids on casuistry set the tone for much that followed him in the seventeenth-century Puritan movement. They have been mined for much of their theological and pastoral usefulness. Remarkably, though, until now no one has given careful attention to the exegetical dimension of Perkins's work. Now that lacuna has been filled by this insightful and clear work by Andrew Ballitch. Not only was Perkins a theological and practical giant, he was also a skilled and careful interpreter of Scripture as Ballitch shows us in this illuminating book.

—**Shawn D. Wright**, professor of church history,
The Southern Baptist Theological Seminary

William Perkins was a towering figure in the Elizabethan era and played a pivotal role in securing the Reformation in England, shaping the development of Reformed theology on the continent, and defining the nature of pastoral ministry on both sides of the Atlantic. What is often forgotten, however, is that Perkins was above all else an exegete. This is what makes the present volume such a welcome one. Here Dr. Andrew Ballitch engages in a first-class analysis of Perkins's exegetical method. His research is clear and concise and makes a valuable contribution to the study of Perkins, the Elizabethan church, and pre-modern biblical exegesis.

—**J. Stephen Yuille**, vice president of academics,
Heritage College & Seminary, Cambridge, ON;
associate professor of biblical spirituality,
The Southern Baptist Theological Seminary, Louisville, KY

THE GLOSS & THE TEXT

William Perkins on Interpreting Scripture with Scripture

STUDIES IN HISTORICAL & SYSTEMATIC THEOLOGY
H
S
S
T

THE GLOSS & THE TEXT

William Perkins on Interpreting Scripture with Scripture

ANDREW S. BALLITCH

STUDIES IN HISTORICAL AND SYSTEMATIC THEOLOGY

The Gloss and the Text: William Perkins on Interpreting Scripture with Scripture
Studies in Historical and Systematic Theology

Copyright 2020 Andrew S. Ballitch

Lexham Press, 1313 Commercial St., Bellingham, WA 98225
LexhamPress.com

All rights reserved. You may use brief quotations from this resource in presentations, articles, and books. For all other uses, please write Lexham Press for permission. Email us at permissions@lexhampress.com.

Print ISBN 9781683593911
Digital ISBN 9781683593928
Library of Congress Control Number 2020933101

Lexham Editorial: Todd Hains, Claire Brubaker, Abigail Stocker
Cover Design: Bryan Hintz
Typesetting: Justin Marr

To my treasured wife, Darcy.

CONTENTS

FOREWORD

Christians live on the basis of Scripture—so for the Puritans, as for all Protestants of the sixteenth and seventeenth centuries, Scripture was central. William Perkins (1558–1602) was a premier theologian in the English Puritan theological tradition, and constant interpretation of Scripture was the task to which he dedicated himself throughout the whole range of his writings.

This focal concern on biblical interpretation makes Andrew Ballitch's study so important. Ballitch's study is invaluable in giving clarity to William Perkins's approach to Scripture and its appropriate interpretation. No other work delves into this topic as thoroughly, sensitively, and with greater insight than this one.

By understanding Perkins's approach and seeing how it was implemented, we gain insights into the wider world of Reformed theology and biblical interpretation. Continental Reformed theology was still developing—especially through the work of John Calvin's successor, Theodore Beza—and it was Perkins who conveyed this emerging Reformed thought to England. From views on election and predestination, to conversion and the spiritual life, to preaching and biblical interpretation, Perkins's views helped shape a Protestant religious culture that became strongly established in the early seventeenth century. Relatedly, the widespread translations of Perkins's works throughout Europe shows Perkins's popularity and testifies to the extensive reception of his interpretation of the Christian faith among other European Protestant traditions. His theology was undergirded by his biblical interpretation, and his experiential emphases in faith were supported by his interpretation of the overall message of Holy Scripture. So Perkins became a trusted resource for theologians and for preachers throughout Europe and New England.

Biblical interpreters—especially preachers—must use the best tools and resources available to understand biblical texts. This is so God's word can be proclaimed and the lives of those who read Scripture and hear the Christian gospel preached will be blessed by the Holy Spirit. As Ballitch shows, Perkins did so in a manner consistent with his convictions that God speaks through Holy Scripture.

Donald K. McKim
Germantown, Tennessee
January 2020

PREFACE

My initial exposure to William Perkins came through J. I. Packer and his lectures on the history and theology of the Puritans. Two things caught my attention. First, Packer emphasized the importance and influence of Perkins, a man I had never before encountered. Second, Packer argued that Perkins popularized a Bezan aberration of Calvinism. In particular, his supralapsarianism seemed scandalous.

Yet as I began to read Perkins himself, few stereotypes held up. He affirmed a supralapsarian ordering of the divine decrees, but he preached evangelistically. He sustained a view of the atonement in which Christ's satisfaction was only for the elect, but he pointed those who struggled with assurance to the cross and the comforting promises of the gospel therein. He spurned the label "Puritan," but he was counted by many as a forerunner to Nonconformists and Dissenters.

Ultimately, it became clear to me Packer was right: Perkins was undeniably influential—hence my surprise at finding relatively little written about him. I was especially struck by the scarcity of work on Perkins's interpretation of Scripture. Given that those who do remember Perkins do so for his powerful preaching, most of which was resolutely expository, this dearth of scholarship is unfortunate. I am fascinated with the history of biblical interpretation—and in the work of Perkins there are many untapped wells, opportunities for much fruitful labor. Moreover, as a balanced, precritical proponent of *sola Scriptura*, Perkins provides a helpful perspective in today's hermeneutical discussions.

But this project is about more than my own interests. I want to take this opportunity to acknowledge my most significant debts, both tangible and intangible. First, my parents have faithfully encouraged me and supported me in countless ways, instilling in me two critical academic virtues from a young age: self-discipline and the ability to teach myself. My father-in-law and childhood pastor, Doyle Peyton, faithfully preached the Reformed faith to me during my formative years and therefore planted the seeds of a love for theology. The most voracious reader I know, he had a treasure trove on his bookshelves for a hungry high school junior with a newly perceived sense of ministerial calling; in God's providence, this trove included the Puritans. My college theology professor at Spring Arbor University, Ken Brewer, took an interest in me as a mentor and was the first person to push me toward a PhD. For the many hours he spent with me over the better part of three years, I will be forever grateful. Mark Correll, my European history professor, fanned my love of history by affirming the study of ideas and the importance of historical context.

The Southern Baptist Theological Seminary was the richest of experiences. When I was a master of divinity student, David Puckett took me under his wing and shepherded me through the process of preparing for and applying to doctoral programs. We even had the opportunity to travel to England and Scotland together, walking the streets of Cambridge at a time when I did not yet know how significant these places would be in my studies. More recently, the PhD program was a joy—in no small measure because of Jonathan Pennington's vision and leadership. During my tenure, he created space for camaraderie and interdisciplinary discussions through the 1892 Club and Doctoral Common Room, providing incentive with an abundance of good pour-over coffee. These conversations with fellow students, professors, and guests sharpened me as a scholar, grew me as a person, and provided invaluable feedback on this project at every stage. Of course, fundamental to my training and the first iteration of this project as a dissertation were my professors, specifically the church history faculty: Gregory Wills, Michael Haykin, David Puckett, and Tom Nettles. Stephen Yuille joined the faculty at the beginning stages of this project and has been most kind with his time and expertise in Perkins. Most of all, I am indebted to my adviser and now friend, Shawn Wright, who suggested Perkins the summer before I started my doctoral program. He has generously given of his time for guidance and evaluation, affording me many opportunities to teach and make Perkins practical along the way. These men model for me what it means to be a historian unto the glory of God.

My gratitude also extends to Joel Beeke for his enthusiastic encouragment of my work and insightful recommendations. Also Donald McKim, whose constructive feedback on the first draft of this manuscript and overwhelmingly positive evaluation served as an invaluable motivator. And to Todd Hains and the team at Lexham, thank you for your expertise and guidance in seeing this project from dissertation through to publication.

I am also grateful to the saints at Hunsinger Lane Baptist Church for making Louisville seem like home and giving me the opportunity to support my family as a pastor while writing a dissertation and revising it for publication.

And finally, it is my family for whom I am unspeakably thankful, though as a pastor, teacher, and writer, words are my stock-in-trade. Elizabeth and Etta unknowingly gave up daddy time to Master Perkins—and my wife, Darcy, has sacrificed more on the altar of God's plan for our lives than I ever have. It is to her that I dedicate this work.

Andrew S. Ballitch
Louisville, Kentucky
July 2019

ABBREVIATIONS

—

AUSS	*Andrews University Seminary Studies*
cap.	capitulus (English: "chapter")
CH	*Church History*
CTJ	*Calvin Theological Journal*
SCJ	*Sixteenth Century Journal*
WTJ	*Westminster Theological Journal*

1

INTRODUCTION

William Perkins (1558–1602) has been called "the principle architect of Elizabethan Puritanism," "the Puritan theologian of Tudor times," "the most important Puritan writer," "the prince of Puritan theologians," "the ideal Puritan clergyman," "the most famous of all Puritan divines," "the father of Pietism," "the father of Puritanism," and, alongside John Calvin and Theodore Beza, the third in "the trinity of the orthodox."[1] He was the first writer to outsell Calvin in England and the first English Protestant to gain an audience in England, continental Europe, and North America.[2] But most of all, Perkins earned his renown as a preacher of God's word.

Perkins studied at Christ's College, Cambridge, and the year he received his master of arts degree, 1584, he became both a fellow at Christ's and a

---

1. Joel R. Beeke compiles these descriptions in "William Perkins on Predestination, Preaching, and Conversion," in *The Practical Calvinist: An Introduction to the Presbyterian and Reformed Heritage*, ed. Peter A. Lillback (Fearn, UK: Christian Focus, 2002), 206; and "William Perkins and His Greatest Case of Conscience: 'How a Man May Know Whether He Be the Child of God, or No,'" *CTJ* 41, no. 2 (2006): 255. No critical biography of Perkins has been published. For biographical information, see Thomas Fuller, *Abel Redevivus, Or, The Dead yet Speaking the Lives and Deaths of the Moderne Divines* (London: Tho. Brudenell, 1651); Samuel Clarke, *The Marrow of Ecclesiastical History Contained in the Lives of One Hundred Forty Eight Fathers, Schoolmen, First Reformers and Modern Divines Which Have Flourished in the Church since Christ's Time to This Present Age: Faithfully Collected and Orderly Disposed according to the Centuries Wherein They Lived, Together with the Lively Effigies of Most of the Eminentest of Them Cut in Copper* (London: Robert White for William Roybould, 1654); Benjamin Brook, *The Lives of the Puritans: Containing a Biographical Account of Those Divines Who Distinguished Themselves in the Cause of Religious Liberty, from the Reformation under Queen Elizabeth, to the Act of Uniformity in 1662*, 3 vols. (Pittsburgh: Soli Deo Gloria, 1994); Richard Rogers and Samuel Ward, *Two Elizabethan Puritan Diaries*, ed. M. M Knappen (Gloucester, MA: P. Smith, 1966); Joel R. Beeke and Randall J. Pederson, *Meet the Puritans: With a Guide to Modern Reprints* (Grand Rapids: Reformation Heritage Books, 2006); Joel R. Beeke and J. Stephen Yuille, *William Perkins*, Bitesize Biographies (Welwyn Garden City, UK: EP Books, 2015).

2. Ian Breward, "The Significance of William Perkins," *Journal of Religious History* 4, no. 2 (1966): 113–16.

lecturer at Cambridge's St. Andrew the Great Church. Preaching was fundamental to both of these roles. More than a decade later, in 1595, he resigned his university position to marry, but continued his preaching post at St. Andrew the Great until his untimely death from kidney stones in 1602.

Many of Perkins's early biographers highlight his preaching. Thomas Fuller recalls Perkins's presence in the pulpit, noting two other observations: his life matched his preaching and his sermons connected with the common people.[3] Samuel Clarke recalls Perkins's powerful ministry to prisoners, and in his personal diary, contemporary Samuel Ward praises Perkins as a model preacher.[4] John Cotton attested to the conviction he personally felt under Perkins's preaching.[5] Perkins once appeared before university authorities on suspicion of nonconformity for his preaching.[6] This historically consistent focus on Perkins's preaching ministry fits his self-understanding. According to Benjamin Brook, Perkins "[wrote] in the title of all his books, 'Thou art a Minister of the Word: Mind thy business.'"[7]

Perkins's convictions on the ministry of God's word are best known through his preaching manual, *The Arte of Prophecying*, which became a standard textbook on the subject. The volume articulated a thoroughly Protestant understanding of the nature and authority of Scripture and rooted itself in a thoroughly Reformed hermeneutic. The book also featured a fountain of homiletical advice, as Perkins detailed his method of sermon development and delivery. More than any other, the popularity of this book explains Perkins's enduring significance in the decades and even centuries after his death.[8]

Perkins's business was the ministry of the word, and it extended far beyond his sermons. He carried this commitment to the word into every genre of his writing. This consistency evidences his convictions

---

3. Fuller, *Abel Redevivus*, 433–37.

4. Clarke, *Marrow of Ecclesiastical History*, 852–53; Rogers and Ward, *Two Elizabethan Puritan Diaries*, 120.

5. Brook, *Lives of the Puritans*, 3:151.

6. Brook, *Lives of the Puritans*, 2:131–33.

7. Brook, *Lives of the Puritans*, 2:131.

8. Breward, "Significance of William Perkins," 121.

concerning Scripture itself as well as the nature of his goals as a reformer. It is not an overstatement to say the systematic interpretation of the Bible and the presentation of its results defined Perkins's life in the university and church pulpit. In fact, it is because of this rigorous commitment—whether in his practical materials, theological treatises, or polemical works—that Perkins started with Scripture and always applied it to the task at hand.

THESIS

William Perkins interpreted Scripture with Scripture by using three tools: context, collation, and the analogy of faith. In brief, context is a close reading of the text in terms of the argument and literary features; collation a comparison with other passages; and the analogy of faith the boundaries of the Reformed tradition. Perkins expounded Scripture throughout his works according to this method, which he presents in *The Arte of Prophecying*. This intense scriptural focus emanated from Perkins's belief that Scripture is God's word and therefore the only adequate foundation for the reformation of individuals, the church, and society. As God's word, Scripture determined his hermeneutic—Scripture interprets itself. Though not reflected in most Perkinsian scholarship, Perkins consistently applied this method of biblical interpretation regardless of the genre in which he worked. He pursued this strategy due to both his own convictions concerning Scripture and his urgent commitment to further reformation during the reign of Elizabeth I.

Only the word of God and its faithful exposition—that is, exposition in line with the hermeneutical principles stated in *The Arte of Prophecying*—could accomplish the monumental tasks before sixteenth-century Puritans. Perkins in particular strove to transform an ignorant and immoral people, exhorting them to live up to the Reformation principles England had officially adopted. So, in his preaching and practical works, what did he do? He expounded Scripture. A Cambridge man, Perkins also played a role in educating the clergy for pastoral ministry. So, in his practical works on ministry, what did he do? He explained Scripture. As part of an international Reformed community, Perkins was compelled to defend the precious doctrines of the Reformed tradition. So, in his theological treatises, what did he do? He exposited Scripture. As one aware of the looming political threat the Church of Rome and its allies posed to England and as one unsettled by the ebb and flow of the English Reformation, Perkins was obliged to defend his conception of the Christian faith. So, in his polemics, what did he do? He explicated Scripture. From first to last, the exposition of Scripture dominated Perkins's endeavors.

Perkins participated in a national and international effort to establish Protestantism, more precisely the Reformed tradition. His preaching and popular writing are representative of this endeavor on the English scene, along with contemporaries such as Richard Greenham and Richard Rogers. Perkins participated in university life at Cambridge with Laurence Chaderton, William Whitaker, and others, educating men for pastoral ministry and wrestling with doctrinal precision in dialogue with university men throughout Europe. On the international stage, Perkins contributed Latin theological treatises, numbering him among Reformed divines such as Theodore Beza and Amandus Polanus. Perkins's consistent use of Scripture reflects his and the Reformed tradition's convictions about biblical authority. His method of interpretation—at heart a commitment to use Scripture to interpret itself, a commitment central to the Reformed tradition as a whole—reveals a conviction about Scripture's sufficiency. This study demonstrates that Perkins's works were a contribution to an already existing and rapidly growing Reformed Protestant exegesis that grounded, defended, nuanced, and articulated the movement's doctrine and practice.

Of course, Perkins did not approach biblical interpretation in isolation from his theological heritage. His hermeneutical method shows both continuity and discontinuity with the medieval era. Moreover, Perkins exhibits both dependence and independence in relation to the Reformed tradition in general and his English contemporaries in particular. His pervasive stress on the Bible challenged the perceived scholastic approach to theology in the post-Reformation Reformed tradition. Perkins was a creative man of his times who devoted his multifaceted career as preacher, teacher, theologian, polemicist, and popular author to one thing: the exposition of Scripture for the purpose of further reformation.

HISTORY OF RESEARCH

While significant work has been done on the particulars of Perkins's thought, only two monographs are devoted to him.[9] Treatments of Perkins have generally focused on four aspects of his thinking: how he fits with Puritanism, his role in the development of covenant theology, his relationship to Calvin and the Westminster Standards, and his preaching method. These approaches leave much of his expository material untapped. Moreover, his biblical interpretation—which is the foundation for everything he did—remains largely absent from the discussion.

First, scholars have debated what constitutes a "Puritan," since William Haller, M. M. Knappen, and Perry Miller introduced the Puritans into modern historical scholarship.[10] A number of significant voices have weighed in over the past fifty years or so.[11] Definitions generally fall

9. W. B. Patterson, *William Perkins and the Making of a Protestant England* (Oxford: Oxford University Press, 2014); Donald K. McKim, *Ramism in William Perkins' Theology*, American University Studies, Series VII, Theology and Religion 15 (New York: Peter Lang, 1987).

10. William Haller, *The Rise of Puritanism: Or, The Way to the New Jerusalem as Set Forth in Pulpit and Press from Thomas Cartwright to John Lilburne and John Milton, 1570–1643* (New York: Columbia University Press, 1957); M. M. Knappen, *Tudor Puritanism: A Chapter in the History of Idealism* (Chicago: University of Chicago Press, 1939); Perry Miller, *The New England Mind: The Seventeenth Century* (New York: Macmillan, 1939).

11. H. C. Porter, *Reformation and Reaction in Tudor Cambridge* (Cambridge: Cambridge University Press, 1958); Charles H. George and Katherine George, *The Protestant Mind of the English Reformation, 1570–1640* (Princeton: Princeton University Press, 1961); John F. H. New, *Anglican and Puritan: The Basis of Their Opposition, 1558–1640* (London: Adam & Charles Black, 1964); Christopher Hill, *Society and Puritanism in Pre-Revolutionary England* (London: Secker & Warburg, 1964); Michael Walzer, *The Revolution of the Saints: A Study in the Origins of Radical Politics* (Cambridge, MA: Harvard University Press, 1965); Basil Hall, "Puritanism: The Problem of Definition," in *Studies in Church History 2*, ed. G. J. Cuming (London: Nelson, 1965), 283–96; Patrick Collinson, *The Elizabethan Puritan Movement* (London: Cape, 1967); Peter Lake, *Moderate Puritans and the Elizabethan Church* (Cambridge: Cambridge University Press, 1982); Dewey D. Wallace, *Puritans and Predestination: Grace in English Protestant Theology, 1525–1695* (Chapel Hill: University of North Carolina Press, 1982); John von Rohr, *The Covenant of Grace in Puritan Thought* (Atlanta: Scholars Press, 1986); John Morgan, *Godly Learning: Puritan Attitudes towards Reason, Learning, and Education, 1560–1640* (Cambridge: Cambridge University Press, 1986); Margo Todd, *Christian Humanism and the Puritan Social Order* (Cambridge: Cambridge University Press, 1987); Theodore Dwight Bozeman, *To Live Ancient Lives: The Primitivist Dimension in Puritanism* (Chapel Hill: University of North Carolina Press, 1988); Stephen Brachlow, *The Communion of Saints: Radical Puritan and Separatist Ecclesiology, 1570–1625* (Oxford: Oxford University Press, 1988); Joel R. Beeke, *Assurance of Faith: Calvin, English Puritanism, and the Dutch Second Reformation* (New York: Peter Lang, 1991); Tom Webster, *Godly Clergy in Early Stuart England: The Caroline Puritan Movement, c. 1620–1643* (Cambridge: Cambridge University Press, 1997); John Coffey, *Politics, Religion and the British Revolutions: The Mind of Samuel Rutherford* (Cambridge: Cambridge University Press, 1997);

into three categories: theological, political or ecclesiological, and pietistic. Definitions that depend on a single category to the exclusion of the others are unsatisfactory. Theological definitions do not work because the Puritans were not a theologically distinct group. During the sixteenth century especially, Puritans and other members of the Church of England were theologically indistinguishable. Political definitions, with their emphasis on nonconformity and active opposition to ecclesiastical authority, have little room for Puritans before the Act of Uniformity in 1662 and almost none in Elizabeth I's reign. Pietistic definitions are evaluative to the point of being arbitrary, often including dissenters and figures after the seventeenth century. Therefore, the best definitions incorporate all three categories and do not insist on individual aspects. Such generosity toward the Puritan movement allows for Puritanism's variety and contextual changes over its century and a half of existence.

Definitions of Puritanism have been offered with Perkins specifically in view. Packer summarizes his understanding of Puritanism as "an evangelical holiness movement seeking to implement its vision of spiritual renewal, national and personal, in the church, the state, and the home; in education, evangelism, and economics; in individual discipleship and devotion, and in pastoral care and competence."[12] Perkins fits comfortably within this definition. More recently, W. B. Patterson saw Puritanism as a "radical attack on the established Church from the Protestant side."[13] This definition limits Puritanism to those chafing under the Church of England's officially prescribed worship forms and authority structures, specifically during Elizabeth's rule; the opposition in the vestiarian controversy of the 1560s; the classical movement of the 1570s and 1580s; and those responsible for the Martin Marprelate tracts of the late 1580s and early 1590s. Patterson's central thesis is that Perkins was not a Puritan by virtue of his loyalty to the Church of England. On this last point, Patterson affirms the majority position among scholars. His attempt at revision, however,

Paul R. Schaefer, *The Spiritual Brotherhood: Cambridge Puritans and the Nature of Christian Piety*, Reformed Historical-Theological Studies (Grand Rapids: Reformation Heritage Books, 2011); Patrick Collinson, *Richard Bancroft and Elizabethan Anti-Puritanism* (Cambridge: Cambridge University Press, 2013).

12. J. I. Packer, *An Anglican to Remember: William Perkins; Puritan Popularizer* (London: St Antholin's Lectureship Charity, 1996), 1–2.

13. Patterson, *William Perkins*, 15.

is not helpful. It does not explain why later Puritan, nonconformist, and dissenting groups claimed Perkins as their forefather. Indeed, Perkins was not an active opponent of the established church, but he was an active proponent of further reformation, even if primarily through individual spiritual renewal.

On this point, Ian Breward's comment is instructive: "Attempts to draw confident distinctions between 'anglicans' and 'puritans' during this [Elizabethan] period are hazardous in the extreme." He goes on to offer his own definition, arguing Puritanism "can broadly be applied to those who by reason of their religious experience and theological convictions were dissatisfied with the government and worship of the Church of England, but nonetheless refused to separate."[14] As Patrick Collinson famously wrote, what separated the godly was degree. They were the "hotter sort of Protestants."[15] Perkins fits nicely with these definitions, especially when open political opposition does not become the measure of dissatisfaction and intensity. The most adequate definitions of Puritanism insist that Puritans were orthodox English Protestants from Elizabeth's reign through the seventeenth century who sought further reformation either at the corporate or individual level.[16]

Second, Perkins's covenant theology has received significant attention.[17] Miller popularized the idea that the Puritans developed covenant theology in response to what they saw as deficiencies in Calvin's theology—namely, a lack of motivation for holiness and the impossibility of assurance due to

---

14. Ian Breward, introduction to *The Work of William Perkins*, ed. Ian Breward, Courtenay Library of Reformation Classics 3 (Appleford, UK: Sutton Courtenay, 1970), 14.

15. Collinson, *Elizabethan Puritan Movement*, 26. Peter Lake, in *Moderate Puritans and the Elizabethan Church*, discusses the moderate stream of the Puritan movement of which Perkins was a part.

16. For detailed discussion of defining Puritanism, see Ian Hugh Clary, "Hot Protestants: A Taxonomy of English Puritanism," *Puritan Reformed Journal* 2 (2010): 41–66; Peter Lake, "The Historiography of Puritanism," in *The Cambridge Companion to Puritanism*, ed. John Coffey and Paul Chang-Ha Lim (Cambridge: Cambridge University Press, 2008), 346–72.

17. For an exhaustive review of Reformed thought on the covenant from its origins in the Reformation to the seventeenth-century formulations and how Perkins fits into this narrative, see Andrew A. Woolsey, *Unity and Continuity in Covenantal Thought: A Study in the Reformed Tradition to the Westminster Assembly*, Reformed Historical-Theological Studies (Grand Rapids: Reformation Heritage Books, 2012). For a summary of the rise of covenant thought in English theology, see Michael McGiffert, "Grace and Works: The Rise and Division of Covenant Divinity in Elizabethan Puritanism," *Harvard Theological Review* 75, no. 4 (1982): 463–502.

God's sovereignty.[18] However, many scholars see covenant theology emerging from factors already present in Reformed theology.[19]

Jens Møller and Michael McGiffert argue Perkins and the Puritans picked up the bilateral covenant tradition of the Zurich-Rhineland Reformers as opposed to the unilateral covenant of Geneva.[20] McGiffert sees Perkins's *Golden Chaine* as a charter document of English federalism, which conflated the moral law with the Adamic covenant of works, making the law work in opposing ways depending on which covenant it operated under.[21] Lyle Bierma and others challenge this thesis, seeing agreement between Geneva and the Zurich-Rhineland Reformers and therefore between Calvin and the Puritans. The distinction, Bierma persuasively argues, is a difference of emphasis on divine sovereignty or human obedience respectively. But neither tradition—and this is certainly true with Perkins—emphasized one element of the covenant to the exclusion of the other.[22]

John von Rohr and Young Song propose a diversity-within-unity approach to understanding the relationship of Calvin and the Zurich-Rhineland Reformers.[23] Song, like Bierma, acknowledges diversity of emphasis but appeals to a methodological distinction between Calvin and the Zurich-Rhineland Reformers to account for it. He understands the

18. Miller, *New England Mind: The Seventeenth Century*. See also Hill, *Society and Puritanism*; Norman Pettit, *The Heart Prepared; Grace and Conversion in Puritan Spiritual Life* (New Haven, CT: Yale University Press, 1966).

19. Anthony A. Hoekema, "The Covenant of Grace in Calvin's Teaching," *CTJ* 2, no. 2 (1967): 133–61; Robert Letham, "The Foedus Operum: Some Factors Accounting for Its Development," *SCJ* 14, no. 4 (1983): 457–67; Peter A. Lillback, *The Binding of God: Calvin's Role in the Development of Covenant Theology* (Grand Rapids: Baker Academic, 2001).

20. Jens G. Møller, "The Beginnings of Puritan Covenant Theology," *Journal of Ecclesiastical History* 14 (1963): 46–67; Michael McGiffert, "The Perkinsian Moment of Federal Theology," *CTJ* 29 (1994): 117–48. For more on the two-traditions theory, see Leonard J. Trinterud, "The Origins of Puritanism," *CH* 20 (1951): 37–57; Everett H. Emerson, "Calvin and Covenant Theology," *CH* 25, no. 2 (1956): 136–44; Richard L. Greaves, "The Origins and Early Development of English Covenant Thought," *The Historian* 31 (1968): 21–35.

21. McGiffert, "Perkinsian Moment of Federal Theology," 118. V. L. Priebe also understood the covenant of works to be only the Mosaic law in Perkins's thought ("The Covenant Theology of William Perkins" [PhD diss., Drew University, 1967]).

22. Lyle D. Bierma, "Federal Theology in the 16th Century: Two Traditions?," *WTJ* 45, no. 2 (1983): 304–21; Bierma, "The Role of Covenant Theology in Early Reformed Orthodoxy," *SCJ* 21, no. 3 (1990): 453–62. See also Hoekema, "Covenant of Grace"; Lillback, *Binding of God*.

23. Von Rohr, *Covenant of Grace*; Young Jae Timothy Song, *Theology and Piety in the Reformed Federal Thought of William Perkins and John Preston* (Lewiston, NY: Edwin Mellen, 1998).

former to take a logical and the latter a historical approach to covenant theology.[24] Mark Shaw concludes:

> [Perkins's] covenant theology enabled him to follow a consistent line of co-action which gave strong emphasis to God's sovereign grace in Christ as the ultimate cause of salvation while at the same time emphasizing the necessity of human response. ... He developed a strong linkage between sanctification and justification.[25]

Shaw's evaluation accurately summarizes Perkins's nuanced theology of the covenants. As Andrew Woolsey affirms, "There were both unilateral and bilateral sides to the covenant. The precision and balance of Perkins's theology of the covenant in this respect is quite remarkable."[26]

In the third place, closely related to covenant theology and its development in the Reformed tradition is the issue of continuity between Calvin and later "Calvinists," whose theology received systematic formulation in the Westminster Confession of Faith. The layers of this continuity-versus-discontinuity debate consist of questions about predestination, atonement, preparation, and assurance. Perkins looms large in both positive and negative assessments.[27]

---

24. Song, *Theology and Piety*, 19.

25. Mark R. Shaw, "Drama in the Meeting House: The Concept of Conversion in the Theology of William Perkins," *WTJ* 45 (1983): 71.

26. Woolsey, *Unity and Continuity*, 497.

27. Those who view the relationship negatively include Knappen, *Tudor Puritanism*; Perry Miller, *Errand into the Wilderness* (Cambridge, MA: Harvard University Press, 1956); Karl Barth, *Church Dogmatics* (Edinburgh: T&T Clark, 1961), 3.4.8; Basil Hall, "Calvin against the Calvinists," in *John Calvin*, ed. G. E. Duffield, Courtenay Studies in Reformation Theology 1 (Appleford, England: Sutton Courtenay, 1966), 19–37; William H. Chalker, "Calvin and Some Seventeenth Century English Calvinists: A Comparison of Their Thought through an Examination of Their Doctrines of the Knowledge of God, Faith, and Assurance" (PhD diss., Duke University, 1973); R. T. Kendall, *Calvin and English Calvinism to 1649*, new ed., Studies in Christian History and Thought (Eugene, OR: Wipf & Stock, 1997); Kendall, "Living the Christian Life in the Teaching of William Perkins and His Followers," in *Living the Christian Life* (London: Westminster Conference, 1974); Kendall, "John Cotton—First English Calvinist?," in *The Puritan Experiment in the New World* (London: Westminster Conference, 1976); Kendall, "The Puritan Modification of Calvin's Theology," in *John Calvin, His Influence in the Western World*, ed. W. Stanford Reid (Grand Rapids: Zondervan, 1982), 199–214. Those who see the relationship positively include C. J. Sommerville, "Conversion, Sacrament and Assurance in the Puritan Covenant of Grace to 1650" (MA thesis, University of Kansas, 1963); F. Ernest Stoeffler, *The Rise of Evangelical Pietism* (Leiden: Brill, 1965); Coleman Cain Markham, "William Perkins' Understanding of the Function of Conscience" (PhD diss., Vanderbilt University, 1967); Breward, "Significance of William Perkins"; Ian Breward, "William Perkins and the Origins of

Basil Hall asserts that Calvin's followers altered Calvin's balanced synthesis of complementary doctrines, primarily found in the *Institutes*. Hall blames William Perkins, Theodore Beza, and Jerome Zanchius for this distortion of Calvin.[28] William Chalker bluntly proclaims that for Perkins, "salvation does not consist in knowing God and Christ." He also declares that Calvin and Perkins had a "different conception of the central theme of the gospel."[29] Calvin's gospel was Christocentric, whereas Perkins's was anthropologically oriented, with Christ merely functioning as the means of salvation. R. T. Kendall brought the general thesis of pitting Calvin against the Calvinists to a head when he traced the doctrine of faith from Calvin to Perkins and then to the Westminster Assembly, concluding that the Westminster divines followed Reformed orthodoxy rather than Calvin himself. He drives a wedge between Calvin and the later Reformed tradition on two counts: the extent of the atonement and believers' ground of assurance.[30]

Reformed Casuistry," *Evangelical Quarterly* 40 (1968): 3–20; Charles Robert Munson, "William Perkins: Theologian of Transition" (PhD diss., Case Western Reserve University, 1971); Lionel Greve, "Freedom and Discipline in the Theology of John Calvin, William Perkins, and John Wesley: An Examination of the Origin and Nature of Pietism" (PhD diss., Hartford Seminary Foundation, 1975); Richard A. Muller, "Perkins' A Golden Chaine: Predestinarian System or Schematized Ordo Salutis?," *SCJ* 9 (1978): 68–81; Muller, "Covenant and Conscience in English Reformed Theology: Three Variations on a 17th Century Theme," *WTJ* 42, no. 2 (1980): 308–34; Muller, *Christ and the Decree: Christology and Predestination in Reformed Theology from Calvin to Perkins* (Grand Rapids: Baker Academic, 2008); Beeke, *Assurance of Faith*; Shaw, "Drama in the Meeting House"; Mark R. Shaw, "William Perkins and the New Pelagians: Another Look at the Cambridge Predestination Controversy of the 1590s," *WTJ* 58, no. 2 (1996): 267–301; Joseph A. Pipa, "William Perkins and the Development of Puritan Preaching" (PhD diss., Westminster Theological Seminary, 1985); Song, *Theology and Piety*; Schaefer, *Spiritual Brotherhood*; Woolsey, *Unity and Continuity*. For a summary of interpretations of Perkins's thought, see Mark R. Shaw, "The Marrow of Practical Divinity: A Study in the Theology of William Perkins" (ThD diss., Westminster Theological Seminary, 1981), 4–29.

28. Hall, "Calvin against the Calvinists," 20–29.

29. Chalker, "Calvin and Some Seventeenth Century English Calvinists," 138, 90.

30. Kendall, *Calvin and English Calvinism*, 2. This work was originally published in 1979. For evidence that Calvin affirmed "limited atonement," see W. Robert Godfrey, "Reformed Thought on the Extent of the Atonement to 1618," *WTJ* 37, no. 2 (1975): 133–71; Roger R. Nicole, "John Calvin's View of the Extent of the Atonement," *WTJ* 47, no. 2 (1985): 197–225. For rebuttals to the idea that Calvin equated faith and assurance and Perkins made sanctification the primary ground, see Shaw, "Drama in the Meeting House," 50–65; Beeke, *Assurance of Faith*, 106–15; David Hoyle, *Reformation and Religious Identity in Cambridge, 1590–1644* (Woodbridge, UK: Boydell, 2007), 9; Schaefer, *Spiritual Brotherhood*, 56–59, 92–97. According to Jonathan D. Moore, the particularism Perkins saw in the atonement was based on the intention of God, the application of the atonement's benefits, and the intercession of Christ. See *English Hypothetical Universalism: John Preston and the Softening of Reformed Theology* (Grand Rapids: Eerdmans,

Scholars of Puritanism on the other side of the Atlantic have proposed a similar dichotomy. Janice Knight argues that there were two divergent religious streams within Puritanism. Thomas Hooker, Thomas Shepard, John Winthrop, and most of the clergy in New England represented the first; this group considered Perkins and William Ames as their authorities from old England. According to Knight, John Cotton, John Davenport, and Henry Vane do not represent a fringe group but rather a second mainstream party within Puritanism, one with closer affinity to Calvin. Richard Sibbes and John Preston led this second party's English representatives. Knight argues these two parties diverged over such key doctrines as preparation and sanctification, with the Perkinsian establishment heavily emphasizing both.[31] Dwight Bozeman sees these emphases as resulting from the antinomian backlash in both England and New England.[32] Lisa Gordis argues that not only the antinomian controversy but also the disagreement surrounding Roger Williams and the Halfway Covenant were largely the result of Perkins's method of biblical interpretation, her understanding of which is significant for the present study.[33]

The "Calvin against the Calvinists" thesis has been undergoing revision for decades. Paul Helm responds directly to Kendall by showing continuity between Calvin, Perkins, and Westminster. In the later Reformed tradition, Helm notes increased precision and a tightening of theology, but the content remained consistent.[34] Richard Muller has devoted much of

---

2007), 38–43. This is contrary to those who give predestination primacy in interpreting Perkins's particularism—e.g., Wallace, *Puritans and Predestination*, 55–61.

31. Janice Knight, *Orthodoxies in Massachusetts: Rereading American Puritanism* (Cambridge, MA: Harvard University Press, 1994), 2–4. Knight is self-professedly in the tradition of Perry Miller, *The New England Mind: From Colony to Province* (Cambridge, MA: Harvard University Press, 1953), which was picked up by Teresa Toulouse, "'The Art of Prophesying': John Cotton and the Rhetoric of Election," *Early American Literature* 19, no. 3 (1985): 279–99. For a thorough response to Knight's thesis, see Schaefer, *Spiritual Brotherhood*, 323–28. For other voices heralding primarily continuity, see Everett H. Emerson, *John Cotton* (New York: Twayne, 1965); Alfred Habegger, "Preparing the Soul for Christ: The Contrasting Sermon Forms of John Cotton and Thomas Hooker," *American Literature* 41, no. 3 (1969): 342–54.

32. Theodore Dwight Bozeman, *The Precisianist Strain: Disciplinary Religion & Antinomian Backlash in Puritanism to 1638* (Chapel Hill: University of North Carolina Press, 2004).

33. Lisa M. Gordis, *Opening Scripture: Bible Reading and Interpretive Authority in Puritan New England* (Chicago: University of Chicago Press, 2003). Her exposition of Perkins's interpretive method will be evaluated later.

34. Paul Helm, *Calvin and the Calvinists* (Edinburgh: Banner of Truth Trust, 1982). See also Shawn D. Wright, *Our Sovereign Refuge: The Pastoral Theology of Theodore Beza* (Eugene,

his impressive corpus to changing this discussion entirely, arguing that "the Reformed tradition is a diverse and variegated movement not suitably described as founded solely on the thought of John Calvin or as either a derivation or a deviation from Calvin."[35] Muller and those influenced by him see steady development in the Reformed tradition rather than strict continuity or discontinuity.[36] For this reason, it can be misleading to contrast isolated statements—such as Calvin's claim that Christ is the mirror for contemplating election or Perkins's remark that predestination is the glass for beholding God's majesty.[37] Calvin's claim implies God's decree was Christocentric, whereas Perkins's implies theocentricity. But the categories are not nearly so neat.[38] The development thesis has the dual strength of being more sensitive to historical context and less dogmatically charged.

In the fourth place, *The Arte of Prophecying* has attracted significant attention. The volume is a preaching manual and lays out Perkins's hermeneutical and homiletical principles. It is obvious that his preaching method had an enduring influence, which explains scholars' consistent emphasis on the work. J. W. Blench is often cited for his taxonomy of Elizabethan preaching. He argues for three forms: ancient, new Reformed, and modern. The new Reformed method was popularized by Wolfgang Musculus's commentaries and outlined in *The Arte of Prophecying*. The doctrine-use formula so prevalent in Perkins's sermons distinguishes this homiletic form. Further, Blench argues for three styles of sermons:

OR: Paternoster, 2004); Robert Letham, *The Westminster Assembly: Reading Its Theology in Historical Context* (Phillipsburg, NJ: P&R, 2009); Willem J. van Asselt, *Introduction to Reformed Scholasticism*, Reformed Historical-Theological Studies (Grand Rapids: Reformation Heritage Books, 2011); Woolsey, *Unity and Continuity*.

35. Richard A. Muller, *Calvin and the Reformed Tradition: On the Work of Christ and the Order of Salvation* (Grand Rapids: Baker Academic, 2012), 9. See also Muller, *Christ and the Decree*; Muller, *The Unaccommodated Calvin: Studies in the Foundation of a Theological Tradition*, Oxford Studies in Historical Theology (New York: Oxford University Press, 2000); Muller, *Post-Reformation Reformed Dogmatics: The Rise and Development of Reformed Orthodoxy, Ca. 1520 to Ca. 1725*, 2nd ed., 4 vols. (Grand Rapids: Baker Academic, 2003); Muller, *After Calvin: Studies in the Development of a Theological Tradition*, Oxford Studies in Historical Theology (New York: Oxford University Press, 2003).

36. Carl R. Trueman, "The Reception of Calvin: Historical Considerations," *Church History and Religious Culture* 91, nos. 1–2 (2011): 19–27.

37. Breward, introduction to *Works of William Perkins*, 86.

38. Muller explains that Perkins's infamous supralapsarian work articulating double predestination is a christocentric, pastoral analysis of the order of salvation. See "Perkins' A Golden Chaine."

the plain but uncolloquial, the colloquial, and the ornate.[39] Within the plain style he sees three levels of plainness: the extremely bare and austere, less colorless with tropes, and moderately decorated with tropes and schemata. Blench unfairly categorizes Perkins with the "extreme Puritans," placing him in the plain-style category, which implies his sermons were extremely bare and austere, despite the fact that Perkins did employ rhetoric and illustrations.[40]

Beginning with Miller, some have traced the development of the plain style and the new Reformed method back to Ramism.[41] However, Eugenie Bernstein and Joseph Pipa demonstrate that too much is made of Ramist influence; they argue it was not responsible for the genesis of the Puritan style and form but merely reinforced it. Pipa argues Perkins became the chief instrument by which the new Reformed method of preaching was adopted almost universally by the seventeenth-century Puritans. Pipa analyzes the *The Arte of Prophecying* and concludes that it laid the theoretical and rhetorical foundations for this method.[42] Edward Davidson attests to the extraordinarily consistent application of the new Reformed method among New England clergy.[43] Mary Morrissey dissents from the often-assumed dichotomy between the plain and metaphysical style, which correlate to Blench's new Reformed and modern sermon forms. For Morrissey, the dichotomy persists on the wrong assumption that preaching must be

39. J. W. Blench, *Preaching in England in the Late Fifteenth and Sixteenth Centuries: A Study of English Sermons 1450–c. 1600* (New York: Barnes & Noble, 1964), 100–102, 113.

40. Blench, *Preaching in England*, 168–69. For more on sermons in general during this period, see Larissa Taylor, *Preachers and People in the Reformations and Early Modern Period* (Leiden: Brill, 2001); Arnold Hunt, *The Art of Hearing: English Preachers and Their Audiences, 1590–1640*, Cambridge Studies in Early Modern British History (Cambridge: Cambridge University Press, 2010); Peter E. McCullough, Hugh Adlington, and Emma Rhatigan, eds., *The Oxford Handbook of the Early Modern Sermon* (Oxford: Oxford University Press, 2011).

41. Miller, *New England Mind: The Seventeenth Century*. For agreement with Miller with Perkins in view, see Wilbur Samuel Howell, *Logic and Rhetoric in England, 1500–1700* (New York: Russell & Russell, 1961), 206–7; John Frederick Wilson, *Pulpit in Parliament: Puritanism during the English Civil Wars, 1640–1648* (Princeton: Princeton University Press, 1969), 139; Munson, "William Perkins," 13–14. For an introduction to Peter Ramus and his method, see Walter J. Ong, *Ramus, Method, and the Decay of Dialogue: From the Art of Discourse to the Art of Reason* (Cambridge, MA: Harvard University Press, 1958).

42. Eugenie Hershon Bernstein, "A Revaluation of the Plain Genre of Homiletics in Its Evolution as a Theory of Persuasion from Ramus to John Wilkins" (PhD diss., University of California, 1975); Pipa, "William Perkins."

43. Edward H. Davidson, "'God's Well-Trodden Foot-Paths': Puritan Preaching and Sermon Form," *Texas Studies in Literature and Language* 25, no. 4 (1983): 503.

considered a branch of rhetoric. But before the restoration of the English monarchy, this was not the case. Preaching was categorically different. It was a means of grace that involved the preacher, the hearer, and the Holy Spirit. The content included both interpretation and application, serving didactic and exhortatory functions respectively. The emphasis on plainness came from a desire for effective teaching.[44]

Attention has been given to Perkins's biblical interpretation as it relates to his preaching method, but this has resulted in surface-level treatment or simple restatement of what Perkins himself said.[45] Cursory treatment in this context is understandable, granting that biblical interpretation is only one subset of preaching. That said, some very helpful work has been done on the specifics of Perkins's interpretation of Scripture, including the authority of the literal sense and continuity with certain medieval streams of thought.

For example, John Augustine argues that Perkins attempted to ascribe authority to the word of God rather than himself as an interpreter. Scripture is the immediate word of God. The literal sense is the meaning of any given text, while the three spiritual senses of the *quadriga* are applications of Scripture. The literal sense could be penned in figures and allegories, when a text goes against common sense, the analogy of faith, or good manners.[46] Breward's evaluation of the authority of the Bible for Perkins concurs. Scripture is God's word, so "discussion of inspiration and the nature of the Bible was therefore fundamental to Perkins's whole theology and to his understanding of the pastoral task of proclaiming the gospel." Breward's analysis also agrees with Augustine's understanding of Perkins's interpretation. The perfection and perspicuity of Scripture were corollaries to Perkins's doctrine of inspiration. So, in short, Scripture must interpret Scripture, particularly when the literal sense remains opaque.[47]

---

44. Mary Morrissey, "Scripture, Style and Persuasion in Seventeenth-Century English Theories of Preaching," *Journal of Ecclesiastical History* 53, no. 4 (2002): 686–706.

45. Bernstein, "Reevaluation of the Plain Genre"; Pipa, "William Perkins"; Tae-Hyeun Park, "The Sacred Rhetoric of the Holy Spirit: A Study of Puritan Preaching in a Pneumatological Perspective" (PhD diss., Theologische Universiteit Apeldoorn, 2005).

46. John H. Augustine, "Authority and Interpretation in Perkins' Commentary on Galatians," in *A Commentary on Galatians*, by William Perkins, ed. Gerald T. Sheppard, Pilgrim Classic Commentaries (New York: Pilgrim Press, 1989), xiv–xlvii.

47. Breward, introduction to *Works of William Perkins*, 38, 47–49.

Muller introduces Protestant exegesis as a continuation of a stream of thought in the Middle Ages. He places Perkins in this tradition. Muller observes that Perkins "evidences a preference for a close, literal/grammatical location of the meaning of the text coupled with, as was true of the work of his predecessors in the Reformed tradition, a strong sense of the direct theological address of the text to the church in the present." Muller insightfully expounds Perkins's use of scope and method for exegeting individual verses. Similar to Melanchthon's locus model, Perkins divided the verses, argued the meaning of the parts, then drew out the argument of the text in terms of the grammatical and logical relations of the parts. Further, Perkins preferred a precise verbal reflection in translation, rather than dynamic equivalency.[48]

Muller also identifies the similarities between two genres—commentary and sermon—and illustrates this by showing that the homiletical method in *The Arte of Prophecying* was based primarily on the tradition of the Reformed commentary. All of this fits nicely into Muller's larger project of proving development in the Reformed tradition. He sees both the Reformation and the post-Reformation exegetes as precritical biblical interpreters. The Reformers denied the *quadriga* in favor of the literal sense but housed the spiritual senses within it. Reformed orthodoxy was left to reconstruct and justify Christian dogma in the context of this hermeneutical revolution. Muller has enumerated the Reformed tradition's general methods of exegesis, the dominant principle being the analogy of Scripture.[49]

Some scholars have made less helpful contributions toward understanding Perkins's biblical interpretation in the context of his preaching. Erwin Gane, in a series of three journal articles, addresses exegetical methods of sixteenth-century Anglican, Puritan, and Roman Catholic preachers.[50] The dogmatic axe he has to grind over the doctrine of inspiration is

48. Richard A. Muller, "William Perkins and the Protestant Exegetical Tradition: Interpretation, Style and Method," in *A Commentary on Hebrews 11 (1609 Edition)*, by William Perkins, ed. John H. Augustine, Pilgrim Classic Commentaries (New York: Pilgrim, 1991), 80–84, 87.

49. Muller, *Post-Reformation Reformed Dogmatics*, 2:443–524.

50. Erwin R. Gane, "The Exegetical Methods of Some Sixteenth-Century Anglican Preachers: Latimer, Jewel, Hooker, and Andrewes," *AUSS* 17 (1979): 23–38, 169–88; Gane, "The Exegetical Methods of Some Sixteenth-Century Puritan Preachers: Hooper, Cartwright, and

obvious. He sides with the Anglicans and goes out of his way to attempt to show how they did not affirm verbal inspiration. He argues that Puritan preachers, and Perkins specifically, were "ultra-literalist" as a result of their presuppositions regarding inspiration. Gane uses "ultra" in the sense of "beyond." So, in his mind, they "were not satisfied to give Bible passages their obvious meanings in context ... but sought to see their own era, as well as their own biases, as subjects of the scriptural passages." Gane also levels the charge that "proof-texting" was Perkins's and the Puritans' "characteristic method." He asserts that they used "verses as jumping off points for favorite doctrines" and then proceeded to support these doctrines with isolated references.[51]

More recently, Lisa M. Gordis offers an explanation of the controversies in seventeenth-century New England, for which she holds Perkins's biblical interpretation responsible. Her central thesis is simple: "Privileging God as author and interpreter, Puritan interpretive strategies minimized the role of the human interpreter, relying on methods that in theory allowed the text to interpret itself." This allowed fluidity, which resulted in the controversy surrounding Roger Williams, antinomianism, and the Halfway Covenant. Gordis expounds Perkins's *The Arte of Prophecying* and Richard Bernard's *The Faithful Shepheard* together. During this exposition, she misrepresents Perkins's hermeneutic on at least two fronts. She claims that the analogy of faith was "above" Scripture and that collation necessarily severed verses from their contexts.[52]

Donald McKim has presented the most substantial comment on Perkins's biblical interpretation in his volume *Ramism in William Perkins' Theology*. His primary argument is that Ramism was pervasive and determinative in Perkins's works, and therefore it extends to his exegetical works. Rather than making logical deductions from the text like the scholastics, Perkins discovered arguments in the text. Biblical texts were unfolded, revealing in Scripture the mind of God or intent of the Spirit. McKim sees Ramism as both Perkins's hermeneutic and the key to his exegesis,

Perkins, Pt 1," *AUSS* 19 (1981): 21–36, 99–114; Gane, "The Exegetical Methods of Some Sixteenth-Century Roman Catholic Preachers in England: Fisher, Peryn, Bonner, and Watson," *AUSS* 23, no. 3 (1985): 161–80, 259–75.

51. Gane, "Exegetical Methods of Some Sixteenth-Century Puritan Preachers," 109, 36.

52. Gordis, *Opening Scripture*, 3, 21, 28.

despite what Perkins claims in his preaching manual.[53] He surmises that for Perkins, the Ramist

> system was more than just classificatory logic when applied to Biblical interpretation. It was an attempt to perceive the logical plan in the mind of God that expressed itself through the flow of the Scriptural material. If this plan was uncovered it could therefore in addition reveal the true hermeneutics for Scriptural interpretation. The exact meaning of a text could be ascertained with certainty if the procedure was able to uncover the mind of God behind the text. All other methods of interpreting that text would thus be false.[54]

He also understood the *The Arte of Prophecying* to be consciously written according to Ramist philosophical principles.[55] While McKim has definitively proved Ramist influences on Perkins, he has overstated his case, particularly with regard to Perkins's biblical interpretation.

No complete treatment of Perkins's biblical interpretation has been written to date. While the central role that Scripture played in his thought has been recognized, that exegesis was at the heart of all his efforts has yet to be demonstrated.[56] I intend to fill this gap in the historiography. This project will naturally answer the charges against Perkins of eisegesis, proof-texting, and subverting the authority of Scripture with the analogy of faith or theological consistency and precision. It will also demonstrate that Perkins's stated interpretive method is preferable to Ramism as an elucidation of his exegesis.

METHODOLOGY

I plan to explicate Perkins's exegesis in two movements. I will first survey Perkins's historical context, giving significant attention to how he fits into the development of biblical interpretation both from the medieval period

---

53. McKim, *Ramism in William Perkins' Theology*, 129. See also, Donald K. McKim, "William Perkins' Use of Ramism as an Exegetical Tool," in Perkins, *Commentary on Hebrews 11*, 32–45.

54. McKim, *Ramism in William Perkins' Theology*, 74.

55. For a similar evaluation of *The Arte of Prophecying*, see Howell, *Logic and Rhetoric*, 206–7.

56. Joel R. Beeke and J. Stephen Yuille, "Biographical Preface," in *The Works of William Perkins*, ed. J. Stephen Yuille (Grand Rapids: Reformation Heritage Books, 2014), 1:xix; Breward, introduction to *Works of William Perkins*, 38.

and within the Reformed tradition. With this context as a backdrop, I will expound his method of interpretation as stated explicitly in *The Arte of Prophecying* and other clear statements he made elsewhere regarding his approach to exegesis. Second, the majority of this project will address Perkins's exegesis in the various genres in which he wrote. Perkins drew his identity primarily from preaching, closely followed by his pastoral ministry. He seems to have valued his constructive theology more than his efforts in deconstruction. For these reasons, the argument will proceed in the following order: sermons and commentaries, practical works, theological treatises, then polemical works. I will walk through his works to demonstrate the consistency of Perkins's method of biblical interpretation throughout while noting the differences demanded by various genres.

My goal is to highlight what Perkins actually said and let his own words illuminate his method and then prove his consistency. Therefore I will predominantly utilize Perkins's published works. As necessary, I will also look at works by his contemporaries for context and interact with scholarly treatments of Perkins, Puritanism, and the history of biblical interpretation.

In chapter 2, I will set Perkins's biblical interpretation in its historical context. I will highlight elements of Perkins's hermeneutic consistent with exegesis from the Middle Ages. Specifically, there is continuity with Thomas Aquinas and with the literal exegesis of Nicholas of Lyra and Jacques Lefèvre d'Étaples. The Reformers picked up this medieval stream of interpretation. I will also underscore those elements in both the Protestant Reformers and the Reformed tradition with which Perkins had an affinity. Last, regarding historical context, I will examine works by Perkins's contemporaries on interpreting the Bible and preaching in English; this includes publications by Niels Hemmingsen, Andreas Hyperius, John Whitgift, William Whitaker, Richard Bernard, and John Wilkins. This survey of English writings and translations, by both Englishmen and others, will show that the ideas in Perkins's preaching manual were not innovative but nonetheless significant due to their clarity, brevity, and intended audience. With this context in mind, I will expound Perkins's stated method of biblical interpretation in *The Arte of Prophecying*. I will also support this method with comments from elsewhere in Perkins's works to emphasize consistency in his stated approach. It will become clear that his convictions concerning the nature and authority of Scripture were foundational to his understanding that Scripture must interpret itself through the analogy of faith, context, and collation, all undergirded by reliance on the Spirit. However, Perkins had no problem with the use of commentaries, other helps, and profane learning; in fact, he saw these as essential in the process of interpretation. Perkins proved faithful to a Reformed understanding of exegesis in a clear and reproducible way.

In chapter 3, I will begin looking at Perkins's exegesis in the first of four genres: his sermons and commentaries. I will include these as one genre because all of Perkins's commentaries started as sermons. Also, as Muller has shown, the new Reformed sermon paradigm was closely related to the Reformed commentary.[57] Before addressing Perkins's writings themselves, I will discuss his historical context as it relates to his sermons and commentaries. This discussion will include the Puritan agenda for further reformation of thinking and morals as well as Perkins's part in this effort. It will also explain why faithful exposition was central to the project. I will then demonstrate that Perkins consistently employed his method of biblical interpretation in such expositions. To do so, I will systematically analyze two expositional works penned by Perkins himself on Galatians 1–5 and Philippians 3:7–9; Perkins's series on Jesus' temptation, the Sermon on the Mount, Revelation 1–3, Jude, and Hebrews 11; and Perkins's occasional sermon on Zephaniah 2:1–2.

Chapter 4 will deal with Perkins's practical works. I will again highlight pertinent contextual considerations. Like Perkins's preaching, his practical works furthered the Puritan goal of further theological and moral reformation of the English people. They were also aimed to train clergy. In the Puritan mind, only the word of God was suited to these tasks. I will show that Perkins used his method of biblical interpretation in his practical work by exploring his publications on various aspects of the Christian life, including family, moderation, the mind, vocation, living and dying well, repentance, and the tongue. I will also consider his writings for the benefit of the clergy, including his work on calling and his multiple books

57. Muller, *Post-Reformation Reformed Dogmatics*, 2:506.

on conscience. In his practical works, Perkins consistently implemented his exegetical method.

In chapter 5, I will establish Perkins's consistent application of his method of biblical interpretation in his theological works. I will sketch his historical situation as a member of the international Reformed movement and as a participant in the Cambridge predestination controversy of the 1590s. This context explains many of the emphases in Perkins's theological treatises. As a third-generation Reformer, Perkins was part of the effort to consolidate and systematize the insights of the first- and second-generation Protestants. I will investigate Perkins's catechism and systematic explanation of the Apostles' Creed, showing that even here the explication of Scripture according to his interpretive method remained central. As a fellow at Cambridge and lecturer at St. Andrew the Great, Perkins was well aware of the predestination debates. I will examine his three works dealing with the sovereignty of God in the salvation of individuals and demonstrate that even at the highest level of sophistication in theological debate, Perkins relied on his method of biblical interpretation.

Chapter 6 will account for Perkins's polemics, the last of the four genres in which he wrote. I will first provide a picture of the polemical context, explaining first and foremost that Roman Catholicism was a very real threat both at home and abroad for Perkins. The Protestantism of Elizabethan England was new and volatile. Further, there were significant political and military threats. Perkins lived during attacks from such forces as the Spanish Armada. He also inhabited an age when there was a heightened awareness of the spiritual world, especially the possibility of demonic influence. These realities account for Perkins's attacks on Roman Catholicism, witchcraft, and astrology. With Perkins's writings against the Church of Rome and his treatises aimed at witchcraft and astrologers, I will demonstrate that his polemics were grounded in Scripture, according to his stated method of biblical interpretation.

I will conclude with a summary of my thesis in light of my research. I will also suggest that more work needs to be done in the area of Puritan hermeneutics and exegesis. Specifically, in what way was Perkins's approach to biblical interpretation unique? Also, more attention to Puritan exegesis would help serve as a corrective to the misrepresentation that the

Puritan era was nothing more than the proliferation of Reformed orthodoxy preoccupied with systems and dogmatics rather than the Bible.

A powerful Protestant apologist and zealot for further reformation in England, Perkins exhausted his energy in the pulpit, behind the lectern, and at his writing desk. In every capacity of influence, he expounded Scripture according to his stated method in *The Arte of Prophecying*. As one surveys his voluminous works, this reality becomes apparent, and I hope to prove this claim in the following chapters.

A final note on sources. Facsimiles of Perkins's published works are available through the Early English Books Online database. This database includes first-edition publications of single works as well as the multiple editions of his collected works. Some of Perkins's works were written originally in Latin and then translated. Many were published during his lifetime. The 1631 edition of his works, *The Whole Works of That Famous and Worthy Minister of Christ in the Universitie of Cambridge, M. William Perkins*, is the most recent, has all of the final corrections and edits, and is one of the collections consistently used in Perkins scholarship.[58] This edition will be utilized throughout this book, and when a first edition was published during Perkins's lifetime it will be cited as well, with variations noted. The first seven volumes of *The Works of William Perkins*, published by Reformation Heritage Books, have been released.[59] This is the only modern edition of Perkins's works to date, but as it is updated for modern readability, it will not be used as a primary source.

58. William Perkins, *The Whole Works of That Famous and Worthy Minister of Christ in the Universitie of Cambridge, M. William Perkins*, 3 vols. (London: John Legatt, 1631).

59. William Perkins, *The Works of William Perkins*, ed. Joel R. Beeke and Derek W. H. Thomas, 10 vols. (Grand Rapids: Reformation Heritage Books, 2014–).

2

PERKINS'S EXEGETICAL METHOD

BIOGRAPHICAL CONTEXT

In 1558, William Perkins was born in Marston Jabbett, Bulkington parish, Warwickshire county. His parents, Thomas and Hannah, must have been close to gentry, as he entered Christ's College Cambridge in 1577 as a pensioner, one able to pay the common expenses of his education. During his early student days, Perkins devoted himself to drunkenness. He also seems to have dabbled in the study of astrology and other dark arts, as evidenced by his intimate knowledge of such things in his later polemics against them. His conversion began when "he heard a woman say to a child that was being forward and peevish, 'Hold your tongue, or I will give you to drunken Perkins, yonder,'" as he stumbled through the streets of Cambridge.[1] This event stirred his conscience, and Perkins redirected his attention and energy to the study of divinity. He eventually graduated with his bachelor's in 1581 and his master's in 1584.

Perkins received a traditional scholastic education, Reformed in its theological content and modified by Ramism. His education was made up of three parts: the trivium, the quadrivium, and the philosophies, which included natural, moral, and metaphysical disciplines. The trivium consisted of grammar, rhetoric, and logic. The quadrivium contained music, arithmetic, geometry, and astronomy. At the time, the Ramist method was coming into vogue through the influence of Lawrence Chaderton. Chaderton served as Perkins's tutor, no doubt exposing him to his own Puritan sympathies. Perkins's writings reveal a wide reading in the patristic, medieval, and Protestant traditions as well, yet all this was subordinated

1. Brook, *Lives of the Puritans*, 2:135, 129.

to divine revelation. Scripture was the axiom of all his thinking and the focus of everything he produced.[2]

Perkins was elected fellow of Christ's College in 1584, which launched his academic career. As a fellow, his responsibilities included preaching, lecturing, and tutoring. He also served as dean from 1590 to 1591.[3] Perkins's *Armilla Aurea* (1590), translated as *A Golden Chaine* (1591), established his reputation as a leading theologian. His productivity continued with his analyses of the Lord's Prayer (1592) and the Apostles' Creed (1595).

In 1595 he married a young widow, Timothye Cradocke, from nearby Grantchester; this effectively ended his fellowship at Christ's College as well as his formal academic career, though Perkins continued to write. His *A Discourse of Conscience* (1596) provided the foundation for his groundbreaking work in casuistry. In the crowning jewel of his apologetic work, *A Reformed Catholike* (1597), Perkins defends the established church and challenges the Church of Rome. The challenge was accepted by William Bishop, who responded in *A Reformation of a Catholike Deformed*, which released in two parts, 1604 and 1607. This was not Perkins's only work to provoke scholarly engagement. None other than Jacob Arminius contested his 1598 treatise on predestination, though Arminius did not publish the work during his lifetime out of respect for his opponent's untimely death. Perkins's books became a mainstay of the Cambridge press and continued to appear in significant numbers in the years following his passing.

During his time as a Cambridge fellow, Perkins appeared before the authorities twice to be questioned on his relationship to nonconformity. The first episode took place in 1587, when a three-part complaint was made against Perkins after a sermon he preached in the college chapel. He reportedly taught that it was a corruption for a minister to give himself the elements of the Lord's Supper, that kneeling to receive the sacrament was superstitious and anti-Christian, and that facing east at particular points in the worship service was objectionable. Perkins stood before the vice-chancellor and the heads of the colleges to defend himself. He explained his reservations about such practices but denied the harsh language attributed to him. In the end, the college imposed no penalty, and

2. Beeke and Yuille, "Biographical Preface."
3. Beeke and Pederson, *Meet the Puritans*, 470.

no further complaints are recorded. In 1591, Perkins was called before the Star Chamber as a witness against the defendants Thomas Cartwright and Edmund Snape. All three men, as well as Lawrence Chaderton, were present at a 1589 meeting at St. John's College, Cambridge, where they discussed the Book of Discipline, largely authored by Walter Travers. Perkins confirmed the defendants' presence but testified that this was an isolated meeting and he was unaware of any discussion of the implementation of presbyteries.[4] It is clear that Perkins never openly allied himself with Presbyterians and denounced the separatists; he sought to reform the church from within.[5]

In 1584, Perkins was appointed lecturer at St. Andrew the Great, the church across the street from Christ's College. He held this post for the rest of his life. This appointment resulted from his growing popularity as a prison preacher. One popular story recounts the time Perkins called a frightened man down from the gallows, saying, "Thou shalt see what God's grace will do to strengthen thee." He then "made such an effectual prayer in confession of sins ... as made the pour prisoner burst out into abundant tears." Then the prisoner prayed to "show him the Lord Jesus," which "cleared him up again to look beyond death, with eyes of faith, to see how the black lines of all his sins were crossed, and canceled with the red lines of his crucified saviours precious blood." He returned to the gallows, this time professing his faith with tears of joy.[6] It has been said that under Perkins's prison ministry "many an Onesimus in bonds was converted to Christ."[7]

His post at St. Andrew the Great required a connection with both university and townsfolk. One biographer recalls, "His sermons were not so plain, but that the piously learned did not admire them; nor so learned, but the plain did understand them."[8] His style and subject earned him the admiration of all. Perkins's preaching was powerful: "He used to apply the terrors of the law so directly to the consciences of his hearers, that their hearts would often sink under the convictions; and he used to pronounce the word *damn* with so peculiar an emphasis, that it left a doleful echo in

---

4. Patterson, *William Perkins*, 46–48.
5. Beeke and Yuille, *William Perkins*, 58.
6. Clarke, *Marrow of Ecclesiastical History*, 853.
7. Fuller, *Abel Redevivus*, 433.
8. Clarke, *Marrow of Ecclesiastical History*, 851.

their ears a long time after."[9] Yet "in his older age he altered his voice, and remitted much of his former rigidnesse, often professing that to preach mercie was that proper office of the ministers of the Gospell."[10] During his eighteen-year tenure as lecturer, Perkins preached six major expositional sermon series: Matthew 5–7; Matthew 4; Revelation 1–3; Hebrews 11; Jude; and Galatians 1–5, likely in this order.

The historical record shows that Perkins's life consistently modeled what he preached. "He lived his sermons," meaning "as his preaching was a comment on the text, so his practice was a comment on his preaching."[11] It was preaching and piety like this that set the tone for seventeenth-century Puritanism.

Perkins's personality has been described as "naturally cheerful and pleasant; rather reserved towards strangers, but familiar upon their further acquaintance."[12] The rare physical description paints a picture of one whose "stature was indifferent, complexion ruddy, hayre bright, body inclined to corpulency, which proceeded not from any lazinesse."[13]

Common to his time, Perkins's adult life was riddled with regular ailments—kidney stones in particular. After several excruciating weeks in 1602, the condition took his life at the age of forty-four. At the time, Perkins's wife was pregnant with their seventh child while caring for three and mourning the loss of the others. His will indicates that he was survived by both of his parents, an unknown number of brothers and sisters, and a son-in-law. Christ's College paid for his burial in the churchyard of St. Andrew the Great. His friend James Montague, who later became the bishop of Winchester, preached Perkins's funeral sermon from Joshua 1:2: "Moses my servant is dead."[14]

Little else is known about Perkins because sparse autobiographical material exists and no personal letters are known to have survived. This means his legacy is altogether left to us via his published works. Though Perkins is less known today, his works made an indelible impact in the

9. Brook, *Lives of the Puritans*, 130.

10. Thomas Fuller, *The Holy State* (Cambridge: Roger Daniel for John Williams, 1642), 90.

11. Fuller, *Abel Redevivus*, 436.

12. Brook, *Lives of the Puritans*, 134.

13. Fuller, *Abel Redevivus*, 438.

14. Brook, *Lives of the Puritans*, 134–35.

Christian world—not just in England but across both the channel and the Atlantic. In the Dutch language alone, there were 185 seventeenth-century printings of his individual and collected works. When this is accounted for in addition to his influence on his student William Ames, it becomes clear that Perkins made no small impact on the *Nadere Reformatie*. His writings were also published in Switzerland and Germany; they were translated into Spanish, French, Italian, Irish, Welsh, Czech, and Hungarian.[15] In America, "a typical Plymouth Colony library comprised a large and a small Bible, Ainsworth's translation of the Psalms, and the works of William Perkins, a favorite theologian."[16] Perry Miller notes that "anyone who reads the writings of early New England learns that Perkins was indeed a towering figure in their eyes."[17] Though Perkins would never have claimed the label "Puritan" for himself, his work set a precedent for literature that poured out from seventeenth-century publishers, ensuring him a title, in the eyes of some, as the father of Puritanism.[18]

HERMENEUTICAL CONTEXT

Perkins did not come to the task of biblical interpretation as a blank slate. In fact, he was not even the first Englishman in the Reformed tradition to call for a singular sense of Scripture. Moreover, Protestant exegesis in general neither had a monopoly on the literal sense nor entirely discontinued the logic and intentions of the *quadriga*. Rather, Perkins stood in a long and broadening line of biblical interpreters who took the natural meaning of Scripture's words seriously while also wrestling with the implications of divine inspiration, which included both the reality of the Bible's figures and types and its address to the church throughout the ages. Put simply, Perkins was a precritical interpreter. His approach to Scripture has more in common with patristic and medieval exegesis than what is characteristic of the modern period. These commonalities, especially as they pertain to Scripture's literal sense, will be highlighted by looking briefly at patristic foundations and a few significant medieval antecedents. I will also explore

---

15. Beeke and Pederson, *Meet the Puritans*, 475.

16. Samuel Morison, *The Intellectual Life of Colonial New England*, 2nd ed. (New York: New York University Press, 1956), 137.

17. Miller, *Errand into the Wilderness*, 57–59.

18. Beeke and Yuille, "Biographical Preface," xxxi.

the Reformed tradition and Perkins's contemporary English context in order to further place his ideas in their proper historical situation.

PATRISTIC FOUNDATION

For the early church fathers, the meaning of the biblical text was not the historical or theological referent but the text itself as divine revelation, ordained by God to edify. Meaning was found in the words, not behind them. The patristic era's exegetical project was motivated by Christ; it sought to understand how faith in Jesus brings order and coherence to Scripture as both its interpretive key and the fulfillment of all things.

The fathers had three primary interpretive strategies. The first was intensive reading, which looked at the literal details of Scripture and how they fit into the whole. They used lexical tools, dialectic, and association. The fathers' second interpretive strategy focused on typological interpretation. This method called for moving beyond particular analysis to larger, unifying patterns. They observed types of Christ and Christian practices in the Old Testament and patterns in both Testaments as types for contemporary experience. Finally, patristic interpreters engaged in allegorical interpretation, which is not entirely different from typology. To be sure, it is more explicit, more intentional, and perhaps more strained. Nonetheless, many church fathers used allegory to make sense out of nonsense, add to the literal sense, and indeed save the literal sense. During the patristic period, discipline in exegesis was found via the rule of faith and personal character.[19] The themes of piety and Christ as the interpretive key to the Bible have obvious parallels in Perkins's interpretive method, as do the use of the rule of faith, careful attention to the text, and association.

Discussing patristic biblical interpretation often digresses into a simplistic polarization of Alexandrian and Antiochene exegesis. Frances Young corrects this narrative by bringing attention to interpretive elements familiar to medieval, Reformation, and post-Reformation students. Young argues the difference between the Alexandrian and Antiochene schools is not simply a spiritual versus a literal reading of the text. One cannot sharply contrast allegory and typology in early Christian literature. For example,

19. John J. O'Keefe and Russell R. Reno, *Sanctified Vision: An Introduction to Early Christian Interpretation of the Bible* (Baltimore: Johns Hopkins University Press, 2005).

Origen's *De Principiis*, normally seen as an articulation of his exegetical technique, provides no description of what he did as a text critic, commentator, or preacher. His methodology for these tasks was influenced by the Greco-Roman schools of grammar, rhetoric, and philosophy. This is also where Origen got the "higher sense," or the identification of metaphorical language.

The Antiochenes, represented by Diodore of Tarsus, Theodore of Mopsuestia, and John Chrysostom, shared these techniques and assumptions. They stressed history but not from the same concerns as modern historical critics. They did not contrast historical and theological meaning. History held the obvious narrative meaning of a given text, not a reconstruction of what really happened—and in this formulation they found both morals and dogma. For them, history was a rhetorical genre meant to improve as much as inform. The Antiochenes were anxious about the allegorization of the rule of faith and salvation history. It was part of the wider attack on Origen's spiritualizing of bodily and material life. They were fine with the higher sense as long as it remained grounded in the text, objecting to any hermeneutic that misidentifies and misapplies figures of speech. They rooted the higher sense in hyperbole, as the identification of prophecy, which was a different figure of speech from what Origen and the philosophic tradition used.

The schools are not radically opposed, as is so often alleged; in fact, on closer examination, it becomes clear their difference is one of emphasis and degree. Both pursued a higher sense, but they defined it differently. The real difference is that the Platonist Origen viewed the created order and Scripture as symbolic of the eternal and spiritual world. The Antiochenes thought narrative mattered and that prophetic, moral, or dogmatic meaning was mirrored in it.[20] Perkins's emphases reflect the Antiochenes, putting his method on the same continuum as allegorization. He found prophetic, doctrinal, and ethical meaning—namely, a higher sense—in the text, but he relentlessly tied such meaning to the natural sense.

---

20. Frances Young, "Alexandrian and Antiochene Exegesis," in *The Ancient Period*, vol. 1 of *A History of Biblical Interpretation*, ed. Alan J. Hauser and Duane F. Watson (Grand Rapids: Eerdmans, 2003), 334–54.

A pivotal figure in biblical interpretation from the patristic era to the medieval period was Augustine of Hippo. Augustine's hermeneutic necessitated that every passage of Scripture be edifying. All of the articles of faith and all that Christians are to love and hope for are clearly taught in plain literal passages of Scripture. The difficulty, according to Augustine, rests in the fact that not every text teaches one of these edifying elements in the plain literal sense. As a result, when the interpreter encounters such passages, the task is to interpret it figuratively. While the literal sense takes precedent, interpretation at times must move beyond the literal in order to make a text edifying. Augustine set the trajectory of Scripture leading to faith, hope, and love, which was formalized in the Middle Ages into the spiritual senses of allegory, tropology, and anagogy.[21]

MEDIEVAL ANTECEDENTS

Looking back to Augustine, "the medieval hermeneutical tradition can be characterized as an authentic attempt to establish the *sensus literalis* of Scripture as its principal meaning, and give it a theologically normative role in the formation of Christian theology."[22] This attempt in the Middle Ages included neatly defining the *quadriga*. In the *Glossa Ordinaria*, we find that the four senses of the text are

> *historia*, which tells what happened; *allegoria*, in which one thing is understood through another; *tropologia*, which is moral declaration, and which deals with the ordering of behavior; *anagoge*, through which we are led to higher things that we might be drawn to the highest and heavenly.[23]

This approach resulted in two streams of exegesis: one that gravitated away from the literal sense and one that gravitated toward it.[24] For our purposes, a few major figures from this latter perspective will be the focus.

---

21. James S. Preus, *From Shadow to Promise: Old Testament Interpretation from Augustine to the Young Luther* (Cambridge, MA: Harvard University Press, 1969), 13, 21.

22. Preus, *From Shadow to Promise*, 3.

23. Translated in Muller, *Post-Reformation Reformed Dogmatics*, 2:35.

24. For treatments of medieval exegesis, see Henri de Lubac, *Exégèse mediaevale: Les quatre sens de l'Ecriture*, 4 vols. (Paris: Aubier, 1959–1964); Ceslas Spicq, *Esquisse d'une histoirede l'exégèse latine au moyen âge* (Paris: J. Vrin, 1944).

Thomas Aquinas (d. 1274) accepted the *quadriga* but emphasized the literal sense of Scripture. He affirmed the four senses: "Since it is the literal sense which the author intends, and since the author is God, who comprehends all things in his mind together, 'it is not unfitting that there should literally be several interpretations contained in one scriptural word.'" However, Aquinas agreed that Scripture's "manifold nature does not mean that one word indicates different things, but that things indicated by words can be signs of different things. Thus no confusion results, since all interpretations are based on one, that is on the literal, from which alone we can argue." Yet "sacred Scripture loses nothing thereby, since nothing essential to the faith is contained in the spiritual sense of one passage which is not clearly expressed in the literal sense of another."[25] While Aquinas strives to affirm a single literal sense as primary, he retreats to some degree by conceding that several interpretations may be contained in a biblical word as a result of divine authorship. That said, he does give precedence to the literal sense by arguing that words signify things and that these things are what potentially symbolize spiritual things. It is important that Aquinas reaffirmed the Augustinian conviction that everything essential to faith is expressed somewhere in the canon in the plain literal sense. According to Aquinas, these clear places of Scripture alone are appropriate for theological argumentation because they control the interpretation of the more difficult passages.[26]

At the height of medieval scholasticism, Aquinas claimed the historical sense provides the foundation for all other levels of interpretation, at times even insisting that the literal meaning is the sole meaning.[27] It is worth noting the Victorine school in the previous century insisted on the literal meaning as the foundation for all interpretation, claiming the Bible leads one through the letter to the spirit. For example, Hugh of St.

---

25. Thomas Aquinas, *Nature and Grace: Selections from the Summa Theologica of Thomas Aquinas*, ed. and trans. A. M. Fairweather, Library of Christian Classics (Philadelphia: Westminster, 1954), 49.

26. Thomas Prügl, "Thomas Aquinas as Interpreter of Scripture," in *The Theology of Thomas Aquinas*, ed. Rik van Nieuwenhove and Joseph Wawrykow (Notre Dame, IN: University of Notre Dame Press, 2005), 393–94.

27. Richard A. Muller, "Biblical Interpretation in the Era of the Reformation: The View from the Middle Ages," in *Biblical Interpretation in the Era of the Reformation: Essays Presented to David C. Steinmetz in Honor of His Sixtieth Birthday*, ed. Richard A. Muller and John L. Thompson (Grand Rapids: Eerdmans, 1996), 10.

Victor (d. 1141) believed spiritual meaning arises from things signified by the words of Scripture, not the words themselves; therefore, the interpreter must grasp the things signified by the words before spiritual significance can be accessed accurately. This emphasis on the literal sense and the distinction between the signification of words and things was picked up and ultimately formalized by Aquinas.[28]

For Aquinas, a word could only signify one thing, but that one thing could signify spiritual things, thus solidifying the relationship between the literal sense and the other three senses. So in his schema, all the senses are founded on the literal sense—not because the words have multiple meanings, but because the referents of the words belong to biblical history, which broadens their meaning to include spiritual significance. As a result, Aquinas's exegetical procedure was to analyze words and phrases in their context, aiming at units of meaning in the text and thus emphasizing the literal sense as the basis of theology. He occupied himself in his commentaries with expositing the literal sense, identifying the intent of the text.[29] A man of his time, Aquinas utilized the scholastic practice of dividing the text in order to identify the author's argument.[30] These hermeneutical assumptions and exegetical practices stand in a tradition that leads to the interpretive models of the Reformation era by way of exegetes such as Nicholas of Lyra (d. 1349).[31]

Lyra followed Aquinas closely in his definition of the four senses of Scripture. He also similarly stressed the literal sense as foundational and had harsh things to say against contemporary allegorizers.[32] Lyra is known as a champion of the literal sense in the Middle Ages due to his knowledge

28. Beryl Smalley, *The Study of the Bible in the Middle Ages*, 2nd ed. (Oxford: Blackwell, 1952), 83–106; Muller, *Post-Reformation Reformed Dogmatics*, 2:35.

29. Muller, *Post-Reformation Reformed Dogmatics*, 2:36; Eleonore Stump, "Biblical Commentary and Philosophy," in *The Cambridge Companion to Aquinas*, ed. Norman Kretzmann and Eleonore Stump (Cambridge: Cambridge University Press, 1993), 258–59.

30. Prügl, "Thomas Aquinas as Interpreter of Scripture," 403–4. This is important to note because it demonstrates that textual division for the purpose of identifying an argument did not originate with Ramism.

31. Muller, "Biblical Interpretation," 10. For a recent, in-depth study of Aquinas's hermeneutics and exegesis, see Piotr Roszak and Jögen Vijgen, eds., *Reading Sacred Scripture with Thomas Aquinas: Hermeneutical Tools, Theological Questions and New Perspectives*, Textes et Études du Moyen Âge 80 (Turnhout: Brepols, 2015).

32. Preus, *From Shadow to Promise*, 67.

of Hebrew and appropriation of Rashi; he is also known for his concept of the double-literal sense. In the second prologue to his *Postilla litteralis*, his literal commentary on Scripture, he writes, "Just as a building leaning off [its] foundation is inclined to collapse, so a mystical interpretation disconnected from the literal sense is considered to be unsuitable and unfitting." He goes on, "For this reason it is necessary for the person who wishes to be proficient in the study of Sacred Scripture to begin with an understanding of the literal sense."[33] Lyra does not dismiss the spiritual sense. In fact, the thrust of his first prologue to *Postilla litteralis* insists there are indeed rich, spiritual, underlying meanings to the text of Scripture. But this concession presupposes the literal sense as the foundation.[34] Lyra's emphasis on the literal sense drove him to learn Hebrew and also to the Jewish exegesis of Rabbi Solomon (d. 1105), who is commonly referred to as Rashi.[35] Though knowledge of Hebrew was rare in Europe during the Middle Ages, especially outside Jewish communities, nothing highlighted thus far makes Lyra unique.

Lyra's original contribution to biblical interpretation is his double-literal sense. He introduces this idea in the second prologue of *Postilla litteralis*, specifically in his discussion of Tyconius's third rule for interpreting Scripture, the distinction between the spirit and the letter.[36] He writes, "Sometimes the same word has a double-literal sense."[37] He argues for this concept via 1 Chronicles 17:13: "I will be to him a father, and he shall be to me a son." Here, the Lord is speaking of Solomon, who is his son by adoption, so this is the literal meaning. But Hebrews 1:5 applies this verse to Christ

---

33. Nicholas of Lyra, *Postilla litteralis*, trans. James George Kiecker, in "The Hermeneutical Principles and Exegetical Methods of Nicholas of Lyra, O.F.M., Ca. 1270–1349" (PhD diss., Marquette University, 1978), 59. Part of Kiecker's project is the translation of Lyra's prologues. For a discussion of individual passages from Lyra's *postilla*, see Philip D. W. Krey and Lesley Smith, eds., *Nicholas of Lyra: The Senses of Scripture*, Studies in the History of Christian Thought 90 (Leiden: Brill, 2000).

34. Kiecker, "Hermeneutical Principles," 57.

35. For Lyra's use of Rashi, see Eugene H. Merrill, "Rashi, Nicholas de Lyra, and Christian Exegesis," *WTJ* 38 (September 1975): 66–79.

36. Tyconius was a fourth-century Donatist writer whose seven rules for the interpretation of Scripture are quoted and explained by Augustine in *Christian Doctrine*, conferring on the rules a measure of authority.

37. Nicholas of Lyra, *Postilla litteralis*, trans. Kiecker, "Hermeneutical Principles," 66. The rule is one of Tyconius's seven rules, which were given authority by Augustine.

in order to prove his superiority to the angels. This is *also* the literal meaning, as Christ is God's Son by nature. From here, Lyra recalls Augustine's statement to Vincent the Donatist—one Aquinas utilized as well—to make the point that doctrinal proofs cannot be made from spiritual senses. But in Hebrews, the apostolic writer is doing just that, proving that Christ is greater than the angels based on 1 Chronicles 17:13. Ergo, the double-literal sense: one historic and one prophetic.[38] In the end, Lyra emphasized both historical and Christological readings of the Old Testament.[39] Ironically, this allowed future commentators to dispense with the historical-literal meaning for the more edifying literal interpretation.

Jacques Lefèvre d'Étaples (d. 1536)—known as Jacobus Faber Stapulensis in Latin—rejected the twofold literal sense and posited the prophetic literal sense as the only valid one. In his introduction to his commentary on the Psalms, published in 1508, he decries the historical literal sense as the "killing letter" and laments the influence of rabbinic exegesis on Christian interpretations of the Old Testament. He says,

> Therefore I went immediately for advice to our first leaders, I mean the Apostles, the Gospel writers, and the prophets, who first entrusted the seed to the furrows of our soul and opened the door of understanding of the letter of Sacred Scripture, and I seemed to see another sense of Scripture: the intention of the prophet and of the Holy Spirit speaking in him. This I call the "literal" sense but a literal sense which coincides with the Spirit. No other letter has the Spirit conveyed to the prophets or to those who have open eyes (not that I should want to deny the other sense, the allegorical, tropological, and anagogical, especially where the content of the text demands it).[40]

38. Kiecker, "Hermeneutical Principles," 66, 78–79.

39. Muller, *Post-Reformation Reformed Dogmatics*, 2:57. Kiecker's thesis is that Lyra offers a spiritual interpretation and calls it literal; thus, he should not be confused with modern exegesis ("Hermeneutical Principles").

40. Jacobus Faber Stapulensis, *Quincuplex Psalterium*, translated in Heiko A. Oberman, *Forerunners of the Reformation: The Shape of Late Medieval Thought* (Cambridge: James Clarke, 2002), 298.

Lefèvre followed Lyra in his departure from Aquinas, anchoring the literal sense of the New Testament in the human author rather than the divine. Yet the human author is only an instrument, so Paul, for example, should be studied as an inspired spokesman, not merely a historical figure. For Lefèvre, the intention of the prophet or apostle is identical to the intention of the Holy Spirit. The true literal sense is the spiritual sense, and the true spiritual sense is the literal one. This means that when the text requires allegory because of the presence of a figure, then such allegorization is legitimate. But outside this, allegory is the wrong spiritual sense. Lefèvre's concern for the text itself was a humanist concern to establish the "true" or "original" text. However, interpretation was not available merely through grammar, for the Spirit responsible for Scripture is an essential exegetical tool.[41] Far from rejecting the spiritual sense of Scripture, Lefèvre merged it with the literal, in many cases denying the historical literal sense all together.[42]

Lefèvre spent the last ten years of his life associated with Lutheranism and in exile, editing, translating, and publishing biblical materials.[43] He read Luther's Ninety-Five Theses and *The Babylonian Captivity of the Church* with approval and openly pleaded for reform. Sounding quite like a Protestant Reformer, he said,

> let this be in all things the only zeal, comfort, desire: to know the Gospel, to follow the Gospel, to promote the Gospel everywhere. Let all firmly hold to what our Fathers and the primitive Church, red with the blood of the martyrs, felt: to know nothing but the Gospel, since to know that is to know everything.[44]

He admired Zwingli, Farel, and Calvin, but like his contemporary Erasmus, he never openly identified with either the Reformation or the Counter-Reformation.[45] However, Lefèvre's emphases on Christ as the center and

41. Oberman, *Forerunners of the Reformation*, 287–88.

42. Preus, *From Shadow to Promise*, 141.

43. Theodor Harmsen, *"Drink from This Fountain": Jacques Lefèvre d'Étaples, Inspired Humanist and Dedicated Editor* (Amsterdam: Bibliotheca Philosophica Hermetica, 2004), 32–33.

44. Quoted in Oberman, *Forerunners of the Reformation*, 291.

45. Oberman, *Forerunners of the Reformation*, 294.

meaning of Scripture and the internal agreement of Scripture place him in the stream of the Reformers' theological interpretation.[46]

The foundation has now been laid to observe what Muller calls the "fundamental continuity of exegetical interest that remained the property of pre-critical exegesis as it passed from the medieval fourfold model into other models that, in one way or another, emphasized the concentration of meaning in the literal sense of the text."[47] Preus demonstrates that Luther led a kind of theological recovery of the Old Testament in the Protestant Reformation and, in the process, outdid tradition in his christological interpretations.[48] Muller shows that Calvin's literal interpretation of the Old Testament prophecies of the kingdom include the reestablishment of Israel post-exile and establishment in Christ's redemptive work, reform of the church, and final victory of the kingdom in Christ's second coming. Here we see faith, love, and hope. What ought to be believed, done, and hoped for are all three present. This looks a lot like the four senses of Scripture, despite a hermeneutic far more grammatical, philological, and focused on the literal meaning. Even this humanist emphasis on philological and textual examination of Scripture, the Renaissance shift adapted by the Reformers, had medieval precedent. The presuppositions of divine inspiration and the canon's authority over tradition were no more inventions of the Reformers than the drive toward the letter of the text and its grammatical meaning. The transition, as will become apparent, was from the spiritual senses beyond the literal sense to spiritual meaning entirely in the literal sense.[49]

46. Muller, *Post-Reformation Reformed Dogmatics*, 2:61.

47. Muller, "Biblical Interpretation," 12.

48. Preus, *From Shadow to Promise*, 267.

49. Muller, "Biblical Interpretation," 11–12.

THE REFORMED TRADITION

Huldrych Zwingli (1484–1531) stands at the beginning of the Reformed tradition and is eclipsed only by Luther among the early Protestant Reformers.[50] In Zwingli, Scripture has the position of sole authority.[51] He mastered the biblical languages, which he thought essential to exegesis, a conviction evidenced by his use of the Hebrew and Greek Bible during debates and from the structure of "the prophecy" gatherings in Zurich. That said, Zwingli appealed to the fathers, councils, and popes to support his views and to show they were not his alone. He also did not dispense with the *quadriga*. Though stressing the natural sense, Zwingli understood the moral sense always followed because all Scripture teaches, admonishes, or consoles. While he did not carefully distinguish between allegorical and typological, Zwingli found the mystical sense in the symbolism of the historical or natural sense. Further, he had a positive view of non-Christian writers, particularly ancient philosophers, an unusual opinion compared to Luther and later Reformed tradition. But any authority these thinkers enjoyed was derived by and placed under the independent authority of Scripture.[52] Zwingli's guiding principles for biblical interpretation proceeded from both his humanist education and his Reformed understanding of the Christian faith and the Bible.[53]

---

50. Zwingli, Bucer, Calvin, and Musculus were chosen to represent the Reformed tradition for a number of reasons. First, they represent generational diversity, Zwingli and Bucer being first-generation reformers and Calvin and Musculus second. Second, they represent different continental Reformation centers, including Zurich, Strasbourg, and Geneva. Third, they all have a clear influence on England. All these authors were translated into English during the sixteenth century. Further, Zwingli was father of the Reformed tradition, of which many in the Church of England considered themselves a part. Bucer ended his career in England. Calvin and his Geneva housed many of the Marian exiles, helped publish the Geneva Bible, and were major theological influences on the Cambridge predestinarians. Musculus is recognized to have affected the English practical divinity and its emphasis on application. Other representatives could certainly have been chosen; Bullinger, Vermigli, Beza, and Zanchi are especially good candidates as well, but given limited space, these four seemed the natural choice.

51. Zwingli's *Commentary on True and False Religion*, the most significant dogmatic work in the Reformed tradition before Calvin's *Institutes*, illustrates this (*Commentary on True and False Religion*, ed. Samuel Macauley Jackson and Clarence Nevin Heller [Durham, UK: Labryrinth, 1981]).

52. W. P. Stephens, *Zwingli: An Introduction to His Thought* (Oxford: Clarendon, 1992), 40, 30–33.

53. Fritz Büsser argues that Zwingli was indebted to Erasmus for more than humanist method and tools but that he took up Erasmus's biblical theology and merely developed it ("Zwingli the Exegete: A Contribution to the 450th Anniversary of the Death of Erasmus,"

Scripture comes from the Holy Spirit and cannot be understood apart from Spirit-given understanding. Zwingli writes, "We do not need human interpreters, but his anointing, which is the Spirit, teaches us all things." The "canker at the heart of all human systems" is that

> we want to find support in Scripture for our own view, and so we take that view to Scripture, and if we find a text which, however artificially, we can relate to it, we do so, and in that way we wrest Scripture in order to make it say what we want it to say.[54]

Without the Spirit's help, interpreting the Bible to support one's preconceptions is inevitable. Zwingli's emphasis on the Spirit as the single divine author meant that differences and inconsistencies within the text were only apparent, and even such apparent discrepancies extended only to nonessential matters. Divine authorship extended to the whole of the canon, which allowed Zwingli to emphasize sanctification alongside justification and avoid devaluing the Old Testament.[55] These presuppositions also determined Zwingli's practice of exegesis.

For Zwingli, Scripture interprets itself as a result of its internal consistency, which itself stems from the doctrine of inspiration. But what is the mechanism for this self-interpretation? Peter Stephens sums it up well:

> Zwingli uses a number of principles of interpretation in common with his contemporaries, in particular setting disputed passages in their context and comparing passages of scripture, together with the analogy of faith and the traditional fourfold use of scripture. All these modify a simple literalist interpretation of a passage, but, more important for Zwingli, they are part of what it means to let the Spirit (or scripture), rather than men, interpret scripture.[56]

---

in *Probing the Reformed Tradition: Historical Studies in Honor of Edward A. Dowey, Jr.*, ed. Elsie Anne McKee and Brian G. Armstrong, trans. Bruce McCormack [Louisville, KY: Westminster John Knox, 1989], 175).

54. Huldrych Zwingli, "Of the Clarity and Certainty of the Word of God," in *Zwingli and Bullinger*, ed. and trans. Geoffrey W. Bromiley, Library of Christian Classics (Philadelphia: Westminster, 1953), 88.

55. Stephens, *Zwingli*, 36, 63, 140.

56. W. P. Stephens, *The Theology of Huldrych Zwingli* (Oxford: Oxford University Press, 1986), 64.

Zwingli was not a strict literalist, for he recognized the distinction between words and their meaning, which in the case of Scripture needed to be illuminated by the Spirit via Scripture itself.

Zwingli's interpretation of Christ's institution of the Lord's Supper illustrates his method. After discounting alternate views, Zwingli says, "Our present task is to indicate that interpretation of the words: 'This is my body,' which best harmonize with the rest of scripture and the three articles of the Creed. … O Lord open thou our eyes."[57] He immediately moves to a discussion of figurative language in Scripture and then looks at the passage's context. Zwingli compares taking verses out of context to "breaking off a flower from its root and trying to plant it in a garden. But that is not the way: you must plant it with the roots and the soil in which it is embedded."[58] Looking to the context of Christ's phrase, he concludes,

> "This is my body," means, "The bread signifies my body," or "is a figure of my body." For immediately afterwards in Luke 22 Christ adds: "This do in remembrance of me," from which it follows that the bread is only a figure of his body to remind us in the Supper that the body was crucified for us.[59]

This interpretation accounts for the immediate context and the larger context of the whole of Scripture and does not violate the Apostles' Creed, which speaks of Christ in heaven, all the while acknowledging the essential role of the Spirit. This interpretive method, even on this passage particularly, is almost identical to that employed by Perkins.

Martin Bucer (1491–1551), an early Reformer in the German Reformed tradition, is remembered as one who sought union between the two streams of the Magisterial Reformation. He was influenced by Erasmus and humanism and was present at Luther's Heidelberg Disputation. He mentored Calvin and gained international renown from his position at Strasbourg.[60] He spent the last two years of his life in exile as Regius Professor of Divinity at Cambridge, where he helped Thomas Cranmer

57. Huldrych Zwingli, "On the Lord's Supper," in Bromiley, *Zwingli and Bullinger*, 223.

58. Zwingli, "Of the Clarity and Certainty," 87.

59. Zwingli, "On the Lord's Supper," 225.

60. N. Scott Amos argues that humanism extended beyond Bucer's exegetical method to his theological method as well (*Bucer, Ephesians and Biblical Humanism: The Exegete as*

shape the English Reformation.[61] In the Tetrapolitan Confession of 1530, prepared by Bucer and affirmed by him until his death, he writes, "Preachers are to teach from the pulpit nothing else than is either contained in the Holy Scriptures or hath sure ground therein."[62] Bucer did not write explicitly on how to interpret the Bible, but he was an inexhaustible exegete. One scholar quips, "In all his commentaries one observes an eagerness to inform of everything readers conceivably might wish to know and considerable that they would never have thought to require."[63] The length of Bucer's commentaries results from his doing theology in their midst, and in his exegesis he elaborates doctrinal and moral propositions.[64] Despite the fact that Bucer wrote no treatise on interpretation and his commentaries are known to be burdensome, his exegesis proved significant in his context and ultimately revealed his exegetical method.

Bucer's systematic exegesis comes through in his commentary on the Gospel of John. Here he divides the chapters, then comments in three ways. First, he paraphrases the text. Then he makes detailed textual and philological remarks. Finally, he adds observations, which consist of points on theology and application. While Bucer rarely cites his sources, he often names the authorities he uses in his prefaces. Bucer does not hesitate to utilize tradition but explicitly indicates his reliance on authors such as John Chrysostom, Augustine, Erasmus, Brenz, and Melancthon.[65] In the preface to his Psalms commentary, he claims to "have endured to the best of my ability to give the right interpretation to each unit, in accordance above all with the historical context." He goes on, "I am thus able to anchor more

---

Theologian, Studies in Early Modern Religious Tradition, Culture and Society 7 [Cham, Switzerland: Springer, 2015], 6).

61. Donald K. McKim, ed., *Dictionary of Major Biblical Interpreters*, 2nd ed. (Downers Grove, IL: IVP Academic, 2007), 247–48.

62. Arthur C. Cochrane, ed., *Reformed Confessions of the 16th Century* (Philadelphia: Westminster, 1966), 56.

63. R. Gerald Hobbs, "How Firm a Foundation: Martin Bucer's Historical Exegesis of the Psalms," *CH* 53, no. 4 (1984): 480.

64. Bernard Roussel, "Bucer Exégète," in *Martin Bucer and Sixteenth Century Europe: Actes Du Colloque de Strasbourg (28–31 Août 1991)*, ed. Christian Krieger and Marc Lienhard, Studies in Medieval and Reformation Thought (Leiden: Brill, 1993), 1:47.

65. Irena Backus, "Church, Communion and Community in Bucer's Commentary on the Gospel of John," in *Martin Bucer: Reforming Church and Community*, ed. David F. Wright (Cambridge: Cambridge University Press, 1994), 63. See also, Roussel, "Bucer Exégète," 45.

solidly in the historical foundation those things that are interpreted of our Saviour Christ and of the Church."[66] To Bucer, the truth of the historical is the foundation of spiritual meaning. This is in seeming contradiction to his sharp rejection of allegorism:

> For my part, although this abuse is ancient and although today it is enjoyed by learned and well-established people quite extravagantly, I have no doubt that it is the most blatant insult to the Holy Spirit and the cunning infliction of Satan to lure us away from the true and efficacious teaching and examples of Christ in the direction of fruitless human inventions.[67]

In his comments on Psalm 6, Bucer says,

> I know that almost everyone interprets allegory here, dragging off to the spirit the things that the Seer sings deprecating illness and death. But where no necessity compels to allegory, and more certain conjectures do not invite … I would follow the simple interpretation of these things.[68]

Bucer was reluctant to interpret allegorically unless inescapably constrained by the text. But he was not against spiritual interpretation, although he saw it as typology and application. Indeed, events in history carry a certain shadow of Christ and the church, and Scripture addresses the people of God in all ages.[69]

In this period, it is often instructive to look at how an individual exegetes Christ's institution of the Lord's Supper. Bucer is no exception. It is simplistic to understand his doctrine on Christ's presence as a synthesis of Luther and Zwingli, but his view does affirm less than the former and more than the latter. Bucer interprets Christ's words in the context of the new covenant. For this reason, "Everything that Christ did and said in the

66. Hobbs, "How Firm a Foundation," 480.

67. Martin Bucer, "Un Traité d'exégèse pratique de Bucer," translated in McKim, *Dictionary of Major Biblical Interpreters*, 249.

68. Hobbs, "How Firm a Foundation," 489–90.

69. The Tetrapolitan Confession speaks directly to the fact that Scripture furnishes the man of God with all doctrine for belief and direction for practice (Cochrane, *Reformed Confessions of the 16th Century*, 56).

Supper, though done and said by means of bodily signs and words, was nevertheless spiritual in nature, and said and done with a view to eternal life."[70] He concludes in opposition to consubstantiation:

> "This is my body; This is my blood," when carefully assessed both by the analogy of faith and by their immediate context in the passage itself, undoubtedly give utterance and expression to something greater and more majestic in the minds of the saints than merely the conveying of proof that Christ is really in the bread, to be eaten by the teeth in a manner in which he can be eaten by the ungodly.[71]

Bucer makes a similar conclusion, adding the evidence of "exhaustively studying the Scriptures which either contain some reference to the subject or otherwise give a comprehensive statement of the standard of the Christian faith."[72] In these statements, he notes his interpretive argument is based on context, other passages, and the analogy of faith.

Beyond the context of the new covenant, 1 Corinthians 10:16–17 indicates that the rightful use and receiving of the sacrament includes fellowship with the rest of the body, the Son, and the Father himself. At this point comparison is extended further than other accounts of the institution. Communion includes "the Father and the Son and with all the saints of which John speaks in the first chapter of his Epistle, and that unity with the Father, the Son, and all the saints which the Lord prayed for us in John 17."[73] Christ's words of institution are a metaphor, a figure of a divine mystery that can only be known and understood by faith. This fact guards against not only Luther's attempt to translate the metaphor into proper terms but also the Zwinglian reduction of the mystery to symbol. The Reformed conclusions about Christ's body being bounded and circumscribed and in heaven according to the analogy of faith are correct. However, this reality is consistent with Christ's spiritual presence:

70. Martin Bucer, *Common Places of Martin Bucer*, ed. and trans. David F. Wright, Courtenay Library of Reformation Classics 4 (Appleford, UK: Sutton Courtenay, 1972), 324.

71. Bucer, *Common Places*, 326.

72. Bucer, *Common Places*, 335.

73. Bucer, *Common Places*, 388.

> The presence of Christ in this world, whether offered or attested by the word alone or by the sacraments as well, is not one of place, or sense, or reason, or earth, but of spirit, of faith, and of heaven, in so far as we are conveyed thither by faith and places together with Christ, and apprehend and embrace him in his heavenly majesty, even though he is disclosed and presented by the dim reflection of words and sacraments discernable by the senses.[74]

What we have here is an articulation of Christ's presence in the Lord's Supper akin to the well-known conception in Calvin. Bucer is part of the Reformed tradition of exegesis, which means he makes use of the analogy of faith, context, and collation. He also employs spiritual interpretation sparingly, folding it into the natural sense.

John Calvin (1509–1564) was one of the most significant Reformers of the second generation and a loud voice in the Reformed tradition—in no small part because of his biblical interpretation, the enterprise to which he devoted his life. Calvin's three primary endeavors—sermons, commentaries, and the *Institutes*—must not be seen in isolation from one another. The theology of the *Institutes* proceeds out of his exegesis in sermons and commentaries, even as he avoids the unwieldy commentaries of Bucer. In what has been termed the "hermeneutical circle," the "*Institutes* enhances Calvin's work of exposition by providing a broad frame of reference within which to understand individual texts."[75] The *Institutes* "uncovered the architectonic structure of the Bible, the underlying plan of the whole, that placed the details in their proper context."[76] In this way, the *Institutes* acts as a detailed analogy of faith, both drawn from Scripture and intended to help others interpret Scripture. Calvin's exegesis, like virtually all of the Reformers, proceeded on the humanist insight that understanding depended on original languages and historical and literary contexts. Calvin himself mastered Latin, Hebrew, and Greek. Further, with the Renaissance humanists, he gave primacy to patristic interpretation and viewed the

---

74. Bucer, *Common Places*, 391.

75. David C. Steinmetz, "John Calvin as an Interpreter of the Bible," in *Calvin and the Bible*, ed. Donald K. McKim (Cambridge: Cambridge University Press, 2006), 291.

76. Steinmetz, "John Calvin as an Interpreter of the Bible," 291.

Middle Ages as largely a departure from the patristic consensus, a consensus that of course supported Protestantism.[77]

Calvin left no extended treatment of his hermeneutics or interpretive method, but he did leave clues as to his primary interpretive principles. These principles include lucid brevity and the natural sense. Calvin discusses his preference for clarity and concision in the preface to his Romans commentary. He says that he felt "lucid brevity constituted the particular virtue of an interpreter," and while he acknowledges differences of opinion, he is "incapable of being moved by a love of abbreviation."[78] This does not mean that everything Calvin wrote was short. Instead, he was disciplined in letting the text determine the necessary length of his commentary.[79] In his preface to the homilies of Chrysostom, Calvin also reveals his inclination toward expounding the natural sense. Here Calvin argues that tradition, including the church fathers, should not be accepted uncritically. He favors Chrysostom because he "took great pains everywhere not to deviate in the slightest from the genuine plain meaning of Scripture, and not to indulge in any license of twisting the straightforward sense of the words."[80] Calvin understands the expositor must concern himself with the text, and he assumes one can understand what the author intends to communicate therein. This explains his meticulous care for detail and his emphasis on Hebrew and Greek. These are necessary avenues that lead to the natural sense.[81] In his commentaries, Calvin faithfully and consistently sticks to the point of the text, refraining from indulging in unrelated theology.[82] Calvin's preaching went beyond scriptural exposition to include application,

---

77. Steinmetz, "John Calvin as an Interpreter of the Bible," 291.

78. John Calvin, *The Epistles of Paul the Apostle to the Romans and to the Thessalonians*, trans. Ross Mackenzie, Calvin's Commentaries 8 (Grand Rapids: Eerdmans, 1960), 1.

79. Steinmetz, "John Calvin as an Interpreter," 289.

80. W. Ian P. Hazlett, "Calvin's Latin Preface to His Proposed French Edition of Chrysostom's Homilies: Translation and Commentary," in *Humanism and Reform: The Church in Europe, England, and Scotland, 1400–1643; Essays in Honour of James K. Cameron*, ed. James Kirk, Studies in Church History 8 (Oxford: Blackwell, 1991), 145–46.

81. T. H. L. Parker, *Calvin's New Testament Commentaries*, 2nd ed. (Louisville, KY: Westminster John Knox, 1993), 92.

82. Parker, *Calvin's New Testament Commentaries*, 192.

exhortation, and reproof. The nature of preaching made diffuseness and repetition necessary.[83]

Calvin takes the opportunity presented by Galatians 4:21–26 to passionately dismiss the concept of fourfold biblical interpretation. According to Calvin, Paul quotes the history in 4:22–23 as a response to those who would prefer to live under the law. So Paul quotes from the law, but as "the story which he cites seems to have nothing to do with the question, he gives it an allegorical interpretation." Calvin immediately attacks Origen, saying that he and many others "have seized this occasion of twisting Scripture this way and that, away from the genuine sense. For they inferred that the literal sense is too meagre and poor and that beneath the bark of the letter there lie deeper mysteries which cannot be extracted but by hammering out allegories." This speculation was preferred by the world and "with such approbation the license increased more and more, so that he who played this game of allegorizing Scripture not only was suffered to pass unpunished but even obtained the highest applause." For Calvin, this unfortunate turn became "a trick of Satan to impair the authority of Scripture," which God met with judgment by allowing the clear meaning to be buried under false interpretations. Calvin understood Scripture to be "the most rich and inexhaustible fount of all wisdom," but he denied that its riches lay in multiple meanings. The true meaning is the natural and obvious meaning. Moses did not write history so that it would be turned into allegory. Paul is pointing out in what way the history speaks to the present question. Calvin sees this figurative representation of the church as warranted because Abraham's family was the true church at that time. He cites Chrysostom, who understood allegory as application and distinct from the natural meaning. According to Calvin, Paul sees this history as figurative of the two covenants.[84]

None of the Reformers wanted to lose the flexibility of reference afforded to allegory, for the biblical text must be allowed to speak to the church. Though "Calvin will not move from grammatical and historical

---

83. T. H. L. Parker, *Calvin's Preaching*, 1st American ed. (Louisville, KY: Westminster John Knox, 1992), 79.

84. John Calvin, *The Epistles of Paul the Apostle to the Galatians, Ephesians, Philippians and Colossians*, trans. T. H. L. Parker, Calvin's Commentaries 11 (Grand Rapids: Eerdmans, 1965), 84–85.

sensus to an allegorical *sensus*," what he will do is "develop the *complexus* of ideas presented in a text to cover an extended meaning virtually identical in content to that covered by allegory or trope but more closely governed by the grammatical and historical *sensus* of the text."[85] While Calvin would allow only an extremely limited use of allegory, he "wanted to find, if possible, the rich range of spiritual meanings inside the letter of the text rather than behind or beyond it."[86] He commonly accomplished this in two primary ways. First, through analogies rooted in common humanity and a common covenant in both Testaments, parallels could be made between people in Scripture and people in the present, especially in application. For example, in Psalm 137, Israel under Babylon represents the church under the papacy. Second, Calvin makes generous use of typology in order to see Christ in the Old Testament. David Steinmetz powerfully concludes that "the literal sense was for Calvin what the allegorical sense had been for Origen, a *sensus plenior*, a generous, big-bellied letter filled with spiritual significance and unfailingly edifying. It was never reducible to a bare narrative of events."[87] The old "Judaizing Calvin" thesis and the oft-related idea that Calvin was something of a modern interpreter are untenable, even as they remain in vogue to some.[88] When it came to spiritual readings, Calvin was certainly more reserved than traditional interpreters, even among his contemporaries. But he simply did not unconditionally reject them. Like Perkins after him, Calvin used Scripture to interpret itself by carefully reading it in context, a context that included the whole canon in its original languages.

---

85. Richard A. Muller, "The Hermeneutic of Promise and Fulfillment in Calvin's Exegesis of the Old Testament Prophecies of the Kingdom," in *The Bible in the Sixteenth Century*, ed. David C. Steinmetz, Duke Monographs in Medieval and Renaissance Studies 11 (Durham, NC: Duke University Press, 1990), 73. Muller goes on to explain that *complexus* is a technical term in rhetoric, indicating a connection in discourse as important to the meaning of the text as the grammatical *sensus*.

86. David C. Steinmetz, *Calvin in Context* (New York: Oxford University Press, 1995), 270.

87. Steinmetz, *Calvin in Context*, 274.

88. Debora Shugar, "Isaiah 63 and the Literal Senses of Scripture," in *The Oxford Handbook of the Bible in Early Modern England, c. 1530–1700*, ed. Kevin Killeen, Helen Smith, and Rachel Willie (Oxford: Oxford University Press, 2015), 156–57. David Puckett argues that Calvin was uncomfortable with many Jewish and Christian readings of the Old Testament (*John Calvin's Exegesis of the Old Testament* [Louisville, KY: Westminster John Knox, 1995], 16.

Wolfgang Musculus (1497–1563), another disciple of Bucer, served as the preacher and reformer of Augsburg. Musculus's influence, however, stemmed from the writing ministry that occupied the last years of his life as professor of Bible at Berne. He translated many patristic resources and published learned commentaries.[89] His *Loci communes* (1560) offered a doctrine of Scripture that Muller evaluates as occupying "a place of preeminent importance in the first codification of the teaching of the Reformation."[90] This estimation is defended on the grounds that Musculus both incorporates scholastic theology and anticipates the Reformed orthodox statement of the doctrine. For Musculus, the Scriptures are unrivaled in their authority:

> The first rulers of the church saw well, and therefore did attribute the highest authoritie unto holy scriptures, by the direction which the minds of all godly men shoulde be stayed in the obedience of faith, so that they should beleeve those things which be set forth in them to be of all moste true, and whensoever they should forsake this rule, they should be subject unto all level of errors.[91]

Such unequaled authority is derived from Scripture's nature as the word of God. Musculus writes, "Holy scriptures are brought forth not by mans will and wisdom, but given from God for oure salvation, and containe the word not of men, but of God, to get convenient authoritie in our mynds, no otherwise than if God should talke with us face to face." Musculus goes on to ground Scripture's authority as the word of God in the doctrine of inspiration: "That most high and everlasting authoritie of the Canonical scripture commeth from none other, but from God as the author of it. And the holy writers wrote not by the motion of the church, but by the instinct of the holy spirite."[92] Musculus's genius consisted in his ability to bring together old and new.

---

89. Craig S. Farmer, *The Gospel of John in the Sixteenth Century: The Johannine Exegesis of Wolfgang Musculus*, Oxford Studies in Historical Theology (New York: Oxford University Press, 1997), 6–7.

90. Muller, *Post-Reformation Reformed Dogmatics*, 2:77.

91. Wolfgang Musculus, *Commonplaces of Christian Religion*, trans. John Man (London: Henry Bynneman, 1578), 355.

92. Musculus, *Commonplaces of Christian Religion*, 356, 364.

Craig Farmer concludes that Musculus's commentaries reveal

> a judicious appropriation of patristic and medieval exegetical ideas and methods of interpretation, a critical use of humanist biblical scholarship, and an emphasis on moral and allegorical modes of exposition—an emphasis that distinguishes his exegesis from that of most of his contemporaries.[93]

These realties unfolded in his exegetical method, consisting of four major components: *lectio, explanatio, quaestio*, and *observatio*. Musculus would quote several verses and offer a general summary. He would then quote phrase by phrase and offer detailed explanations. This is where he utilized original languages and other humanist tools. Then Muculus would often respond to questions, although *quaestio* was dropped frequently. Finally, Musculus observed doctrines in the text as well as other legitimate applications and allegories.[94] After explaining the literal meaning, he would draw out the spiritual meaning. He speaks of a threefold searching that closely approximates the spiritual senses of the *quadriga*. Scripture must be read christologically and interpreted morally; it should also nurture hope.[95] This method resulted in a simple organization but extensive commentaries.

Despite warning against the excesses of medieval allegory, Musculus makes selective use of the tradition by both presenting and at times reinterpreting allegorical readings.[96] For Musculus, the biblical commentary is a theological genre with expressly theological purposes. So humanist tools and the literal-grammatical meaning they unearth are only the first step in mining interpretation that edifies faith and promotes piety. For example, in opposition to humanist commentators on Jesus' sea miracle, an allegorical image defines the course of Musculus's interpretation. The stormy sea represents the satanic opposition that plagues the followers of

93. Farmer, *Johannine Exegesis of Wolfgang Musculus*, 8.

94. Jordan J. Ballor, *Covenant, Causality, and Law: A Study in the Theology of Wolfgang Musculus*, Refo500 Academic Studies 3 (Göttingen: Vandenhoeck & Ruprecht, 2012), 82.

95. Craig S. Farmer, "Wolfgang Musculus's Commentary on John: Tradition and Innovation in the Story of the Woman Taken in Adultery," in *Biblical Interpretation in the Era of the Reformation*, 221.

96. Craig S. Farmer, "Wolfgang Musculus and the Allegory of Malchus's Ear," *WTJ* 56, no. 2 (1994): 285–301.

Christ, especially ministers of the gospel as symbolized by the disciples. Accordingly, Musculus draws out multiple moral lessons concerning fear, courage, haughtiness, obedience, and carnality.[97] His liberal use of allegory distinguishes his exegesis from his contemporaries.

Musculus also constructively uses moral interpretation, a feature of spiritual exegesis so pronounced that it became a distinctive mark of his exposition.[98] The foundation for his emphasis on application is the profitability of Scripture for doctrine, trial, redress, and instruction, as outlined in 2 Timothy 3:16.[99] For instance, one of Musculus's chief concerns in his 1 and 2 Corinthians commentary is to "describe and defend a distinctively Protestant, indeed reformed, conception of the pastoral office." Here "commentary-writing serves as a platform for instructing ministers and ministerial candidates as to the duties, priorities, and difficulties that accompany the pastoral calling."[100] His emphasis on application, coupled with his accessibility in sixteenth-century England, makes him a predecessor of the doctrine-use formula of English plain-style preaching.[101] As we will see, simplicity of method and the importance of application were part of the English tradition, the milieu to which Perkins prominently contributes.

CONTEMPORARY ENGLISH WORKS

Six works will provide a sampling of Perkins's contemporary English context, showing how Perkins's method was unique, what similarities existed with what came before, and some of its influence. The first two are translations of authors Niels Hemmingson and Andreas Hyperius, both of

97. Farmer, *Johannine Exegesis of Wolfgang Musculus*, 180.

98. Farmer, *Johannine Exegesis of Wolfgang Musculus*, 9.

99. Musculus, *Commonplaces of Christian Religion*, 381.

100. Scott M. Manetsch, "(Re)constructing the Pastoral Office: Wolfgang Musculus's Commentaries on 1 & 2 Corinthians," in *On the Writing of New Testament Commentaries: Festschrift for Grant R. Osborne on the Occasion of His 70th Birthday*, ed. Stanley E. Porter and Eckhard J. Schnabel, Texts and Editions for New Testament Study 8 (Leiden: Brill, 2013), 255.

101. Patrick O'Banion persuasively argues that Jerome Zanchi deserves a share of responsibility for English practical divinity. He demonstrates that Perkins was not neatly separated from the continental Reformed in his emphasis on application. He memorably says that, if one can "describe William Perkins as the father of pietism, then Zanchi, 39 years Perkins's senior and a major influence on his thinking, must be regarded as its grandfather" ("Jerome Zanchi, the Application of Theology, and the Rise of the English Practical Divinity Tradition," *Renaissance and Reformation / Renaissance et Réforme* 29, no. 2/3 [2005]: 110–11).

whom are included as influences in *The Arte of Prophecying*.[102] Two polemical pieces by John Whitgift and William Whitaker precede Perkins's work, and two preaching manuals written by Richard Bernard and John Wilkins follow Perkins's footsteps. Since hermeneutics was not a discipline as such in the sixteenth century, it is not surprising that one must turn to works on preaching, sermons, and commentaries to find interpretive rules and methods outlined. Further, Perkins was the first Englishman to publish a preaching manual, so one must turn to other genres by Englishmen to compare what came before. The following selections lay the foundation for understanding Perkins's preaching manual and the method of biblical interpretation found in its immediate historical context.

Hemmingson's *The Preacher, or Method of Preaching* (1574) belongs in historical surveys of the development of exegetical method on its own merit.[103] The translator states that the purpose of the work is to equip the minister to plainly and orderly break and distribute the word of God unto the people. To this end, the preacher should have proficiency in the liberal arts, especially rhetoric and logic; seek God in fear and humility; and go no further than the Bible, confident that all of Scripture will agree. Hemmingson's volume defends the necessity of piety and the authority of Scripture while implying the analogy of faith and collation. As he enumerates different kinds of interpretation, he emphasizes the importance of the original languages and literary context. At one point, Hemmingson differentiates between teaching and exhortation. Teaching should explain the text in "plaine and common speache, not having any respect to his owne commendation for his eloquence." Exhortation, on the other hand, should account for different kinds of hearers and consist of persuasion, rebuke, and comfort.[104] In Hemmingson we find similar principles of interpretation to Perkins and an emphasis on plain style and application that is characteristic of most Puritan preaching.[105]

---

102. Perkins, *Works*, 2:673. The list of influential authors is not included in the first edition (William Perkins, *Prophetica* [Cambridge: Johannis Legatt, 1592], n.p.).

103. Kenneth G. Hagen, "'De Exegetica Methodo': Niels Hemmingsen's *De Methodis* (1555)," in *Bible in the Sixteenth Century*, 188.

104. Niels Hemmingsen, *The Preacher, or Methode of Preachinge*, trans. John Horsfall (London: Thomas Marsh, 1574), 8, 12–13, 18–19, 53.

105. For expositions of Hemmingson's theology and his influence on the Reformed tradition, see Henrik Frandsen, *Hemmingius in the Same World as Perkinsius and Arminius: Niels*

In *The Practice of Preaching* (1577), Hyperius offers similar principles and emphases as Perkins. Preachers are companions with God in the building of his church. They ought to be furnished with learning, purity, and the power of the Spirit in teaching. While the fathers and other commentators are helpful, preaching ultimately relies on Scripture. According to Hyperius, sermons should be brief, perspicuous, and consist only of lawful parts. There are seven lawful parts: reading of canonical books, invocation, introduction, outline or proposition, confirmation, confutation, and conclusion. Confirmation is the statement of doctrine, which Hyperius refers to as the exposition of common places tailored to the audience. He also argues it is the most worthy part of any sermon. In Hyperius's schema, the conclusion accompanies exhortation. Application, however, is primarily present in the confirmation part of the sermon, the whole of which Hyperius bases on 2 Timothy 3:16. Here he finds doctrine, redargution, institution, correction, and consolation, all from which common places are drawn. While Hyperius does not give significant attention to questions of exegesis, the principles of piety, education, and the primacy of Scripture are apparent. Hyperius does spend substantial time drawing teaching and application from the text, "one of the chief and principle virtues of a faithful teacher."[106] Here especially, we see affinity with Perkins.[107]

In his polemical exchange with Thomas Cartwright, a leader in the Puritan political and ecclesiastical movement, John Whitgift conceded the importance of preaching. In *The Defense of the Answer*, he notes that untrained ministers should not preach but rather read sermons, acknowledging that this was less than ideal. Whitgift believed that one learned

Hemmingsen 1513–2013 (Praestoe, Denmark: Grafik Werk Praestoe, 2013), and Mattias Skat Sommer, "Niels Hemmingsen and the Construction of a Seventeenth-Century Protestant Memory," *Journal of Early Modern Christianity* 4 (2016): 135–60.

106. Andreas Hyperius, *The Practise of Preaching, Otherwise Called the Pathway to the Pulpet Conteyning an Excellent Method How to Frame Diuine Sermons, & to Interpret the Holy Scriptures according to the Capacitie of the Vulgar People*, trans. John Ludham (London: Thomas East, 1577), 3–36, 58, 140, 156.

107. For expositions of Hyperius's preaching manual, see Edward Cecil Meyer, "The First Protestant Handbook on Preaching: An Analysis of the *De formandis concionibus sacris seu de iterpretationescripturarum populair libri II* of Andreas Hyperius in Relation to Medieval Homiletical Manuals" (PhD diss., Boston University, 1967); Graham Allan David Scott, "La première Homilétique Protestante: Le 'De formandis concionibus sacris seu de interpretatione scriptuarum populari libri II,' 1553 et 1562, d'André Gérard Hyperius (1511–1564), introduction, traduction, et notes (PhD diss., Protestant Faculty of the University of Strasbourg II, 1971).

and edifying sermon was better than many unlearned. Reading Scripture was still edifying and effectual, he reasoned, though preaching was the most ordinary and useful means God used to work in hearts. Throughout his defense of reading Scripture and homilies, Whitgift also argues that preaching is best because it explains the text to the unlearned.[108] On this latter point, Perkins and the Puritans would certainly agree.

William Whitaker, in his 1588 *Disputation on Holy Scripture*, systematically discusses biblical interpretation, which in his estimation is a key difference between Protestants and the Church of Rome. In his prolegomena to the question, "Whence the true interpretation of scripture is to be sought?," Whitaker leads by denying the fourfold sense. He argues, "There is but one true and genuine sense of scripture, namely, the literal or grammatical, whether it arise from the words taken strictly, or from the words figuratively understood, or from both together." The three spiritual senses are applications or accommodations of the text. Only from the literal sense can arguments be made, as the literal sense agrees with the mind, intention, and dictate of the Holy Spirit. When a preacher finds this meaning, according to Whitaker, "The supreme right, authority, and judgement of interpreting the scriptures, is lodged with the Holy Ghost and the scripture itself."[109] The Spirit is the illuminator, which accounts for the internal persuasion, while Scripture is its own interpreter, accounting for the external persuasion.

After these preliminary considerations and statements of principle, Whitaker moves to the practice of exegesis. He provides eight means for finding the true sense of Scripture. First and foremost, prayer, faith, and holiness—in short, personal piety—are essential to right interpretation. Second, proficiency in the original languages of Hebrew and Greek is required "to understand the words which the Holy Spirit hath used." Third is consideration of the words themselves, whether they are proper or figurative and modified. Closely related is the fourth means, consideration of context, which includes "the scope, end, matter, circumstances,

108. John Whitgift, *The Defense of the Aunswere to the Admonition against the Replie of T.C.* (London: Henry Binneman, for Humfrey Toye, 1574), 251, 568–74.

109. William Whitaker, *A Disputation on Holy Scripture: Against the Papists, Especially Bellarmine and Stapleton*, trans. William Fitzgerald (Cambridge: University Press, 1849), 402, 406, 409–10, 415.

antecedents, and consequents of each passage." Fifth, each text must be compared with another, the less plain with the more plain. Sixth, comparison also extends to dissimilar passages. Seventh, all expositions should accord with the analogy of faith, which Whitaker defines as "the constant sense of the general tenour of scripture in those clear passages of scripture, where the meaning labours under no obscurity."[110] This consists in the Apostles' Creed, Lord's Prayer, Decalogue, and catechism. Whitaker interprets the words of Christ's institution of the Lord's Supper in accordance with the creed's statement that Christ ascended into heaven as an example. After all these other means of interpretation, Whitaker recommends a cautious use of commentators and theologians. He overlapped with Perkins at Cambridge University and wrote just a few years before Perkins's *The Arte of Prophecying*, and there are remarkable parallels between Whitaker's *Disputation on Holy Scripture* and Perkins's famed preaching manual, especially on the doctrine of Scripture, interpretive principles, and tools of exegesis.

The success of Perkins's *The Arte of Prophecying* resulted in a proliferation of preaching manuals, many of which incorporated Perkins's insights. In his dedicatory epistle for *The Faithful Shepheard* (1607), Bernard quotes Perkins, concluding that his preaching method is a modest contribution, but "a mite in the Lord's treasury." Bernard reveals his dependence on Perkins, though he does some refinement. Sermons should consist of three main parts: exposition, doctrine, and application. Bernard takes the reader through the logical steps of developing a faithful sermon. He encourages plain style and the doctrine-use philosophy of preaching. Like Perkins, he emphasizes application, even enumerating different kinds of hearers, though he combines the humbled and believers for a total number of six rather than Perkins's seven. Bernard actually distinguishes between uses and application, a distinction not found in Perkins. There are primarily four uses of Scripture based on 2 Timothy 3:16, but application is one step closer to the hearers than use. Application is more specific and requires

110. Whitaker, *Disputation on Holy Scripture*, 466–72. David Sytsma notes fundamental continuity between Whitaker and Aquinas in both hermeneutics and exegetical practice ("Thomas Aquinas and Reformed Biblical Interpretation: The Contribution of William Whitaker," in *Aquinas among the Protestants*, ed. David VanDrunen and Manfred Svensson [Hoboken, NJ: Wiley-Blackwell, 2018), 49–74].

the minister to know both himself and his hearers.[111] Bernard develops Perkins's ideas on sermon preparation and delivery, but little development exists in regard to the interpretation of Scripture.

Bernard's method of biblical interpretation mimics Perkins's. The requirements for proper interpretation are a knowledge of grammar; facility in Hebrew, Greek, and Latin; training in rhetoric and other liberal arts; a grasp of theology and the whole of Scripture; and access to good books. For Bernard, like Perkins, all Scripture is either plain or obscure, and the necessities for proper interpretation help one arrive at the true meaning of obscure passages. Plain passages need no explanation, and all doctrine necessary for salvation can be found in such passages.[112] Every passage of Scripture has one true and natural sense, even the unclear passages.

Bernard defines the literal sense as "that which the holie Ghost principally intendeth." So there is only one true and right interpretation. While godly meaning may come from various readings, the proper sense and genuine interpretation agrees with the purpose and scope of the Spirit's intention. One finds this proper sense, the literal sense, with three tools: the analogy of faith, which includes the Apostles' Creed, Lord's Prayer, Ten Commandments, and doctrine of the sacraments; the circumstances of place or context; and finally, by comparing Scripture with Scripture, both like and unlike. Scripture by nature cannot contradict itself. Therefore, when used properly, these three tools result in correct interpretation by letting Scripture interpret itself.[113]

Wilkins, in his *Ecclesiastes, or A Discourse concerning the Gift of Preaching* (1646), views preaching as a particular art. Preaching takes prerequisite abilities beyond academic preparation in languages, sciences, and divinity, including "right understanding of sound doctrine" and "an ability to propound, confirm, and apply it unto the edification of others." According to Wilkins, university training especially overlooks application. As a gift, preaching is "an expertnesse and facility in the right handling and dividing

111. Richard Bernard, *The Faithfull Shepheard, or the Shepheards Faithfulnesse: Wherein Is for the Matter Largely, but for the Maner, in Few Words, Set Forth the Excellencie and Necessitie of the Ministerie; a Ministers Properties and Dutie; His Entrance into This Function and Charge; How to Begin Fitly to Instruct His People; Catechising and Preaching; and a Good Plaine Order and Method Therein* (London: Arnold Hatfield for John Bill, 1607), 9–11, 60–73.

112. Bernard, *Faithfull Shepheard*, 26, 35–38.

113. Bernard, *Faithfull Shepheard*, 28–30.

the word of Truth, as may approve us to be workmen that need not be ashamed." Wilkins adopts the plain style, doctrine-use formula of preaching, suitable to which are the three chief parts of the sermon: explication, confirmation, and application. Here, Wilkins shares Perkins's preaching method and philosophy. He also utilizes Perkins's tools to arrive at a text's true sense or proper meaning. He focuses on the original language and context but asserts that interpretation must contradict neither the analogy of faith nor other Scriptures.[114]

Clearly, Wilkins was familiar with Perkins's writings. Not only did he recommend *The Arte of Prophecying*, he includes many of Perkins's other works in his lengthy catalog of recommended authors and resources. In particular, Wilkins recommends his expositions of Galatians, Jude, and Revelation and lists him among the most eminent in England for preaching and practical divinity.[115] He commends his works on numerous topics: casuistry, the Lord's Prayer, the Apostles' Creed, the Decalogue, polemics against the Church of Rome, patristics, predestination, mortality, free will, knowledge of God, idolatry, witchcraft, preaching, family, justice and equity, callings, the gift of tongues, faith, assurance, and repentance.[116] Wilkins's appreciation for Perkins is clear, and it manifests itself in his proposed methods of preaching and biblical interpretation.

CONCLUSION

Before moving to Perkins, a few conclusions are in order about the exegesis of the English Puritans as they stand within both the Reformed tradition and the history of literal biblical interpretation stretching as far back as the Middle Ages and the patristic era. In the Puritan mind, the disciplinary or ecclesiastical means of understanding Scripture were exegetical techniques of both humanistic and scholastic influence. These means operated within the bounds of certain precritical presuppositions—namely,

---

114. John Wilkins, *Ecclesiastes, Or, A Discourse Concerning the Gift of Preaching as It Fals under the Rules of Art Shewing the Most Proper Rules and Directions, for Method, Invention, Books, Expression, Whereby a Minister May Be Furnished with Such Abilities as May Make Him a Workman That Needs Not to Be Ashamed: Very Seasonable for These Times, Wherein the Harvest Is Great, and the Skilfull Labourers but Few* (London: M. F. for Samuel Gellibrand, 1646), 1, 3–5, 8–9.

115. Wilkins, *Ecclesiastes*, 2, 39, 42, 43, 45.

116. Wilkins, *Ecclesiastes*, 48, 48, 49, 49, 53, 59, 67, 70, 71, 81, 83, 83, 83, 85, 89, 89, 91, 91, 92, 103, 103.

the coherent and consistent message of Scripture and its contemporary relevance.[117] The Puritans strove for mastery of the original languages and labored to get Scripture's grammar and syntax right. They were sensitive to context, both historical and literary, and accounted for genre and rhetorical devices.[118] But even as they approached each text like this—an approach many would consider narrow—we must not presume their affinity with modern interpreters. While the Puritans sought the scope of the text—its author's focus, design, target, and intention—this was determined by biblical context rather than historical situation. They did give attention to historical situations, using language of occasion and circumstance, but these still found their explanation in the context of what comes before and after in the text.[119] Meaning was located in the text for the Puritans, not behind it.

The Puritans' precritical presuppositions are clearer still in their analogies of faith and Scripture. The analogy of faith, when given explicit content, usually included the Apostles' Creed, the Lord's Prayer, and the Decalogue, all robustly interpreted but also limiting the possible meanings the exegete could consider. That God cannot lie or contradict himself, that Scripture is divine, and that the core of Christian doctrine flows faithfully from the Bible are undergirding suppositions. The analogy of Scripture operates on a similar idea. Because of its divine author, Scripture cannot contradict itself. Therefore, Scripture is the best interpreter of itself. This legitimizes the process of bringing clarity to a text by comparing it with other portions of Scripture, both similar and dissimilar.[120] In fact, the broader scope of the Bible—including the biblical covenants and Christ as the substance of the whole—theologically ensures its unity. For most Puritans, federal theology offered a framework for understanding the sweep of biblical history. The old and new covenants represented by the two Testaments are one in substance and differ only in their administration.

117. Henry M. Knapp, "Understanding the Mind of God: John Owen and Seventeenth-Century Exegetical Methodology" (PhD diss., Calvin Theological Seminary, 2002), 62.

118. Thomas D. Lea, "The Hermeneutics of the Puritans," *Journal of the Evangelical Theological Society* 39, no. 2 (June 1996): 276–81; Muller, *Post-Reformation Reformed Dogmatics*, 2:484–89.

119. Knapp, "Understanding the Mind of God," 80–83.

120. Knapp, "Understanding the Mind of God," 63–75; Joel R. Beeke and Mark Jones, *A Puritan Theology: Doctrine for Life* (Grand Rapids: Reformation Heritage Books, 2012), 36; Muller, *Post-Reformation Reformed Dogmatics*, 2:490–94.

The christological focus of the whole Bible flows from this covenant theology. Christ is the scope of Scripture, and everything points to him. This broad scope of Scripture makes Puritan exegesis more open to allegorical and typological interpretation.[121]

Typology cannot be neatly separated from allegory, but it clearly differs in degree. The former is intrinsic to the literal sense, while the latter is extrinsic to it, even as both depend on single divine authorship.[122] Typology is "a method of interpretation where one explains Old Testament events, persons, and practices, as prefiguring the coming person and ministry of the Messiah and his covenant people."[123] In other words, types presuppose reliable history. For example, Jonah really did spend three days in the belly of a great fish. Types also deal with the comparison of facts, which means they cannot be applied indiscriminately. Even if the Puritans often explicitly reject multiple senses, they are keen to press a fuller sense with multiple layers of meaning and applications.[124] Protestant allegory became a specialized type of the literal sense, and tropology and anagogy were often applied forms of the same meaning. Even the most vehement opponents of the *quadriga* could not get away from figurative language in the text.[125] Further, no one wanted to forfeit the text's direct address to their contemporary situation. The elucidation of Scripture for the sake of piety, declaring doctrine, and formulating theology was the enterprise of the medieval church, the Reformers, and the Protestant orthodox.[126]

THE ARTE OF PROPHECYING

Perkins's *The Arte of Prophecying* was not revolutionary in its presentation of interpretive method, not even in England. Though his preaching manual addressed the preparation and delivery of sermons, which

121. Beeke and Jones, *Puritan Theology*, 28–32; Muller, *Post-Reformation Reformed Dogmaticsd*, 2:492.

122. Brian Cummings, "Protestant Allegory," in *The Cambridge Companion to Allegory*, ed. Rita Copeland and Peter T. Struck (Cambridge: Cambridge University Press, 2010), 179.

123. Knapp, "Understanding the Mind of God," 264.

124. Beeke and Jones, *Puritan Theology*, 34–35, 40.

125. Cummings, "Protestant Allegory," 184. Cummings actually ties the theory of Protestant allegory to Perkins, whom he identifies as uniquely positioned to unite the arts of theology and rhetoric into single analysis, which he attempted in *The Arte of Prophecying*.

126. Muller, *Post-Reformation Reformed Dogmatics*, 2:501.

included sustained attention to proper exegetical method, his contributions to homiletics and biblical interpretation were not new. Rather, Perkins remained consistently in the tradition outlined above. That said, what his work lacked in originality, it made up for with clarity, concision, and accessibility. He offered a usable, understandable, and repeatable summary of a Reformed method of interpretation. Perkins's renowned preaching ministry and his international stature as a leading Reformed theologian helped give *The Arte of Prophecying* traction. Following that, its widespread use ensured an enduring influence.

BIBLICAL AUTHORITY

Perkins affirmed *sola Scriptura*, the Reformation doctrine that placed the source and norm of all theological discourse in Scripture alone. In Perkins's understanding, Scripture held absolute authority by its very nature as the word of God. Perkins devotes the third chapter of *The Arte of Prophecying* to the word of God, the object of preaching. His convictions concerning Scripture serve as a foundation for most of what follows: his method of biblical interpretation, his definition of the phrase "word of God," his description of its excellency, his equation of it with Scripture, and his limitation of it to canonical Scripture.

Perkins describes the word of God as "the wisdom of God concerning the truth, which is according unto godlinesse descending from above."[127] As the wisdom of God from above, the word of God is most excellent, a reality manifest in both its nature and operation. By nature, the word of God is both perfect and eternal. Its perfection consists of its sufficiency and purity. Scripture is sufficient in that "the word of God is so complete, that nothing may bee either put to it, or taken from it, which appertaineth to the proper end thereof."[128] The word is pure in that "it remaineth entire in it selfe, voide of deceit and errour."[129] This reference to Scripture's lack of

127. Perkins, *Prophetica*, cap. III; Perkins, *Whole Works*, 2:646. Perkins cites Jas 3:17 and Titus 1:1 in support of this definition.

128. Perkins, *Prophetica*, cap. III; Perkins, *Whole Works*, 2:646. The biblical warrant cited is Ps 19:7; Deut 12:32; Rev 22:18–19.

129. Perkins, *Prophetica*, cap. III; Perkins, *Whole Works*, 2:646. Psalm 12:6 is Perkins's biblical support. This contradicts the anti-inerrancy thesis of Jack Bartlett Rogers and Donald K. McKim, *The Authority and Interpretation of the Bible: An Historical Approach* (San Francisco: Harper & Row, 1979).

error is intentional as it is the necessary inference of Perkins's doctrine of inspiration, which will be highlighted in the coming paragraphs. The eternity of the word also manifests its excellency, a reference to Jesus' teaching in Matthew 5:18 about the word of God not passing away until everything is accomplished. Perkins believes God's word is excellent according to its nature but also according to its operation. The word's excellent operation is its discernment of the spirit of man and its binding of the conscience.[130] In the former, it serves as a mirror, revealing the thoughts and intentions of the heart; in the latter, the word constrains the conscience either to accuse or excuse before God. These functions make God's word utterly unique and therefore attest to its excellency.

Perkins equates the word of God with holy Scripture. He does write that "the word is in the holy Scripture," but unpacks what he means in the next sentence when he describes Scripture as "the word of God written in a language fit for the Church by men immediately called to be *Clerkes*, or *Secretaries* of the holy Ghost."[131] In his exposition of the Apostles' Creed, Perkins affirms that

> Divine, are the books of the old and new Testament, penned either by Prophets or Apostles. And these are not onely the pure *word of God*, but also the *scripture of God:* because not onely the matter of them; but the whole disposition thereof, with the style and phrase was set downe by the immediate inspiration of the holy Ghost.[132]

This statement reveals Perkins's verbal plenary conception of inspiration, a view exhibited throughout his works by interchangeable references to the Spirit and humans as authors of Scripture. For example, regarding Psalm 15 and 1 John on the topic of assurance, Perkins states that they are

130. Perkins, *Prophetica*, cap. III; Perkins, *Whole Works*, 2:647. Perkins cites Heb 4:12; Jas 4:12; Isa 33:22, respectively.

131. Perkins, *Prophetica*, cap. III; Perkins, *Whole Works*, 2:647, emphasis original. Perkins cites 2 Pet 1:21 as support. This contradicts the Barthian interpretation of Perkins of Augustine, "Authority and Interpretation."

132. William Perkins, *An Exposition of the Symbole or Creed of the Apostles according to the Tenour of the Scriptures, and the Consent of Orthodoxe Fathers of the Church* (Cambridge: Iohn Legatt, printer to the Vniuersitie of Cambridge. And are to be solde by R. Bankworth at the signe of the Sunne in Pauls Church-yard in London, 1595), 3; Perkins, *Whole Works*, 1:122, emphasis original.

"parcels of Scripture penned by the Holy Ghost for this end."[133] The canonical status of the books of the Old and New Testaments comes from this reality of inspiration. They serve as a rule for determinations and judgments in all church controversy. Perkins summarizes the whole of canonical Scripture in syllogistic form:

> (a) The true Messias shall be both God and man of the seede of David; he shall be borne of a Virgin; he shall bring the Gospel forth of his Fathers bosome; he shall satisfie the Law; he shall offer up himselfe a sacrifice for the sins of the faithfull; he shall conquer death by dying and rising againe; he shall ascend into heaven; and in his due time he shall return unto judgement. But (b) Jesus of Nazareth the Son of Mary is such a one: He (c) therefore is the true Messias.[134]

The major premise is "the scope or principal drift" of the writings of the prophets; the minor premise comprises the work of the apostles and evangelists.[135] Similarly, in *How to Live Well*, Perkins states, "The scope of the Whole Bible is Christ with his benefits, and he is revealed, propounded, and offered unto us in the maine promise of the word: the tenour whereof is, that God will give remission of sinnes and life everlasting to such as will believe in Christ."[136] This is key because it underscores the unity of Scripture in Perkins's thinking, which in his estimation is only possible through divine authorship.

In his *Cases of Conscience*, Perkins provides six arguments that Scripture is indeed the word of God.[137] First, God is the author of Scripture. One knows this because Scripture speaks of things no one could know except God himself. Therefore, the Bible is the only book that reveals God's will.

---

133. Perkins, *Exposition of the Symbole*, 446; Perkins, *Whole Works*, 1:286.

134. Perkins, *Prophetica*, cap. III; Perkins, *Whole Works*, 2:647.

135. Perkins, *Prophetica*, cap. III; Perkins, *Whole Works*, 2:647.

136. William Perkins, *How to Liue, and That Well in All Estates and Times, Specially When Helps and Comforts Faile* (Cambridge: Iohn Legat, printer to the Vniuersitie of Cambridge, and are to be sold at the Crowne in Pauls Churchyard by Simon Waterson, 1601), 77–78; Perkins, *Whole Works*, 1:484.

137. Perkins enumerates a similar list, but in thirteen points, in his Galatians commentary (*Whole Works*, 2:170) and in *How to Liue*, in five points (*How to Liue*, 70–77; *Whole Works*, 1:483–84).

Moreover, if God did not author it, then it would have been exposed and disproved long ago. The human authors were penmen of the Holy Spirit, for they do not hide their flaws and direct all glory to God. Second, the matter of Scripture proves that it is God's word by elucidating the corruption of humankind through sin and exposing and condemning its particular manifestations. Moreover, Scripture contains the articles of faith, which are far above human reason. It makes predictions that are precisely fulfilled hundreds of years later. Finally, biblical prose is plain and simple yet full of grace and majesty. Third, the effects of Scripture manifest its nature as the word of God. The message of the gospel is contrary to human nature, yet the preaching of it results in conversion. Another effect is the comfort and relief Scripture brings to the conscience. Fourth, the properties of Scripture demonstrate it to be the word of God. It is ancient, providing continuous history from creation, while other histories extend back only to the time of Israel's return from Babylonian captivity. A further property of Scripture is its unity, which simply means the Bible agrees with itself in matter, scope, and end; there are no contradictions. Fifth, the total opposition of Satan and wicked people in belief and practice attest to Scripture's status as the word of God. Sixth, numerous testimonies serve as witnesses to Scripture as God's word: martyrs, heathen writers, and miracles. The testimony of the Holy Spirit is "the argument of all arguments, to settle and resolve the Conscience, and to seale up the certaintie of the word of God." This witness of the Spirit is obtained through "resigning our selves to become truly obedient to the doctrine taught" and "praying unto God for his Spirit, to certifie our consciences, that the doctrine revealed is the doctrine of God."[138] For Perkins, ample evidence exists that points to Scripture as the word of God, but the work of the Spirit ultimately proves this reality to believers.

The way Perkins divides and describes the canonical books leaves clues as to why he interprets the Bible in certain ways. He follows the ordering of books found in the Geneva Bible and provides a summary statement of the contents of each. Perkins sees continuity between the people of God in the Old Testament and the New, which manifests itself in his references to

---

138. Perkins, *Whole Works*, 2:56. Perkins goes on in *Cases of Conscience* to respond to fourteen allegations against the text of Scripture.

both the "church" and the "Church of the Jewes" under the old covenant. He splits up the Old Testament into historical, dogmatic, and prophetic books. According to Perkins, the Bible contains fifteen historical books, Genesis through Job, which are "stories of things done, for the illustration and confirmation of that doctrine which is propounded in other books."[139] The dogmatic books "teach and prescribe the Doctrine of Divinity"; they include Psalms, Proverbs, Ecclesiastes, and Song of Solomon. Finally, the prophetic books offer "predictions, either of the judgements of God for the sins of the people, or of the deliverance of the Church, which is to be perfitted at the coming of Christ." Further, in such predictions, "they doe mingle the doctrine of repentance, and doe almost alwayes use consolation in Christ to them that doe repent."[140] The prophets include Isaiah through Malachi, for a total of thirty-nine Old Testament canonical books. Perkins's division and brief comments on the Old Testament make clear that he believes the Hebrew Scriptures seek to describe more than their historical situation but are addressed to the church and even include Christ himself.

The New Testament, then, plainly propounds the doctrine of the new covenant in histories and epistles. The historical writings include the four Gospels, Acts, and Revelation. The Gospels record a history of the life, deeds, and doctrine of Christ. Before citing Jerome's influential man, lion, ox, and eagle description, Perkins makes some observations of his own. He understands Luke to frame the perfect history or ordering of events, which is why he harmonizes the Gospels according to Luke.[141] The book of Revelation is history for Perkins, but "propheticall history concerning the condition of the Church from the age in which John the Apostle lived unto the end of the world," which indicates his paradigm for understanding apocalyptic literature. The epistles consist of the thirteen Pauline letters and Hebrews through Jude. Perkins includes James, describing it as "concerning works to be joyned with faith"; of 1 John, Perkins says it concerns "the signes of

139. Perkins, *Prophetica*, cap. III; Perkins, *Whole Works*, 2:647. Perkins cites 1 Cor 10:11 and Rom 15:4 as warrant for his description. There are eighteen historical books if the Samuel, Kings, and Chronicles duplicates are counted separately.

140. Perkins, *Prophetica*, cap. III; Perkins, *Whole Works*, 2:648.

141. For Perkins's harmony, see William Perkins, *Specimen Digesti, Sive Harmoniae Bibliorum Veteris et Novi Testamneti* (Cantabridgiae: Ex officiis J. Legat, 1598), prolegomena; Perkins, *Whole Works*, 2:678.

fellowship with God."[142] Here, relatively early in his career, both his soteriological formulation and the assurance of faith include the necessity of works.

Not only is canonical Scripture the word of God, but this inspired authoritative status is limited to canonical Scripture. Perkins offers a number of proofs to back up this claim. The inward testimony of the Holy Spirit brings about a surety that Scripture alone is the word of God. The Spirit speaks in the Scriptures, "not only telling a man within his heart, but also effectually persuading him, that these books of Scripture are the word of God."[143] Perkins enumerates ten further proofs, but these are merely proofs of declaration or testification. They are not effectual like the witness of the Spirit. These proofs include the perpetual consent of the church, affirmation by enemies of the faith, antiquity, fulfillment of prophecy, matter, unity, miraculous preservation, simple majesty of the words, and the fact that writers included their own blemishes. Perkins also includes Scripture's effectual operation on human beings, despite it being contrary to their reason and affections. The apocryphal books, on the other hand, should not be reckoned canonical because they were not written by the prophets, penned in Hebrew, or referenced by the New Testament writers; they also contain false information and contradictions to Scripture. Thus the word of God is limited to the sixty-six books of canonical Scripture.[144] Perkins summarizes his conviction that Scripture is the source and norm of theological discourse well in his exposition of the Apostles' Creed. He states,

> the authoritie of these books is *divine*, that is, absolute and soveraigne: and they are of sufficient credit in and by themselves, needing not the testimony of any creature; not subject to the censure either of men or Angels; binding the consciences of all men at all times, and being the onely foundation of our faith, and the rule and canon of all truth.[145]

142. Perkins, *Prophetica*, cap. III; Perkins, *Whole Works*, 2:649.

143. Perkins, *Prophetica*, cap. III; Perkins, *Whole Works*, 2:649. Perkins cites Isa 59:21 as evidence. This work of the Spirit is similar to what one finds in Calvin.

144. Perkins, *Prophetica*, cap. III; Perkins, *Whole Works*, 2:650.

145. Perkins, *Exposition of the Symbole*, 3; Perkins, *Whole Works*, 1:122, emphasis original.

Perkins consistently argues that Scripture alone is absolutely authoritative as the word of God, a commitment that determines his method of biblical interpretation.

BIBLICAL INTERPRETATION

In chapter 4 of *The Arte of Prophecying*, Perkins transitions to the interpretation of Scripture, which is part of the preparation for preaching and begins with a five-part suggestion for the private study of divinity. Perkins's suggestions for the private study of Scripture are significant because they anticipate his stated method of biblical interpretation. First, Perkins recommends one "diligently imprint both in thy minde and memorie the substance of Divinitie described, with definitions, divisions, and explications of the properties." Perkins does not propose coming to Scripture without presupposition or expectancy; on the contrary, one's mind should have creeds, confessions, and a grasp of theology firmly in mind. This will manifest itself in Perkins's interpretation as an emphasis on the analogy of faith. Perkins's second suggestion is to read Scripture in a certain order, "using a grammaticall, rhetoricall, and logicall Analysis, and the helpe of the rest of the Arts." Perkins recommends reading the text of Scripture in context and using all of one's learning and rational powers. This anticipates his interpretive method's attention to circumstances of place. Further, the order Perkins advocates is important. One should start with the New Testament, specifically Romans and then John, which are "the keyes of the new Testament."[146] Proceeding to the Old Testament, one should begin with the dogmatic books, particularly Psalms; then the Prophets, especially Isaiah; and finally end with the historical books, chiefly Genesis.[147] Perkins is clear that this implies primacy of order, not differing levels of authority, and it is in line with Protestant emphases at large. Perkins largely adheres to this in his citation throughout his works. Third, Perkins recommends the utilization of orthodox writers, with special attention given to ancient ones. This practice, too, is apparent in Perkins's own work. Fourth, Perkins says to keep commonplace books, a discipline that aids the comparison of

146. Perkins, *Prophetica*, cap. IV; Perkins, *Whole Works*, 2:650–51.

147. Perkins concludes this Old Testament order of emphasis from the fact that the New Testament writers quote from Psalms and Isaiah with the most frequency (Perkins, *Prophetica*, cap. IV; Perkins, *Whole Works*, 2:651).

Scripture with its similar and dissimilar passages. Finally, "before all these things God must earnestly bee sued unto by prayer, that he would blesse these meanes, and that he would open the meaning of the Scriptures to us that are blinde."[148] Such primacy given to prayer and reliance on God anticipates Perkins's understanding of the Spirit as the principal interpreter of the Bible. These five suggestions for private study serve to equip the interpreter to competently handle the Scriptures.

According to Perkins, interpretation is "the *Opening* of the words and sentences of the Scripture, that one entire and natural sense may appeare." After describing the *quadriga* of the Church of Rome, he concludes that "her device of the foure-fold meaning of the Scripture must be exploded and rejected." Perkins goes on: "*There is one onely sense, and the same is the literall*. An allegory is only a certaine manner of uttering the same sense. The Anagogie and Tropologie are waies, whereby the sense may be applied."[149]

Two things need to be highlighted at this point. First, while Perkins strongly dismisses the *quadriga*, the three spiritual senses do not disappear in his determination of meaning. Second, Perkins uses the language of "natural sense" in his definition of interpretation then moves to "literal sense" in his response to the exegesis he equates with the Church of Rome. Therefore, the literal and natural senses are used interchangeably, the former being an inherited designation and the latter being more helpful for our purposes. Natural sense allows for the necessary flexibility when accounting for rhetorical devices and figures. It distances us from the historical-critical method, rigidity of language, and fixation on human authorial intent—three missteps often implicitly implied in the modern use of the term "literal." For Perkins, interpretation requires arriving at the natural sense of the words on the page, words in the case of Scripture that were authored by God the Holy Spirit and are addressed to the church throughout the ages.

Perkins further comments on the topic of multiple senses in his exposition of Galatians 4:24, where Paul says, "These things are said by allegory." Again, after recounting the *quadriga*, Perkins claims,

---

148. Perkins, *Prophetica*, cap. IV; Perkins, *Whole Works*, 2:651. Perkins cites Ps 119:18 and Rev 3:18 in support of this necessary reliance on God.

149. Perkins, *Prophetica*, cap. IV; Perkins, *Whole Works*, 2:651, emphasis original.

> But I say to the contrary, that there is but one full and intire sense in every place of Scripture, and that is also the literall sense, sometimes expressed in proper, and sometimes in borrowed or figurative speeches. To make many senses of Scripture is to overturne all sense, and to make nothing certaine. As for the three spiritual senses (so called) they are not senses, but applications or uses of Scripture.[150]

In this case, with Paul's reference to Abraham's family, there "are not two senses, but two parts of one full and intire sense. For not only the bare history, but also that which is thereby signified, is the full sense of the holy Ghost."[151] This passage illustrates that Scripture was not only written in proper terms but also in divine figures and allegories. Perkins lists Song of Solomon, Daniel, Revelation, Old and New Testament parables, and individual psalms as more examples of divine figures or allegories in Scripture. At times, the text demands a figurative reading, and in certain places there are multiple referents in a single sense; in short, the spiritual senses are folded into the literal or natural sense.

How does one distinguish between a proper and figurative reading? Perkins offers a rule: "If the proper signification of the words be against common reason, or against the analogy of faith, or against good manners they are not then to be taken properly, but by figure."[152] For Perkins, the meaning of Scripture cannot be irrational, immoral, or contrary to the analogy of faith. This means there is still room for a range of interpretations and in no way necessitates the Church of Rome's magisterium or authoritative tradition. Commenting on the same Galatians passage, Perkins asserts, "The church hath no divine and infallible authority distinct from the authority of Scriptures (as the Papist teach) but onely a ministry, which is to speake in the name of God, according to the written word." Describing *how* this operates in interpretation, Perkins declares,

> Scripture is both the glosse and the text; And the principal meanes of the interpretation of Scripture, is Scripture it selfe. And it is a

150. Perkins, *Whole Works*, 2:298.

151. Perkins, *Whole Works*, 2:298.

152. Perkins, *Whole Works*, 2:298. Perkins uses Christ's words "I am the vine" and "this is my body" to illustrate this point.

> meanes, when places of Scripture are expounded by the Analogy of faith, by the words, scope, and circumstances of the place. And the interpretation which is suitable to all these, is sure, certaine, and publike: for it is the interpretation of God.[153]

This method of biblical interpretation, which allows Scripture to interpret itself, is developed in *The Arte of Prophecying*.

After addressing the singular sense of Scripture in *The Arte of Prophecying*, Perkins transitions to how one arrives at this sense. Two related concepts are that "the principall Interpreter of Scripture, is the holy Ghost" and "the supreme and absolute meanes of interpretation, is the Scripture it selfe."[154] These are interrelated because Perkins has already expressed the necessity of reliance on the Spirit and that the word of God is limited to canonical Scripture. Beyond this, that the Spirit is the divine author of Scripture makes him the best interpreter of it. Perkins describes a threefold method for interpreting Scripture according to Scripture: "The meanes subordinated to the Scripture, are three; the analogie of faith, the circumstances of the place propounded, and the comparing of places together."[155] He goes on to define each of the three tools.

First, "the *Analogy* of faith is a certaine *abridgement* or *summe* of the Scriptures, collected out of the most manifest and familiar places."[156] This includes the Apostles' Creed, a clear statement of belief, and the Ten Commandments, a distillation of love. It does not entail a reductionist

---

153. Perkins, *Whole Works*, 2:301. This contradicts McKim's claim that for Perkins, Ramism was key to God's interpretation (McKim, *Ramism in William Perkins' Theology*, 74).

154. Perkins, *Prophetica*, cap. IV; Perkins, *Whole Works*, 2:651. Perkins quotes 2 Pet 1:20 and Neh 8:8 respectively in support of these concepts.

155. Perkins, *Prophetica*, cap. IV; Perkins, *Whole Works*, 2:651. The participle "subordinated" here should not be understood as subservience or secondary importance. Perkins's Latin phrase is "Scripturae subordinata media sunt tria." Here the lexical form *ordino*, meaning "to order or arrange," is prefixed with *sub-*, meaning "under." *Subordinata* literally means "to order under" and does not necessitate inferiority. The analogy of faith, circumstances of place, and comparing of places are subordinated means of interpretation to Scripture, meaning they are ordered under, come second, or ordained to aid Scripture. They are the means by which Scripture interprets itself. This is clear from Perkins's rules for plain and difficult passages. An alternative meaning must be given when the literal connotation of the words is contrary to the analogy of faith, and this alternative must agree with other passages and the context (Perkins, *Whole Works*, 2:654). These three means are how Scripture interprets itself, they are from Scripture, and they are in no way of secondary rank.

156. Perkins, *Prophetica*, cap. IV; Perkins, *Whole Works*, 2:651–52, emphasis original.

understanding of the creed and Decalogue but rather a robust interpretation of both. Perkins himself expounds upon both the creed and the Decalogue at length elsewhere. Therefore, the analogy of faith as Perkins implements it is akin to systematic theology. Richard Muller defines the analogy of faith as "the use of a general sense of the meaning of Scripture, constructed from the clear or unambiguous loci, as the basis for interpreting unclear or ambiguous texts." This accurately reflects Perkins's employment of the analogy of faith. It is distinguished from the more basic analogy of Scripture, which is "the interpretation of unclear, difficult, or ambiguous passages of Scripture by comparison with clear and unambiguous passages that refer to the same teaching or event."[157] In summary, the analogy of faith is a distillation of the meaning of Scripture, a complex Reformed theology that serves as an interpretive grid, while the analogy of Scripture speaks to the unity of the Bible.[158] The analogy of Scripture allows for the comparing of places, but before getting to collation, Perkins defines his second tool: context.

The circumstances of place propounded are "who? to whom? upon what occasion? at what time? in what place? for what end? what goeth before? what followeth?"[159] Interrogating a text with this series of questions forces consideration of historical context, grammar, and immediate context—indeed, the words of the text itself.

Third, "collation or comparing of places together, is that whereby places are set like parallels one beside another, that the meaning of them may more evidently appeare."[160] Perkins goes on to describe collation in a number of ways. It may include comparing the place with other places where the passage is cited, perhaps verbatim or with alteration. Collation includes the comparing of places that are either like or unlike. This exercise presupposes the analogy of Scripture, which itself depends on divine

157. Richard A. Muller, *Dictionary of Latin and Greek Theological Terms: Drawn Principally from Protestant Scholastic Theology* (Grand Rapids: Baker Academic, 1985), 33.

158. There is a level of circularity in the analogy of faith. While much of its content comes from clear propositions in Scripture, there are elements that proceed from the interpretation of an individual tradition. For instance, a Lutheran analogy of faith will differ from a Reformed one on the communication of attributes between the natures of Christ. So to a degree, Perkins's analogy of faith presupposes biblical interpretation.

159. Perkins, *Prophetica*, cap. IV; Perkins, *Whole Works*, 2:652.

160. Perkins, *Prophetica*, cap. IV; Perkins, *Works*, 2:652.

inspiration, which makes Scripture utterly authoritative and therefore the standard for its own interpretation.

Perkins's method of biblical interpretation uses Scripture to interpret itself through the analogy of faith, context, and collation. This order is significant, and whenever summarizing his method, Perkins remains true to it. The analogy of faith does not so much determine the meaning of a text as it rules out aberrant interpretations. It places the boundaries within which accurate interpretation can take place. For example, when Christ institutes the Lord's Supper with the words "this is my body," the interpretive options are limited by the fact that Christ ascended into heaven and remains at the right hand of the Father. Therefore, any reading that results in consubstantiation is out of bounds.

Circumstances of place—or context—is where the heavy lifting of exegesis happens, including grammatical, rhetorical, historical, and literary analysis. All contextual exegesis persists on an intense awareness that the meaning of words are largely determined by their surroundings. To again use the institution of the Lord's Supper as an example, Christ's words are a metonymy of the subject for the adjunct; the bread is a sign of Jesus' body. This is fitting in this instance because the narrative says he broke the bread. He certainly did not break his own body with his hands, but the breaking of the bread was a symbol. Jesus says it is given for the disciples. Again, the bread cannot be said to be given for them, but rather it symbolizes Jesus' giving of himself. Christ ate the bread but did not eat himself. The meal is to be continued in remembrance of Jesus until he returns, which implies he is not corporally present.

Collation then verifies or qualifies a given interpretation by comparison with similar and dissimilar passages. That the bread of the Lord's Supper is a sign of Jesus' body accords with other texts of Scripture. For instance, Genesis 17:10 teaches that circumcision is a sign of the covenant. Acts 22:16 asserts that baptism symbolizes the washing away of sins. In John 6:35, Jesus himself uses the "bread of life" as a representative symbol.[161]

While this order is significant for understanding Perkins's method, it does not follow that his exegesis always neatly respects this systematic, step-by-step process. Further, Perkins does not always make the operation

161. Perkins, *Prophetica*, cap. V; Perkins, *Whole Works*, 2:654–55.

of these tools explicit in his exegesis. What will become apparent in the analysis of Perkins's interpretation in the following chapters is that when Perkins interprets Scripture—which he does in almost everything he writes—he does so using at least one element from his threefold method. Sometimes he uses a combination or even all of them.

Perkins adds nuance and further direction to his interpretive method in the fifth chapter of *The Arte of Prophecying*. Places of Scripture are either "Analogicall and plaine, or Crypticall and darke," and Perkins proposes rules for determining which of these two is the case. First, he writes, "If the natural signification of the words of the place propounded doe agree with the circumstances of the same place, it is the proper meaning of the place." At this point, he asserts the perspicuity of Scripture: "every article and doctrine concerning faith and manners, which is necessary unto salvation, is very plainly delivered in the Scriptures." Perkins's second rule is:

> If the native (or natural) signification of the words doe manifestly disagree with either the analogie of faith, or very perspicuous places of Scripture: then the other meaning, which is given of the place propounded, is natural and proper, if it agree with contrary and like places, with the circumstances and words of the place, and with the nature of that thing which is treated of.[162]

An example of this is the interpretation of "this is my body" outlined above. Here, the analogy of faith limits certain interpretive options, the circumstances of place determine meaning, and collation affirms the interpretation—just as this rule for handling unclear passages promotes.

From his rule for handling unclear passages, Perkins draws six further conclusions, three of which require significant attention. Conclusion one is "the supply of every word which is wanting, is fitting for the place propounded, if it agrees with the analogie of faith, and with the circumstances and words of the same place."[163] In essence, there are times when words must be added to make sense of statements, but these are implied by the text.

162. Perkins, *Prophetica*, cap. V; Perkins, *Whole Works*, 2:654.

163. Perkins, *Prophetica*, cap. V; Perkins, *Whole Works*, 2:655.

Second, "if that other exposition of the place propounded doe change one noune (or name) for another, then the words of the place containe in them a trope, or borrowed speech."[164] Often, the natural sense is not the literal meaning strictly defined. Perkins enumerates some key examples from Scripture. Anthropomorphisms occur when biblical authors metaphorically project human attributes onto God. Sacramental metonymy offers the sign for the thing signified, which is crucial for the Reformed understanding of the Lord's Supper. Synecdoche in the communication of properties protects orthodox Christology. When evil things are accomplished by God, this must be viewed as his operative or working permission. Things begun and being fulfilled are at times spoken of as complete. Moral commands against specific sins include all the sins of that kind.[165] Threats and promises always include conditions of repentance and faith respectively. Things said of one person of the Trinity do not exclude the other divine persons, for the outward works and all attributes are to be understood inclusively. When God is considered absolutely, the three persons are comprehended, but when the term "God" is used in conjunction with another person of the Trinity it designates the Father. It is not rare for Scripture to use a general word for a more specific term, such as the case of "all" for "many" and vice versa. Perkins presents an exhaustive and sophisticated breakdown of figurative biblical language.[166]

Perkins's third conclusion is "Grammaticall and Rhetoricall proprieties of words signify diversity with those words." Again, Perkins enumerates some key examples with illustrations from Scripture. An ellipsis signifies brevity or swiftness of affections. "Exallage of the preterperfect tense" identifies a time past for a time in the future as in the oracles of

164. Perkins, *Prophetica*, cap. V; Perkins, *Whole Works*, 2:656.

165. Perkins expands on this in his five rules for interpreting the Decalogue in his *Golden Chaine*. These principles are (1) the negative assumes the positive and vice versa; (2) the affirmative bind at all times but not to all times, while negative bind at and to all times; (3) under the vice expressly forbidden are included all sins of that kind; (4) the smallest sins are entitled the same as the sins expressly forbidden; and (5) every command assumes the exception, "unless God command the contrary" (William Perkins, *Armilla Aurea Id Est, Theologiae Descriptio Mirandam Seriem Causarum & Salutis & Damnationis Juxta Verbum Dei Proponens: Eius Synopsim Continet Annexa Tabula. Editio Tertia Recognita & Aucta. Accesit Practica Th. Bezae pro Consolandis Afflictis Conscientiis* [Cantabridgiae: Ex officina Johannis Legatt. Extant Londini apud Abrahamum Kitson, ad insigne Solis in Camiserio D. Pauli, 1592], 74–75; *Whole Works*, 1:32).

166. Perkins, *Prophetica*, cap. V; Perkins, *Whole Works*, 2:656–58.

the prophets. Pleonasm occurs in several forms. When a substantive is repeated in the same case, it indicates force and emphasis, a multitude, distribution, or diversity and variety. Repetition of a substantive when one is governed by another denotes significance and certainty in the singular and excellency in the plural. Repetition of an adjective and sometimes of a substantive as well shows exaggeration or increase. Repetition of the verb provides either emphasis or vehemence. Repetition of a conjunction designates earnestness. Finally, repetition of a sentence as a whole implies distribution or emphasis or is done for the sake of exposition. Tropes enlarge the sense and nourish faith. Irony signifies a just consequence of sin. Interrogation suggests earnest observation, denial, forbidding, or affections. Concession or yielding intimates a denial and reprehension. Clearly, Perkins offers a thorough and erudite presentation of grammatical and rhetorical forms.[167]

Perkins's fourth conclusion is, "If the Opposition of unlike places shall be taught to be, either not of the same matter, but of name only, or not according to the same part, or not in the same respect, or not in the same manner, or not at the same time, a reconciliation or agreement is made."[168] For example, David's request for judgment according to his righteousness in Psalm 7:8 seems to contradict Isaiah's statement that fallen humanity's righteousness is as filthy rags in Isaiah 64:6. These are reconciled by recognizing the contradiction is not in the same respect. David speaks of a righteousness of cause or action, while Isaiah refers to the righteousness of a person.

Perkins goes on to provide a number of cautions in the reconciling of places. First, the biblical authors wrote of things that preceded them according to the custom of their own time. For instance, Moses references Bethel in writing about Abraham (Gen 12:8) even though it was named Luz in Abraham's day (Gen 28:19). Second, allegories should be expounded according to the scope of the passage in which they are found. Third, places and persons in Scripture sometimes have multiple names or distinct persons and places have a single name. Fourth, some accounts leave out names of princes or the number of years they reigned because of the

167. Perkins, *Prophetica*, cap. V; Perkins, *Whole Works*, 2:658–59.

168. Perkins, *Prophetica*, cap. V; Perkins, *Whole Works*, 2:659.

ruler's wickedness. Fifth, time is spoken of either completely or incompletely, and the parts are understood inclusively or exclusively. For example, Matthew 17:1 claims that after six days Jesus led his disciples to the mount of transfiguration, while Luke 9:28 speaks of eight days. The reconciliation is that Matthew references exclusively the days between and Luke includes the partial day before and after. Sixth, in royal chronologies, occasionally a son's reign overlaps with that of his father. Seventh, the hours of the day in the east are divided into twelves and then also in quadrants. This accounts for Mark and John's supposed conflict regarding the time of the crucifixion. Eighth, the lesser number is to be counted under the greater or more complete number. Ninth and last, filiation can be either natural or legal. All of these considerations must be kept in mind when reconciling what seem to be contradictory places of Scripture.[169]

Perkins finishes by offering his fifth and sixth conclusions. Conclusion five is "when the naturall sense of the place (propounded) is given by the foresaid helpes, a signification of a word signifying divers things shall bee given, which is fitting to the place."[170] In short, meaning is determined by context when a word has multiple definitions. Perkins's last conclusion is:

> if a word given in a Bible, whether it be an Hebrew or a Greek; if first it doe agree with Grammaticall construction, and with other approved copies: if also it doe agree in respect of the sense with the circumstances and drift of the place, and with the analogie of faith, it is proper and natural.[171]

This final conclusion verifies the practice of textual criticism. Context and a close reading of the text are essential to Perkins's method.

CONCLUSION

One may conclude that at its most basic level, Perkins's method of biblical interpretation is that Scripture must interpret itself. This method is based on the authority of Scripture derived from its nature as the word of God. Right interpretation for Perkins leads the reader and exegete to the single,

169. Perkins, *Prophetica*, cap. V; Perkins, *Whole Works*, 2:659–61.

170. Perkins, *Prophetica*, cap. V; Perkins, *Whole Works*, 2:662.

171. Perkins, *Prophetica*, cap. V; Perkins, *Whole Works*, 2:662.

natural sense of the words on the sacred page. Scripture interprets itself through the analogy of faith, context, and collation. None of these three rise above Scripture, for even the analogy of faith is an extension of clear biblical teaching and only authoritative insofar as it remains consistent with Scripture. The tools are to be used individually or in tandem based on the demands of the biblical text. The analogy of faith, a robust interpretation of the creed and Decalogue, operates as a theological system and sets the boundaries of interpretation. Context is usually the determiner of meaning. As we saw, attention to the circumstances of place must account for a complex landscape of figures as well as grammatical and rhetorical forms. Collation, made possible by the unity of biblical teaching articulated in the analogy of Scripture, verifies and nuances the interpretation. Via this method, Perkins interprets Scripture with Scripture. The rest of this book will demonstrate that he consistently implemented this method throughout his works.

3

—

EXEGESIS IN SERMONS AND COMMENTARIES

Perkins thundered against England, exhorting his countrymen to repentance from the opening verses of Zephaniah 2. His nation, like Israel, was not worthy to be beloved. Englishmen had every advantage but refused to wholly turn to God. In a particularly potent paragraph, Perkins cries,

> Looke at the outward face of our Church, at the signes of God's love, which are amongst us, and at God's dealing with us; and behold, we are a most beautiful Church, a glorious Nation, a Nation to be admired and wondered at: but looke at the lives of our ordinarie professors, looke at our sinnes, and at our requiting of God's love; and we are a people of Sodom, as full of iniquities as they were, whose sinnes are so many, so rife, and so ripe, that at the last they will even bring down fire and brimstone, or some other strange judgement upon us, if repentance doe not prevent it, or the cries and prayers of holy men stay not Gods hand. So then let us all here assembled, grant and confesse, that wee are a Nation, so farre from being worthy to be beloved, as that wee are most worthy to bee hated, and to have all the wrath of God powred upon us.[1]

It is no mystery why, in the publication title, the editor included "powerful" as a modifier before "exhortation to repentance"! Preaching itself was one of God's tools to bring about repentance, which, if ineffective, would be followed by judgment. Perkins compares preaching and judgment to two fans used by God to drive away chaff. He claims that "when the gospel is preached to a Nation or Congregation, it fannes them, and

1. Perkins, *Whole Works*, 3:422.

tries them, and purgeth them, and so severs them, that a man may see a manifest difference of the chaffe and the wheat, that is, of the godly man and the wicked man." In England, "the Gospell hath beene preached these five and thirtie yeares: and is daily more and more, so that the light thereof did never shine more gloriously, since the Primitive Church: yet for all this, there is a general ignorance."[2] Though given matchless grace, Perkins said his countrymen had responded in unrepentance, which, if left unchanged, would undoubtedly result in judgment.

What were the sins of the English people? Superstition, ignorance, and immorality. Superstition came primarily through the worship of the Church of Rome, witchcraft, and astrology, as will be discussed in chapter 6. Ignorance in the context of catechism is considered in chapter 5. Chapter 4 addresses the economic issues of the age, which resulted in an increase of the wandering poor. The unemployed who had the ability to work were considered idle—a moral failing. Such rogues and vagabonds were all predatory in the Elizabethan mind.[3] Moreover, economic pressures delayed entrance into adulthood—a substantial obstacle in a society that did not value youth. Instead, many saw youth as a liability, an age of independence and immorality. In order to become an adult, a man needed a wife, a house, or a decent job, the interdependency of which made them hard to come by. These problems affected women, too, as single women who worked to support themselves were considered suspect.[4] In short, cynical estimations of society's trajectory were common.

Evidence suggests Perkins's perception of immorality was to a degree consistent with reality. Elizabeth's reign saw some of the highest murder and execution rates in recorded English history. It also witnessed a dramatic rise in felony prosecutions from around 1580, with a spike in executions in the 1590s.[5] Perkins was no stranger to crime and punishment. After his ordination, he ministered at the Cambridge jail for his first preaching post. A biographer recalls at least one instance of Perkins ministering to

2. Perkins, *Whole Works*, 3:424–25.

3. Steve Hindle, "Poverty and the Poor Laws," in *The Elizabethan World*, ed. Susan Doran and Norman Jones (London: Routledge, 2011), 302.

4. Paul Griffiths, "Tudor Troubles: Problems of Youth in Elizabethan England," in Doran and Jones, *Elizabethan World*, 318–19.

5. K. J. Kesselring, "Rebellion and Disorder," in Doran and Jones, *Elizabethan World*, 372–74.

a man on his way to the gallows.[6] Bastardy rates and denunciations for witchcraft, slander, and sexual deviance were also on the rise. There were thirty-five significant riots in London between 1581 and 1602 as well as food riots in the countryside during the 1590s. While the only serious rebellion was the Northern Rising of 1569, Elizabeth's reign was not a period of domestic tranquility.[7]

Perkins considered preaching to be the primary remedy for the problems of superstition, ignorance, and immorality.[8] Given his convictions about the nature and authority of Scripture, it makes sense that he would give primacy to preaching as both God's chosen method of building his church and the center of every Christian's worship and devotion. The preacher echoed and explained God's word for salvation and sanctification. Preaching derived its power in that it aimed at the mind through rationality, the conscience through addressing specific sins, and the heart through passionate and zealous pleading.[9] At times, the government forbade preaching;

---

6. Beeke and Yuille, *William Perkins*, 73.

7. Kesselring, "Rebellion and Disorder," 375–81.

8. For more on Puritan preaching, see R. Bruce Bickel, *Light and Heat: The Puritan View of the Pulpit; And, the Focus of the Gospel in Puritan Preaching* (Morgan, PA: Soli Deo Gloria, 1999); Joel R. Beeke, *Puritan Evangelism: A Biblical Approach* (Grand Rapids: Reformation Heritage Books, 1999); Murray A. Capill, *Preaching with Spiritual Vigour: Including Lessons from the Life and Practice of Richard Baxter* (Fearn, UK: Mentor, 2003); Eric Josef Carlson, "The Boring of the Ear: Shaping the Pastoral Vision of Preaching in England, 1540–1640," in *Preachers and People in the Reformations and the Early Modern Period*, ed. Larissa Taylor, A New History of the Sermon 2 (Leiden: Brill, 2001), 249–96; Lori Anne Ferrell and Peter E. McCullough, eds., *The English Sermon Revised: Religion, Literature and History 1600–1750* (Manchester: Manchester University Press, 2000); Mariano Di Gangi, *Great Themes in Puritan Preaching* (Guelph, Canada: Joshua Press, 2007); Alan Fager Herr, *The Elizabethan Sermon: A Survey and a Bibliography* (New York: Octagon Books, 1969); Peter Lewis, *The Genius of Puritanism* (Grand Rapids: Reformation Heritage Books, 2008); D. M. Lloyd-Jones, *The Puritans: Their Origins and Successors* (Edinburgh: Banner of Truth Trust, 1987), 372–89; Anders Robert Lunt, "The Reinvention of Preaching: A Study of Sixteenth and Seventeenth Century English Preaching Theories" (PhD diss., University of Maryland College Park, 1998); Irvonwy Morgan, *The Godly Preachers of the Elizabethan Church* (London: Epworth, 1965); Hughes Oliphant Old, *The Age of the Reformation*, vol. 4, *The Reading and Preaching of the Scriptures in the Worship of the Christian Church* (Grand Rapids: Eerdmans, 2002), 251–79; Park, "Sacred Rhetoric"; Joseph A. Pipa, "Puritan Preaching," in *The Practical Calvinist: An Introduction to the Presbyterian and Reformed Heritage*, ed. Peter A. Lillback (Fearn, UK: Mentor, 2002), 163–82; Pipa, "William Perkins"; Leland Ryken, *Worldly Saints: The Puritans as They Really Were* (Grand Rapids: Zondervan, 1986), 91–107; Harry S. Stout, *The New England Soul: Preaching and Religious Culture in Colonial New England* (New York: Oxford University Press, 1986); Cary Nelson Weisiger III, "The Doctrine of the Holy Spirit in the Preaching of Richard Sibbes" (PhD diss., Fuller Theological Seminary, 1984).

9. Beeke and Jones, *Puritan Theology*, 682–85. Arnold Hunt argues that Puritans placed such an emphasis on the sermon preached that many were hesitant about printed sermons

other times, it was enjoined. But in every season, preaching remained under surveillance and criticism.[10] Nonetheless, the Puritan project centered on preaching, and so the "ideal was for every church in the land to have provision for a sermon at all major acts of worship."[11] This came to fruition in the 1570s as the old-guard clergy started to pass away and universities began graduating significant numbers of qualified candidates.[12] Until roughly this time, four out of five pastors were uneducated and merely read homilies once per quarter. In the 1590s, the number of graduate clergy and licensed preachers rose to 50 percent and continued to rise in the seventeenth century.[13] The emphasis on preaching and the effort to create an educated preaching ministry were rewarded with immense success.

But not just any preaching would do, and university education did not necessarily equip preachers for what the Puritans had in mind. The Reformation had scarcely changed the curricula, besides an added emphasis on linguistics.[14] What was not added, and what therefore remained unofficially supplemented, was training in how to preach. In the 1560s and 1570s, these supplements came in the form of prophesyings, in which a minister would deliver a sermon that would in turn be discussed by those in attendance. Critiques dealt with sermon form, delivery, content, and application. This served as a training ground for preachers. Archbishop Edmund Grindal supported this much-needed but unofficial clerical education, but Elizabeth suppressed it in 1576.[15] The impetus for equipping preachers continued in the modified form of clergy conferences and

---

and some viewed them as no sermons at all (*Art of Hearing*, 10). See also James Rigney, "Sermons to Print," in McCullough, Adlington, and Rhatigan, eds., *Oxford Handbook of the Early Modern Sermon*, 201.

10. Herr, *Elizabethan Sermon*, 11.

11. Diarmaid MacCulloch, *The Later Reformation in England, 1547–1603* (New York: Palgrave, 2001), 96; Carlson, "Boring of the Ear," 250.

12. Susan Doran and Christopher Durston, *Princes, Pastors, and People: The Church and Religion in England, 1500–1700* (London: Routledge, 2003), 168.

13. Ian Green, "Preaching in the Parishes," in *Oxford Handbook of the Early Modern Sermon*, 138–39.

14. Carl Trueman, "Preachers and Medieval and Renaissance Commentary," in *Oxford Handbook of the Early Modern Sermon*, 58.

15. Collinson, *Elizabethan Puritan Movement*, 168–239; Patrick Collinson, *Archbishop Grindal, 1519–1583: The Struggle for a Reformed Church* (Berkeley: University of California Press, 1979), 219–82; Peter Iver Kaufman, "Prophesying Again," *CH* 68, no. 2 (June 1999): 337–58.

sponsored lectures.[16] Perkins wrote *The Arte of Prophecying* out of this same motivation. The perceived need for such a preaching manual, given that rhetoric was at the heart of the Cambridge undergraduate curriculum, indicates that both Perkins and the Puritans were after much more than merely persuasive communication.[17]

The Arte of Prophecying definitively presents the plain-style method of Puritan preaching.[18] The method is threefold: interpretation, analysis, and application. I discussed interpretation at length in the previous chapter. The sections devoted to analysis or "resolution" entail drawing out various doctrines from the passage. Perkins uses the metaphor of the Levites cutting up animal sacrifices with precision and careful consideration. Whether explicit or implicit, doctrine must come from the genuine meaning of the text.[19]

Finally, the doctrines are applied. The key for application is determining whether the passage is law or gospel. Law passages point out sin, whereas gospel passages teach what is to be done or believed. Perkins articulates seven spiritual conditions or ways of applying, which correspond to the possible conditions of the hearer: ignorant and unteachable unbelievers, ignorant but teachable unbelievers, knowledgeable but unhumbled unbelievers, the already humbled believers, backsliders, and churches with a mix of believers and unbelievers. Perkins also sees four kinds of application, each derived from 2 Timothy 3:16. Teaching and reproof are mental categories, reforming the mind and recovering it from error. Instruction and correction are practical categories. Instruction enables one to live well in a family, state, or church. Correction transforms ungodliness and

16. Patrick Collinson, "Lectures by Combination: Structures and Characteristics of Church Life in 17th-Century England," in Collinson, *Godly People: Essays on English Protestantism and Puritanism*, History Series (London: Hambledon, 1983), 467–98; Patrick Collinson, Brett Usher, and John Craig, eds., *Conferences and Combination Lectures in the Elizabethan Church: Dedham and Bury St Edmunds, 1582–1590*, Church of England Record Society 10 (London: Boydell, 2003), xxi–xxxii; Haller, *Rise of Puritanism*, 330; Morgan, *Godly Preachers of the Elizabethan Church*, 33–60; Paul S. Seaver, *The Puritan Lectureships: The Politics of Religious Dissent, 1560–1662* (Stanford, CA: Stanford University Press, 1970).

17. Patterson, *William Perkins*, 119.

18. James Thomas Ford, "Preaching in the Reformed Tradition," in Taylor, *Preachers and People in the Reformations and the Early Modern Period*, 75; Pipa, "William Perkins," 127–28.

19. Perkins, *Prophetica*, cap. VI; Perkins, *Whole Works*, 2:662–63. See also Greg Kneidel, "*Ars Praedicendi*: Theories and Practice," in McCullough, Adlington, and Rhatigan, eds., *Oxford Handbook of the Early Modern Sermon*, 17.

unrighteousness into obedience.[20] This sophisticated breakdown allows the application of doctrine from the text to be specific and therefore more effective.[21]

Perkins's manual clearly articulates the doctrine-use plain-style method of Puritan preaching. What made Puritan preaching plain can be summed up by his two requirements for the promulgation of sermons: hiding human wisdom and demonstrating the Spirit. In preparation, a preacher is free to use everything at his disposal, but he should not bring it all with him into the pulpit. Other languages and specialized vocabulary should be avoided. Only those errors that threaten the church should be corrected. Only a few applicable doctrines should be propounded. Only human testimonies that convince the conscience should be cited.[22] In short, "the goal was to teach, not to dazzle."[23] Demonstration of the Spirit manifested itself in the grace of a person, his holiness of heart and blameless life.[24] All of this stood in marked contrast to the overly oratorical preaching celebrated by the educated clergy of his day.[25]

Some have argued that Perkinsian preaching, with its moral demands and focus on predestination, was resisted by English parishioners.[26] But this was simply not the case. Sermons were popular occasions, and well-known preachers generated great excitement.[27] This was certainly true

20. Perkins, *Prophetica*, cap. VIII; Perkins, *Whole Works*, 2:664–69.

21. For a detailed summary of each chapter of *The Arte of Prophecying*, see Pipa, "William Perkins," 84–103.

22. Perkins, *Prophetica*, cap. VI–X; Perkins, *Whole Works*, 2:664, 668–71.

23. Beeke and Jones, *Puritan Theology*, 689.

24. Perkins, *Prophetica*, cap. X; Perkins, *Whole Works*, 2:670.

25. For contrast of the plain style with other forms of preaching, see Blench, *Preaching in England*; Horton Davies, *Like Angels from a Cloud: The English Metaphysical Preachers, 1588–1645* (San Marino, CA: Huntington Library, 1986); Davies, *Worship and Theology in England: From Cranmer to Hooker, 1534–1603* (Princeton: Princeton University Press, 1970); Davidson, "'God's Well-Trodden Foot-Paths,'" 503; Pipa, "William Perkins Preaching"; Ford, "Preaching in the Reformed Tradition."

26. Christopher Haigh, *The Plain Man's Pathways to Heaven: Kinds of Christianity in Post-Reformation England* (Oxford: Oxford University Press, 2007), 124–30, 207; Haigh, "The Taming of Reformation: Preachers, Pastors and Parishioners in Elizabethan and Early Stuart England," *History* 85 (October 2000): 572–88; Peter Iver Kaufman, "The Protestant Opposition to Elizabethan Religious Reform," in *A Companion to Tudor Britain* (Oxford: Blackwell, 2004), 271–88.

27. John Craig, "Sermon Reception," in McCullough, Adlington, and Rhatigan, eds., *Oxford Handbook of the Early Modern Sermon*, 181–82.

with Perkins, whose preaching method was mimicked and whose sermons were printed again and again. This chapter is devoted to Perkins's biblical interpretation in those sermons. I will consider the categories of commentaries penned by Perkins, his expositional series, and his unique occasional sermon on repentance from Zephaniah.[28] It will become clear that, throughout his sermons and commentaries, Perkins remained faithful to his scriptural hermeneutic and the tools of the analogy of faith, context, and collation.

THE TRUE GAINE: PHILIPPIANS 3:7–11

Perkins wrote his exposition of Philippians 3:7–11 in 1601. He published it as a treatise under the title *The True Gaine: More in Worth then All the Goods in the World*. He dedicates the volume to a Sir Edward Dennie, who had mentioned his desire for something to be written that would bring insight into this passage.[29] Perkins delivers this insight by using Scripture to interpret itself, which in this case is primarily through context and, as he illuminates the particulars, collation.

Perkins sets the passage in context by looking at what immediately precedes it. Starting in 3:2, Paul admonishes the Philippians to take heed of certain false apostles who combined circumcision with Christ for salvation, placing confidence in works of the law. He goes on to argue that true circumcision is to worship God in Spirit while putting no confidence in the flesh. Further, Paul does not put any trust in his works, though if anyone could have it would have been him, a Jew from the tribe of Benjamin. In fact, these works are what Paul spurns in 3:7–8. Perkins explains that Paul not only esteemed all pre- and postconversion works as "losses, and deprive himselfe of them, but also cast them away with loathing, in a mind never to seeke the recovery of them." Similarly, Paul's gain is amplified by a threefold gradation, for he claims, "I esteeme the knowledge of Christ an excellent thing: I desire to gaine Christ: and I desire to be found in

28. Handling Perkins's expository material in this order allows a logical flow from written to oral discourse. The hybrid sermon series are discussed in the order that they were likely preached.

29. William Perkins, *The True Gaine More in Worth Then All the Goods in the World* (Cambridge: Iohn Legat, printer to the Vniuersitie of Cambridge, 1601), "The Epistle Dedicatorie"; Perkins, *Whole Works*, 1:645.

him." Verses 9 through 11 explain what "gaining Christ" includes: righteousness, fellowship in Christ's death and resurrection, and attainment of the resurrection.[30]

Perkins then expounds the particulars through collation and the analogy of faith. He uses collation to reinforce Paul's assertion that works are of no value in justification, that salvation by grace and salvation by works cannot stand together. For the former, he cites Isaiah 64:6, which refers to the concept of human righteousness as a cloth to be cast away. He also cites Galatians 2:21, which teaches Christ's death was in vain if righteousness comes via the law. He further appeals to David's plea for the Lord not to judge him, since no one is just in his sight (Ps 143:2). Also, Paul elsewhere asserts that justification is free by the redemption in Christ (Rom 3:24), which excludes any saving role for works. The stark either/or contrast is clear in both Romans 11:6 and Galatians 5:4.[31] Perkins uses a variety of biblical references to further clarify and support the theological points found in these verses.

Collation again explains Paul's phrase "Christ is my Gaine." John 1:16 says that of Christ's fullness "we receive grace for grace." Colossians 2:3 claims that in Christ are "all the treasures of wisdome and knowledge"; a few verses later in Colossians, Paul says Christ's people are "complete in him." First Timothy 2:6 teaches that Christ is "our ransom." From these passages, Perkins concludes that Christ is gain because "Christ our mediatour God & man, is the onely fountaine of all good things, that are, or can be thought on, whether spirituall, or temporal." He goes on to use the analogy of faith to explain how Christ is one's gain, specifically the person-nature distinction in reference to Christ. The person of Christ, with both his divine and human natures, is the gain, for one nature without the other profits no sinner. Christ must be both to stand as mediator, with everything that entails.[32] So in this case, expounding Christ as gain, Perkins utilizes collation and the analogy of faith.

Perkins continues to use collation in his explanation of the excellency of the knowledge of Christ, which he sees in both its content and

30. Perkins, *True Gaine*, 4, 5, 67–121; Perkins, *Whole Works*, 1:647, 659–67.

31. Perkins, *True Gaine*, 15–17, 31; Perkins, *Whole Works*, 1:649–52.

32. Perkins, *True Gaine*, 33, 37–44; Perkins, *Whole Works*, 1:652–54.

its effects. In 1 Timothy 3:16, Paul reduces the mysteries of the knowledge of Christ into six heads: the incarnation, justification of Christ, sight of angels, preaching of Christ to the gentiles, conversion of the world, and Christ's ascension. The effects of this excellent knowledge are at least two. First, by the knowledge of Christ, God is known aright. Hebrews 1:3 calls Christ the brightness of the glory of the Father, Colossians 1:15 says he is the image of the invisible God, and 2 Corinthians 4:6 says God's glory is seen in the face of Christ. Therefore, Perkins concludes the wisdom, power, goodness, justice, and love of God are more clearly manifest in Christ than in either creation or the law. Knowledge of Christ also effects true knowledge of humanity, for the passion narratives reveal our natural standing before God by recounting what Christ suffered in our place. Perkins makes a clear appeal to other Scriptures as he expounds the meaning of "knowledge of Christ."[33]

Perkins remains with collation as he transitions to the specifics of gaining Christ, even using it extensively to explain Paul's statement about fellowship with Christ in his resurrection and death. The virtue of Christ's resurrection lies in its effects, for he raised himself from death to life on behalf of his people. This showed him to be the true and perfect savior, the fulfillment of the prophecy of Psalm 16:10 and Matthew 12:40, and the Son of God according to Romans 1:4. The resurrection declared that Christ made full satisfaction for sins (1 Cor 15:17); it also effected justification (Rom 4:25). Perkins elucidates the resurrection further, arguing that it makes possible at least four important realities: the gift of the Spirit, vivification, preservation, and bodily resurrection at the last day. Perkins also uses collation to explain fellowship with Christ in his suffering and death, specifically as he defined what the sufferings of Christ are. Acts 9:4 indicates Saul's persecution of the church was a persecution of Christ himself. Moreover, Paul claims to have fulfilled the rest of the afflictions of Christ (Col 1:24). Elsewhere in the New Testament, 1 Peter 4:13 exhorts believers to rejoice in partaking in the sufferings of Christ, with the caveat that no one should suffer as an evildoer. From these verses, Perkins concludes "our sufferings are then to be accounted the sufferings of Christ, when they are for good

---

33. Perkins, *True Gaine*, 46–53; Perkins, *Whole Works*, 1:655–56.

cause, and for the name of Christ."[34] Perkins uses collation to explain the complex concept of fellowship with Christ in his death and resurrection in Philippians 3:10, but he does so in service to his exposition of the whole passage. This, plus Perkins's attention to context and the analogy of faith, enables him to use Scripture to interpret itself.

GALATIANS

For three years, Perkins devoted his Sunday lectures to preaching through the first five chapters of Galatians. Ralph Cudworth, who prepared Perkins's commentary for publication shortly after his death, reveals in his letter to the reader that Perkins wrote the commentary with his own hand after the delivery of his sermons.[35] This makes this particular commentary unique for several reasons. It is more accurate than the edited transcripts that were characteristic of this period, while retaining the quality of oral discourse. Perkins also intended the works for print. These factors make Perkins's work on Galatians a sort of hybrid between sermons and a commentary.[36] That the Galatians commentary was the last of Perkins's works also makes it significant.[37] Even in this, his most mature work, we find Perkins interpreting Paul's letter according to context, collation, and the analogy of faith.

Perkins sees the overall argument of Galatians unfolding in three main movements. The occasion of Paul's letter was an attack on his calling and doctrine. False apostles had seduced the Galatian churches by undermining Paul's apostleship and persuading Galatian believers that justification

34. Perkins, *True Gaine*, 92–100, 106; Perkins, *Whole Works*, 1:664–65.

35. Sermons edited for print from this period do include the additions of careful formulation and supporting sources, as they were more open to scrutiny than oral discourse (Hunt, *Art of Hearing*, 148). Perkins was no exception. His sermons were not "published as sermons but were altered into other genres, such as topical or expository treatises, commentaries, or lectures" (Ford, "Preaching in the Reformed Tradition," 78). For a detailed discussion of this process, see Pipa, "William Perkins," 104–14. While such modification poses a significant obstacle to the study of Perkins's homiletics, it is not a problem for the analysis of his biblical interpretation.

36. Paul Smalley describes the commentary in four words: plain, pedagogical, polemical, and practical. This description fits nicely with Perkins's conception of preaching and the larger preaching program of the Puritans (preface to *The Works of William Perkins*, ed. Paul M. Smalley [Grand Rapids: Reformation Heritage Books, 2015], 2:xxii).

37. Perkins, *Whole Works*, 2:157. The first edition was published two years after Perkins's death. Cudworth did prepare it for publication and append a commentary on Gal 6, but he left no evidence of misrepresentation. He limited his work to minor editorial adjustments, leaving even inconsistencies in spelling, which was not standardized until the 1617 edition.

came both through Christ and the law. Paul's response defends his calling as an apostle in Galatians 1–2. Second, in Galatians 3:1–5:12 Paul answers the question of how a person can stand righteous before God, defending the doctrine of justification by Christ alone. Last, Paul prescribes rules for the good life in 5:13–6:18. In his exposition of Galatians, Perkins remains faithful to his method of using Scripture to interpret itself. Below, as evidence, I will offer an example of interpretation according to context, collation, and the analogy of faith from each of the three stages of Paul's argument.

CONTEXT

Within Paul's defense of his apostleship, he recounts his interaction with Jesus' other apostles. Perkins explains this by providing context. In Galatians 1, Paul provides the narrative of his immediate and extraordinary calling from God. Starting in the next chapter, he begins to defend the legitimacy of this calling. In order to do this, Paul had to demonstrate his teaching was in line with the other apostles. Recounting his interactions in Jerusalem and Antioch, he engages an implied objection to the contrary. Paul went to Jerusalem, conferred with the apostles, and received their approval. The only case of dissension arose between Paul and Peter at Antioch, over Peter's hypocritical capitulation to the circumcision party. Therefore, the point of division was entirely Peter's fault.[38] Perkins explains Paul's accounts in Galatians 2 according to the context of the previous chapter and the overall argument of the epistle.

In Galatians 3, Paul begins to defend justification by faith without works, focusing on the righteousness of Abraham, which Perkins interprets according to the context of Genesis. The occasion of Abraham's belief was the renewal of God's promise of descendants at the beginning of Genesis 15. This promise of his prosperity functioned as the object of Abraham's faith, and it was founded on the more principal promises of God's all-sufficiency (Gen 17:1) as well as the fact that God himself was Abraham's reward (Gen 15:11). With the eye of faith, Abraham saw in the promise of physical descendants a pledge of redemption. The property of Abraham's faith was belief against hope, for he and Sarah were too old to have children and Sarah

38. Perkins, *Whole Works*, 2:187, 198.

was barren besides. But context is key to understand Perkins's treatment of Abraham's justifying faith.[39]

Galatians 5:13 marks Paul's transition to rules for the good life, and Perkins's commentary terminates at the end of chapter 5. The rules are twofold: not to use Christian freedom as an opportunity for the flesh, and to serve one another in love. Galatians 5:14 claims the whole law is summed up in loving one's neighbor as oneself. The context of 5:13–14 makes sense of the warning about biting and devouring in 5:15. What may seem peculiar and detached, according to Perkins, is another reason for the second rule. The caution is drawn from the dangerous effect of not serving one another in love.[40] In short, "Contentions breed the desolation of the Church: therefore doe service one to another by love."[41] This is yet another example of Perkins's close attention to context in his biblical interpretation.

COLLATION

Perkins uses collation to arrive at the meaning of "dying to the law" in Galatians 2:19. Dying to the law frees one from the dominion of the law, and that in several ways. First, Romans 8:1 teaches freedom from the condemnation of the law. Second, according to Romans 7:8, dying to the law brings freedom from its power to stir up the corruption of the unregenerate heart. Further, Perkins sees freedom from the observation of ceremonies taught by Colossians 2:10. Clearly, he uses various places in Scripture to shed light on this concept of dying to the law. He does the same to illuminate the converse reality, which is living to God. Titus 2:12 explains that living to God means living wise, just, and godly lives. Wisdom includes laboring to be in Christ (Eph 5:15; Luke 21:36) and participation in Christian community (Heb 11:25–26; Ps 84:10). Godliness consists of seven rules, all of which are found in particular passages of Scripture. For instance, God must receive

---

39. Perkins, *Whole Works*, 2:228. John Prime, a contemporary English interpreter of Galatians with Perkins who employs the same hermeneutical tools but not the Puritan plain style, also interprets Abraham's faith in the larger context of Genesis, though he does not argue that Abraham saw a pledge of redemption in the promise of physical descendants (*An Exposition, and Observations upon Saint Paul to the Galathians Togither with Incident Quaestions Debated, and Motiues Remoued* [Oxford: Printed by Ioseph Barnes and are to be sold by T. Cooke in Pauls Church-yard at the signe of the Tygers head, 1587], 104–8).

40. Similarly, Prime understands 5:15 as the "inconvenience of not loving" (*Exposition, and Observations*, 256).

41. Perkins, *Whole Works*, 2:323.

praise and thanks in all things, even for miseries and afflictions (Job 1:22). Finally, living justly requires making God in Christ one's treasure and portion. This is how Paul was content in any estate (Phil 4:11), which is what enables one to love one's neighbor.[42] In his explanation of dying to the law and living to God, Perkins employs a variety of biblical passages, striving to let Scripture interpret itself.

Perkins also uses collation to explain the bondage and freedom referenced in Galatians 5:1. The nature of humanity's spiritual bondage is threefold. First, there is bondage under sin, spoken of in Romans 7:14. This sin includes both guilt and corruption, which means people are drawn to sin, they cannot but sin, and everything they do is sin. The second part of the bondage is subjection to temporal and eternal punishment. This includes slavery to Satan (2 Tim 2:26; 2 Cor 4:4; Heb 2:14), to an evil conscience (Gen 4:7), and to the fear of the wrath of God (Heb 2:15). The third part of bondage is the obligation to the ceremonial law, which Perkins understands as a special bondage on the Jews according to Acts 15. From here, Perkins continues with collation to expound Christian freedom. This liberty consists of deliverance from misery and freedom in good things, both of which Perkins breaks down into four parts. First, he details a deliverance from the curse that comes from breaching the law per Romans 8:1. Second, he highlights the Christian's deliverance from the obligation to perfect righteousness according to the law, an obligation implied in the covenant of works and therefore part of the analogy of faith. A third deliverance is from the ceremonial law, as explicitly taught in Colossians 2:15–20. The final deliverance is from the dominion of sin according to Romans 6:14.

Again, Perkins also splits liberty in good things into four discreet parts. The first liberty is freedom to the voluntary service of God, cited in 1 Timothy 1:9. Freedom to use all God's creatures is another liberty. Titus 1:15 and Romans 14:14 teach that the unclean regulations are obsolete. Further, the Christian has freedom to go to the Father in prayer and be heard per Romans 5:2 and Ephesians 3:12. Finally, the Christian has liberty to enter heaven at death, a freedom made possible by Christ, according to

42. Perkins, *Whole Works*, 2:212–14. Prime's comments on these verses are much shorter, and while he does some doctrinal exposition of dying to the law and living to Christ, he does not use collation as a tool (*Exposition, and Observations*, 86–90).

Hebrews 10:19. Perkins extensively employs various particular passages of Scripture to define the terms "bondage" and "freedom."[43]

Perkins explains the lust of the flesh and Spirit referenced in Galatians 5:17 with the help of passages from elsewhere in the canon. The lust of the flesh shows itself in two other places. According to Romans 7:21–23, it defiles and represses any good inclinations of the spirit; according to James 1:14, it tempts, entices, and draws away the mind, filling it with wicked thoughts and rebellious proclivities. The lust of the Spirit also reveals itself through two actions. First, in 1 John 3:9, the Spirit curbs and restrains the flesh as grace keeps the regenerate from sin. Second, the Spirit acts to bring good thoughts and tendencies to the mind, engendering actions agreeable to the will of God. Isaiah 30:21 supports this claim. These competing lusts are the reason for the spiritual war described in the second half of Galatians 5, and Perkins uses collation to describe their specific actions.[44]

ANALOGY OF FAITH

Perkins uses the analogy of faith to handle the theological difficulty presented by the fact that Paul circumcises Timothy in Acts 16:3 and refuses the circumcision of Titus in Galatians 2:3, both of whom were Greeks. Circumcision at this point in the history of redemption was a thing indifferent. According to Perkins, from the rite's institution to the death of Christ, it was obligatory for proper worship of God; it was a sacrament. After the establishing of the church in the New Testament, God abolished circumcision as a sacrament. But in the time between, circumcision became a matter left to the liberty of the people of God—not a sacrament, not a part of God's worship, but a free ceremony to be used only for the edification of men. Perkins concludes that Paul condescended to the weakness of the Jews in his circumcision of Timothy but refused to circumcise Titus so he might not offend the godly or hinder Christian liberty.

43. Perkins, *Whole Works*, 2:306–7. Prime comes to some of the same conclusions about bondage and freedom but does not utilize collation (*Exposition, and Observations*, 240–45).

44. Perkins, *Whole Works*, 2:327. Prime handles Gal 5:13–18 as an interpretive unit and does not address the specifics of the desires of the flesh and Spirit (*Exposition, and Observations*, 251–57).

This interpretation is founded on the accepted precept, drawn from the whole witness of Scripture, that circumcision was a thing indifferent.[45]

Perkins also appeals to the analogy of faith to describe how Christ can be both made a curse and sent by the Father as the Son. Galatians 3:13 references Christ being made a curse. Perkins explains this with orthodox Christology. Christ was not cursed by nature, for he is God. Neither was he cursed by fault, for he never sinned. Rather, Christ became a curse voluntarily as part of his mediatorial role in the eternal covenant of redemption. In time, he took the guilt of sin at his baptism and the punishment for sin on his cross. Jesus Christ as God the Son incarnate was cursed, yet the curse fell not on his divine nature but only his humanity.[46] Galatians 4:4 presents another potential difficulty in that the Father sends the Son, which could imply a division in the Godhead. To combat this, Perkins appeals to orthodox Trinitarianism. Was the Son sent by his own consent? Perkins answers, "Yea, the decree of the father is the decree of the sonne and holy Ghost: because as they are all one in nature, so are they all one in will. All the persons then have a stroke in this sending yet for orders sake, the father is said to send, because he is first." But how can the Father send the Son if they are one? Perkins responds again,

> *Nature* and *Person* must be distinguished. *Nature* is a substance common to many, as the godhead. A *Person* is that which subsisteth of itselfe, and hath a proper manner of subsisting, as the father begetting the sonne begotten, the holy Ghost proceeding. Now the father and the sonne are one indeed for nature or Godhead, but they are not one for person. Nay thus they are really distinct. The father is not the sonne, nor the sonne the father.[47]

45. Perkins, *Whole Works*, 2:190. Prime does not reference the circumcision of Timothy but asserts that Paul's refusal to submit Titus to circumcision revolved around the issue of Christian liberty (*Exposition, and Observations*, 39–41).

46. Perkins, *Whole Works*, 2:238. Prime offers clear presentation of penal substitution but does not raise the question of how the Son of God could be said to be made a curse (*Exposition, and Observations*, 117–18).

47. Perkins, *Whole Works*, 2:271. Prime outlines orthodox Trinitariansim and Christology in this context but to interpret what is meant by "God's Son" rather than the act of sending; an example of the analogy of faith nonetheless (*Exposition, and Observations*, 140–42).

Here Perkins utilizes the analogy of faith, specifically the classical formulations of the person of Christ and the Trinity, to interpret texts that might seem problematic at first glance.

Finally, Perkins elucidates Paul's comment in Galatians 5:23 about there being no law against the fruit of the Spirit by referencing the Christian's relationship to the law, a relationship that needed no further explanation or defense. He argues this relationship is relevant in two ways. First, the law does not condemn such positive acts of obedience. Second, the law is not what compels the fruit of the Spirit in the life of the believer, because they freely obey God.[48] Christian freedom is a major theme throughout Galatians and is highlighted continually in Perkins's commentary. Further, the whole of Scripture emphasizes Christian freedom, which establishes the doctrine as a part of the analogy of faith. Perkins draws on this to allow Scripture to interpret itself, which remains the larger goal of interpretation throughout Perkins's entire commentary.

CHRIST'S SERMON ON THE MOUNT

Thomas Pierson published *A Godly and Learned Exposition upon Christ's Sermon on the Mount* at the request of Perkins's executors. The work started as Perkins's sermon series in Cambridge on Matthew 5–7, in which he interpreted Jesus' address in light of the rest of Scripture. For Perkins, Jesus in the Sermon on the Mount sought "to teach his disciples, with all that believe in him, to lead a godly, holy, and blessed life."[49] This is the scope and point of the sermon. The Jewish leaders had corrupted the true meaning of Moses and the prophets, so Jesus intended to make that true meaning clear.[50] The unchanging message of Scripture is the imperative to love God. This imperative lies at the heart of the Mosaic law such that in the Sermon on the Mount Jesus was not instituting a new law, social gospel, or standard to live by in some future kingdom. Instead, he was revealing

48. Perkins, *Whole Works*, 2:340. Prime does not raise the same question in his discussion of Gal 5:23 (*Exposition, and Observations*, 267–78).

49. Perkins, *Whole Works*, 3:1.

50. Perkins saw direct correlation between the scribes and Pharisees and the Church of Rome. This connection explains the polemical nature of his exposition ("Preface," in *Works of William Perkins*, 1:xxxvii).

the nature of true godliness.[51] For Perkins, Jesus' Sermon on the Mount is the "key of the whole Bible: for here Christ opens the sum of the Old and New Testament."[52] He tells his people how to live a blessed life according to the law of God.

Luke's account provides the immediate time and setting of Jesus' sermon. Perkins understands the discourse in Luke 6 to be the same actual sermon found in Matthew 5–7. The time was the second year of Christ's ministry. After he cured the man with a withered hand on the Sabbath, Jesus went up into the mountain because the scribes and Pharisees were trying to kill him. He spent the night there in prayer and then elected the twelve disciples. Matthew includes the account of the calling of the twelve in chapter 10 because that was the occasion of their commission to preach. But according to the context found in Luke, the actual timeline is that Jesus calls his disciples on the mountain before the sermon. He went down and performed miracles but had to retreat again because of the crowds. He then preached the Sermon on the Mount to his disciples with the multitude in the audience.[53] This understanding of the purpose and context is crucial for understanding how Perkins handles the sermon as one extended discourse and how he interprets individual parts in the context of the whole.

---

51. J. Stephen Yuille, *Living Blessedly Forever* (Grand Rapids: Reformation Heritage Books, 2012), 19. This point and purpose of the Sermon on the Mount was echoed by Perkins's contemporaries. See William Burton, *Ten Sermons Vpon the First, Second, Third and Fourth Verses of the Sixt of Matthew Containing Diuerse Necessary and Profitable Treatises, Viz. a Preseruative against the Poyson of Vaine-Glory in the 1 & 2, the Reward of Sincerity in the 3, the Vncasing of the Hypocrite in the 4, 5 and 6, the Reward of Hypocrisie in the 7 and 8, an Admonition to Left-Handed Christians in the 9 and 10 : Whereunto Is Annexed Another Treatise Called The Anatomie of Belial, Set Foorth in Ten Sermons Vpon the 12, 13, 14, 15 Verses of the 6 Chapter of the Prouerbs of Salomon* (London: Richard Field for Thomas Man, 1602), 1.

52. Perkins, *Whole Works*, 3:1. The understanding of the Sermon on the Mount as the key to the whole Bible as Jesus swept away the accretions added to the Old Testament by Israel's religious leaders goes back to William Tyndale in the English Protestant interpretive tradition (William Tyndale, *An Exposicion Vppon the V. Vi. Vii. Chapters of Mathew Which Thre Chaptres Are the Keye and the Dore of the Scripture, and the Restoringe Agayne of Moses Lawe Corrupte by the Scrybes and Pharises: And the Exposicion Is the Restoringe Agayne of Christes Lawe Corrupte by the Papistes : Item before the Booke, Thou Hast a Prologe Very Necessarie, Contaynynge the Whole Somme of the Couenaunt Made Betwene God and vs, Vppon Which We Be Baptised to Kepe It: And after Thou Hast a Table That Leadeth the by the Notes in the Mergentes, Vnto All That Is Intreated of in the Booke* [Antwerp: J. Grapheus, 1533], prologue).

53. Perkins, *Whole Works*, 3:1–2.

INTERPRETATION OF THE PARTS IN THE CONTEXT OF THE WHOLE

Perkins organizes the sermon into three sections: a preface, the matter, and the conclusion. The preface comprises the brief introduction of the first two verses. The matter, or the body, includes twelve heads of doctrine, by which Perkins organizes the major movements of his sermons. He sees five marks of godliness: blessedness, repentance, righteousness, sincerity, and contentment.[54] These marks are followed by seven heads that describe the state of the faithful. The matter begins with the Beatitudes. For Perkins, blessedness means "true happiness before God, is ever joined, yea covered many times, with the cross in this world." The disciples were promised happiness but seemed to get more misery. Jesus asserts that happiness is not carnal joy, which arises from one's circumstances, but spiritual joy, which arises from one's relationship with God. The Beatitudes, then, are "rules for happiness."[55]

Perkins systematically walks through each beatitude and asks two questions: Who is blessed? And why? The promises are fulfilled partly in this life but primarily in the next. The first rule for happiness is poverty of spirit, which Perkins defines as proper self-perception in light of sin. Those who follow this rule possess at present the kingdom of grace, which will culminate in the kingdom of glory. The second rule for happiness is mourning or great distress over "an inward feeling of their spiritual want."[56] It is not just grief in Perkins's understanding but grief over sin. Seeking God's forgiveness in Jesus Christ comforts those who experience such mourning.

Meekness, another characteristic of the happy, is "a gift of God's Spirit, whereby a man doth moderate his affection of anger, and bridle in himself impatience, hatred, and desire of revenge." This attribute flows from the first two, for it is manifested in the bearing of the judgment of God and the reproach of men. The meek share in Christ's inheritance, which according to Jesus includes the whole earth. That inheritance is theirs by right, and one day they will possess it in full. Those who hunger and thirst for

---

54. This language for Perkins's five categories is from Yuille's *Living Blessedly Forever* but is not foreign to Perkins's work and both briefly and helpfully characterizes Perkins's understanding of each of his divisions.

55. Perkins, *Whole Works*, 3:3.

56. Perkins, *Whole Works*, 3:5–6.

righteousness long for both outward and inward righteousness. Perkins understands outward righteousness to be justification and inward righteousness as sanctification. Those with such longing are filled because of partial satisfaction in this life and completion in the next. The merciful are happy because they will receive mercy. Perkins stresses that this does not teach a doctrine of merit but that "holy compassion of heart, whereby a man is moved to help another in his misery" is evidence of the mercy he has obtained.[57]

The sixth rule of happiness is purity in heart. Again, Perkins says this is obtained through justification and sanctification, for "the holy in heart" have "their hearts purged from defilement of their sin" and are "in part renewed and sanctified by the Holy Ghost." The heart for Perkins is equivalent to the soul, consisting of the mind, conscience, will, and affections. The beatific vision is by faith through a "sight of the mind when the creature sees God, so far forth as it is capable of his knowledge." It is perception of God "by his effects." But the pure in heart will one day see him "perfectly." Peacemakers are those who are happy because they bring concord and agreement among men, which begins with peace with God. They are happy because their adoption is declared in this world and will be enjoyed fully in eternity. The final rule of happiness is being persecuted for righteousness's sake. Everyone who lives contrary to the world by the previous seven rules will be persecuted, but eternal life is the reward. The paradox and apparent absurdity of the statements found in the Beatitudes only make sense in light of Christ and the cross.[58]

Perkins then argues Matthew 5:13–16 explains how one becomes like those described in the Beatitudes—namely, through repentance. Jesus transitions to the illustration of salt and light, which are the ministry of the apostles. Preaching is compared to salt, the properties of which when "applied to raw flesh, or fresh wounds are principally three: First, it will bite and fret, being of nature hot and dry; secondly, it makes meats savory unto our taste; thirdly, it preserveth meats from putrification, by drawing out of them superfluous moistness." Preaching of the word of God, including both law and gospel, must have the same effect. The law must be

57. Perkins, *Whole Works*, 3:6–12.

58. Perkins, *Whole Works*, 3:14, 16–20.

applied to "rip up men's hearts," to recognize their sin, and to cause them to renounce themselves. The gospel must season corrupt men with grace so that they may be "reconciled to God, and made savory in his sight." For the sake of preservation, Perkins says, "law and gospel must be continually dispensed."[59] Good works, or holiness of life, are compared to light, and Perkins understands them to have a threefold use. They express reverence, obedience, and thankfulness to God; serve as evidence of salvation; and are a testimony to others. With regard to preaching, the comparison to light is important for two reasons. It shows how preaching expels darkness and ignorance; it also shows how God's word is to be handled—namely, to make people aware of sin and the remedy of Christ. These illustrations of salt and light indirectly refer to other ministers and all Christians, but the ministry of the apostles is what Jesus primarily had in view. It is their preaching and good works Jesus referred to, and their goal is to bring people to repentance.[60]

In Perkins's formulation, Jesus goes on the offensive in the rest of Matthew 5 in restoring the moral law to its true sense, describing what it means to be righteous. The Jewish leaders' accusation against Jesus about diminishing the law's importance provides the background of this part of the sermon. Perkins understands Jesus to make three arguments. First, from 5:17, his purpose in coming was to fulfill the whole Old Testament. This is primarily a statement about the moral law, which is made clear by Jesus' emphasis on the Decalogue throughout the rest of the chapter. Jesus fulfills the moral law by restoring it, obeying it, suffering its penalty, and creating faith in his people. Second, in 5:18–19, Jesus promises the moral law is permanent because it reveals God's eternal and unchanging rule for all people. Last, in 5:20, Jesus imposes his own standard, which is higher than the standard of the Jewish leaders.[61] This is unfolded in the six antitheses in Matthew 5. Here, Perkins sees Jesus restoring the moral law from the

---

59. Perkins, *Whole Works*, 3:23.

60. Perkins, *Whole Works*, 3:26–32. The idea that being salt and light refers to the apostles and ministers while only referring to all Christians secondarily is a minority interpretation. However, Calvin also affirmed it (John Calvin, *A Harmony of the Gospels, Matthew, Mark and Luke*, ed. David W. Torrance and Thomas F. Torrance, trans. A. W. Morrison, Calvin's Commentaries 1 [Grand Rapids: Eerdmans, 1972], 175–78).

61. Perkins, *Whole Works*, 3:33–40. Burton, similarly, sees the issue at the heart of sincerity in generosity as motivation (*Ten Sermons*, 6).

corruptions of the Jewish authorities and their focus on externals. Why command what no one can perform? No one can be perfect, but Perkins sees two reasons for the requirement. It points to the individual's need for justification or outward righteousness. It also aids the pursuit of sanctification or inward righteousness.[62]

Perkins sees another shift in Jesus' sermon in Matthew 6: from a description of righteousness to its pursuit through sincerity and contentment. One must be careful to avoid hypocrisy, especially in the areas of giving, prayer, and fasting. Perkins expounds extensively on the Lord's Prayer, which he sees as made up of a preface, six petitions, and a conclusion.[63] The first three petitions focus on God's glory, while the second three focus on the needs of humanity. God's glory is the end of all things, even human needs. The conclusion—that the kingdom, power, and glory eternally belong to God—is the very reason for prayer.[64] The first half of Matthew 6 teaches sincerity, while the second teaches contentment. The imperative is to avoid attachment to worldly things.

Perkins understands Matthew 7 as Jesus' explanation of faithfulness. Jesus describes "the state of those that profess his holy name."[65] This state is made up of the last seven heads of doctrine Perkins finds in the sermon. First, being faithful means avoiding rash judgment.[66] Second, faithfulness requires guarding the word of God through church discipline.[67] Third, the faithful ones are marked by earnest prayer.[68] Fourth, the faithful practice equity and justice.[69] Fifth, Christ exhorts "his hearers and us all effectually, to an earnest care in seeking eternal life."[70] Sixth, faithfulness involves

62. Perkins, *Whole Works*, 3:57, 101.

63. See Kenneth Stevenson, *The Lord's Prayer: A Text in Tradition* (Minneapolis: Fortress, 2004), 222–23, for a discussion of the understanding of the shape of the Lord's Prayer throughout church history. He shows that Perkins's understanding of the prayer was more overtly Calvinistic than the Church of England Prayer Book, which included seven petitions and heavy liturgical use (180–81).

64. Perkins, *Whole Works*, 3:124, 144.

65. Perkins, *Whole Works*, 3:244.

66. Perkins, *Whole Works*, 3:194 (Matt 7:1–5).

67. Perkins, *Whole Works*, 3:207–8 (Matt 7:6).

68. Perkins, *Whole Works*, 3:213 (Matt 7:7–11).

69. Perkins, *Whole Works*, 3:219 (Matt 7:12).

70. Perkins, *Whole Works*, 3:226 (Matt 7:13–14).

discerning and avoiding false prophets.[71] The final mark of faithfulness is doing the Father's will.[72] These seven marks identify those who are faithful—namely, those who profess his holy name.

Perkins sees Jesus' conclusion as an exhortation to be doers of his teaching. It is not enough to hear, read, or learn Jesus' doctrine; one must put it into practice.[73] The house Jesus references in 7:24–27 is a profession of faith. Perkins understands the difference between the wise man and the foolish man—between the foundation of sand and the foundation of rock—as the difference between the "effectual doer" and the "forgetful hearer."[74] The doer is the one who experiences true happiness.

QUALIFICATION IN LIGHT OF THE CANON

Perkins also uses Scripture to interpret itself through the analogy of faith and collation. This allows him to apply the particular demands of the Sermon on the Mount universally, therefore avoiding the extremes of Roman Catholic teaching and Anabaptist ideals. Perkins also consistently applies the Sermon on the Mount to both the spiritual and secular kingdoms. In his exposition of the second beatitude, he demonstrates that it is not those who mourn for any reason who will be comforted but only those who mourn over their sin. In his defense, Perkins cites the examples of Cain, Saul, Ahithophel, and Judas. Each of these men mourned but not with the sorrow of repentance. Perkins again utilizes collation to specify the four ways the Lord comforts those who mourn. First, he cites 1 Corinthians 10:13 and 2 Samuel 7:4 to show God that adjusts sorrows and afflictions according to the mourner's strength. Second, sometimes God removes grief by removing its cause, as in the case of Manasseh in 2 Chronicles 33:13. Third, God gives inward comfort through his word and Spirit, evidenced by Paul in Romans 5:3 and 2 Corinthians 1:4–5. Fourth and finally, God comforts by bringing misery to an end through death. Lazarus was brought solace in death (Luke 16:25), and the thief on the cross was

71. Perkins, *Whole Works*, 3:234 (Matt 7:15–20).
72. Perkins, *Whole Works*, 3:244 (Matt 7:21–23).
73. Perkins, *Whole Works*, 3:258–59.
74. Yuille, *Living Blessedly Forever*, 138–43.

given hope in death. Perkins uses collation to explain both the one blessed and how one is blessed.[75]

Perkins explains the salt metaphor in Matthew 5:13 through context and collation. As mentioned earlier, salt signifies the preaching of the gospel, because such preaching is the principal means by which God works grace in the hearts of his followers. That the salt metaphor comes immediately after the paradoxical blessedness referenced in the Beatitudes is crucial for Perkins's interpretation. The metaphor begins to answer the implicit question of how one may attain the happiness spoken of previously. It is through preaching that people are made pleasing to God in both heart and life, how they are made savory, to follow the salt metaphor. That the apostles, and by extension ministers of the gospel, are the salt of the whole earth, is confirmed by the Great Commission in Matthew 28:18–20. So Perkins uses context and collation to determine the designation "salt of the earth" in Matthew 5:13.[76]

In his discussion of Matthew 5:21–22, Perkins is careful to qualify that not all killing is wrong. He makes this caveat based on the witness of the rest of the canon. God gives men the power to kill in at least three ways. The first is his written word, in which he gives permission to princes and governors. From these legitimate forms of authority, executioners and soldiers derive license to kill malefactors and enemies in lawful war. The second is by an extraordinary commandment. Here Perkins recalls Abraham's directive to sacrifice his son Isaac. The third is by "extraordinary instinct, which is answerable to a special commandment." The biblical reference for this is the slaying of Zimri and Cozbi by Phinehas.[77] Based on the whole of Scripture, Perkins concludes that killing is murder when it is done without warrant from God.

---

75. Perkins, *Whole Works*, 3:6–7. While Perkins's exegesis of the second beatitude looks very different from Tyndale's, the tool of collation is clearly shared (Tyndale, *Exposicion Vppon the V. Vi. Vii. Chapters of Mathew*; this work's pages are not numbered, but the material is clearly organized around the verses and biblical phrases of the Sermon on the Mount).

76. Perkins, *Whole Works*, 3:23. Tyndale also concludes that the "salt" is the preaching of the gospel, but he asserts this and does not defend his conclusion with collation (Tyndale, *Exposicion Vppon the V. Vi. Vii. Chapters of Mathew*).

77. Perkins, *Whole Works*, 3:47. Tyndale does not even address the question of whether all killing is wrong. Instead, he proceeds to discuss biblical examples of hate leading to the death of another, even if the killing was done by someone else (Tyndale, *Exposicion Vppon the V. Vi. Vii. Chapters of Mathew*).

Perkins moderates the idea of literally relying on God for one's daily means of living in several places. In his discussion of the Lord's Prayer, he argues that "give us this day our daily bread" prohibits one from distrustful care, not prudent saving. This is evidenced by the story of Joseph and his storing up of grain in Egypt for the inevitable famine. The apostolic example of providing for the church of Judea is another indication that reliance on God for one's daily bread is not comparable to Israel's wilderness wandering and God's daily provision of manna.[78] Later in Matthew 6, Jesus commands people to not lay up treasures on earth but in heaven. Here Perkins is quick to say Jesus does not discourage saving. The point is to teach a "moderate care and desire of worldly things." He denotes three things Christ does not forbid. First, "diligent labor in a mans vocation" is not forbidden, or else God "should be contrary to himself." Perkins concludes this from Genesis 3:19, "enjoining man to eat his bread in the sweat of his face," and 2 Thessalonians 3:10, "he that will not labor, should not eat." Second, "the fruition and possession of goods" is not forbidden, for they are good things from God, as illustrated by Abraham, Job, and Solomon. Last, simple accumulation is not forbidden, for 2 Corinthians 12:14 says, "The father must lay up for the children"; he also mentions that the temple had a treasury. As a rule, Perkins proposes, "Things necessary for man's person and his calling, a man may seek for and lay up; but for abundance, and for superfluities, no man ought to labor or be careful."[79] The issue is to trust God for one's daily needs, which Perkins concludes from various scriptural qualifications.

Perkins restricts Jesus' words "judge not" in Matthew 7:1 to rash judgment. From the rest of Scripture, it is obvious to Perkins that "this commandment forbids not all kinds of judgment, but must be restrained to unlawful judgment." The kinds of lawful judgment condoned by Scripture are four. One is civil judgment, belonging to the magistrate. Another is ecclesiastical, belonging primarily to ministers. Ministers may judge

---

78. William Perkins, *An Exposition of the Lords Prayer in the Vvay of Catechising Seruing for Ignorant People. Hereunto Are Adioined the Praiers of Paule, Taken out of His Epistles* (London: Adam Islip for Iohn Legat, Cambridge, 1595), 38–40; Perkins, *Whole Works*, 1:340.

79. Perkins, *Whole Works*, 3:163–64. Tyndale does not seem interested in qualifying Jesus' statements in the same way Perkins does. In the case of Matt 6:19, he makes an applicational case against covetousness from various passages of Scripture (Tyndale, *Exposicion Vppon the V. Vi. Vii. Chapters of Mathew*).

and condemn public sin, as Hebrews 11:7 recounts Noah doing. There are also forms of private judgment allowed by Scripture. For example, private admonition is commanded, which includes one Christian lovingly approaching another regarding sin. Finally, there is just dispraise: "when the gross faults of notorious persons are reproved and condemned for this end alone, that others may take warning thereby." The example provided of this type of righteous judgment is Jesus himself. He judged the life and teaching of the Pharisees and concluded his disciples should beware of them. He calls them hypocrites, their doctrine leaven. Further, Jesus calls Herod a fox to discourage his subtlety among others.[80] Because Scripture explicitly approves of some judgment, both public and private, Jesus' words must not be taken too woodenly. For Perkins, it is rash, unlawful judgment that Jesus condemns.

Perkins curbs the promise of answered prayer to those who ask, seek, and knock with two rules. For the promise to be effective, prayer must be done by those who are in Christ and offered according to what Christ commands. Therefore, the promise has four conditions. First, it must be "while the time of grace and mercy remaineth." This is made clear by the parable of the ten virgins. Second, it must not be according to the will of man. The sons of Zebedee were denied their request. According to 1 John 5:14, prayer must be according to the will of God for him to hear it. Third, prayer must be in faith. Perkins employs James 1:5–6 and Mark 11:24 to demonstrate that one must believe God will grant one's request. Fourth and finally, the time and manner of God's accomplishing requests must be deferred to his good pleasure. It was the mistake of Israel in Psalm 78:41 to demand when they would have their request answered. The model is rather David, who waited on the Lord, as he recounts in Psalm 40:1.[81] While it would seem that Jesus' words taken literally would mean that whatever one asks for will be given, Perkins understands that the rest of the Bible demands a different reading.

---

80. Perkins, *Whole Works*, 3:194–95. Tyndale similarly claims that this is not a universal prohibition on judgment then shows through collation that it is a condemnation of hypocrisy (Tyndale, *Exposicion Vppon the V. Vi. Vii. Chapters of Mathew*).

81. Perkins, *Whole Works*, 3:213. Tyndale also defines what true prayer is, citing other Scripture passages (Tyndale, *Exposicion Vppon the V. Vi. Vii. Chapters of Mathew*).

Perkins handles Christ's Sermon on the Mount as a single sermon delivered to the apostles. This results in careful attention to the whole as he interprets the individual parts, which build on one another and form a coherent argument. Perkins uses all three of the tools of his scriptural hermeneutic to interpret the five marks of godliness and the seven characteristics of faithfulness. I have demonstrated this through representative examples of Perkins's exegesis, according to his major divisions of the sermon. Whether looking at the major units of thought or single statements of Jesus, Perkins consistently interprets the sermon with Scripture.

THE COMBAT BETWEENE CHRIST AND THE DEVILL: MATTHEW 4:1–11

Perkins's sermon series on Matthew 4:1–11, preached at Cambridge, was published as *The Combat Betweene Christ and the Devill Displayed: or, A Commentarie upon the Temptations of Christ*.[82] Perkins divides the passage into three main parts: the preparation, the combat, and the happy result. The three temptations of unbelief, presumption, and idolatry make up the body of the work.[83] The context of Jesus' baptism precedes the temptation narrative, especially the Father's declaration that Jesus is the Son of God. This is significant because Satan's temptations attack Jesus at the level of his identity.[84] Perkins is also careful to incorporate insights from the other Gospel accounts of Jesus' temptation. Yet beyond these high-level uses of context and collation, Perkins uses the components of his Scripture hermeneutic in his detailed exposition of Jesus' three temptations.

In the first temptation, Satan tries to overthrow Jesus' faith and then bring him to unbelief, according to Perkins. He cunningly questions Jesus' identity as the Son of God by drawing attention to his hunger, trying to

82. The first edition of this work was compiled and edited by Robert Hill, fellow at St. John's College and longtime acquaintance of Perkins. The executors of Perkins's will charged Thomas Pierson with revising and expanding it based on a more complete copy of notes from the sermons. This final edition came off the press in 1606.

83. The purpose of Christ's temptation was threefold: first, that Christ might defeat the devil as the devil overcame Adam; second, to equip his followers to resist the devil; and third, that he might be a merciful and faithful high priest to those who are tempted ("Preface," in *Works of William Perkins*, 1:xxxv).

84. Perkins, *Whole Works*, 3:371.

undermine the voice from heaven that said he is God's beloved Son.[85] The practice of unbelief, which the devil urged Jesus toward, was to turn stones to bread. Jesus responds to Satan's attack with Deuteronomy 8:3. The "word" in this verse could mean the Second Person of the Trinity, as in John 1:1, the Scripture, as in 1 Peter 1:25; or God's will and decree, as in Hebrews 1:2. Given the context, the last option fits best, for Moses was speaking to Israel about the ordinary and extraordinary means of God's provision. So by quoting Deuteronomy 8:3, Jesus is saying, according to Perkins, "Man doth not preserve this natural life by ordinary meanes only, but withal by Gods good pleasure, will, and decree." Perkins cites Israel's manna, Moses on Sinai, Elijah on Horeb, Daniel, and other examples to support this concept of extraordinary means. Clearly, context and collation are key in Perkins's explanation of Jesus' first temptation as well as Jesus' rebuttal.[86]

In his second temptation, Satan tries to push Jesus to presume on the Father's protection by urging him to jump from the pinnacle of the temple. He again questions Jesus' identity as the Son of God, but the temptation this time is the exact opposite of the first. Context is important because Perkins sees this temptation as building on Satan's initial assault. Whereas Satan failed to overthrow Christ's faith and to cause him to distrust the truth of God's word, now he wants him to take the promise of protection for granted. He borrows from Christ's profession of trust in the Father and asks him to prove it. Satan even quotes Scripture, Psalm 91:11–12, to reinforce the temptation. Perkins demonstrates this is an abuse of Scripture by appealing to context. Satan leaves out the last phrase of 91:11, which functions as the ground of the promise of angelic protection. The angels are charged to

---

85. This is precisely the interpretation according to context found in John Knox's exposition of this narrative (*A Notable and Comfortable Exposition of M. Iohn Knoxes, Vpon the Fourth of Mathew, Concerning the Tentations of Christ: First Had in the Publique Church, and Then Afterwards Written for the Comfort of Certaine Priuate Friends, but Now Published in Print for the Benefite of All That Feare God* [London: Robert Waldegraue, for Thomas Man, dwelling in Pater-noster-row, at the signe of the Talbot, 1583], n.p.). And also on the Marian exiles in Thomas Bentham's interpretation of this passage (*A Notable and Comfortable Exposition, Vpon the Fourth of Mathevv; Concerning the Tentations of Christ Preached in S.Peters Church, in Oxenford; By Thomas Bentham, Fellovv Ov Magdalin Colledge and Afterwards Vyshop of Liechfeeld and Coventrie* [London: Robert Waldegraue, dwelling in Foster-Lane, ouer against Goldsmiths Hall, 1583], n.p.).

86. Perkins, *Whole Works*, 3:381–82, 385. Knox and Bentham also understand the "word" to be God's extraordinary provision as illustrated in Israel's manna (Knox, *Notable and Comfortable Exposition*; Bentham, *Notable and Comfortable Exposition*).

keep in obedience, not to protect against recklessness. So again, context is essential to interpret Jesus' second temptation.[87]

In Satan's final attempt against Jesus, he shows Jesus all the kingdoms of the world and offers them in exchange for worship, thus tempting Jesus to idolatry. Perkins notes Satan's comment recorded in Luke 4:6 about having the kingdoms of the world delivered to him and the power to transfer them to whom he pleases. Collation shows Satan actually lied about this ownership, for Daniel 4:21 teaches that God alone rules over the kingdoms of men and gives them to whomever he wills.[88] Jesus rebuts the tempter once again with Scripture; this time, he quotes Deuteronomy 6:13. Perkins utilizes the analogy of faith to clarify. He understands the twofold division of divine worship as part of accepted Christian doctrine. Inward worship entails devotion of heart and soul with all their faculties to God. This serves as the ground and substance of all divine worship, such that true outward or bodily worship simply testifies to this inner reality. In his exposition of Jesus' third temptation, as in his interpretation of the whole narrative, Perkins uses Scripture to interpret itself according to his express hermeneutical method.[89]

REVELATION 1–3

In 1595, during the ordinary course of his lectures in Cambridge, Perkins preached through Revelation 1–3.[90] His series was published posthumously as *A Godly and Learned Exposition or Commentarie upon the Three First Chapters of Revelation*.[91] Perkins divides the passage up into the preface and

87. Perkins, *Whole Works*, 3:390–92. Bentham's interpretation mirrors Perkins's in its consideration of context, both the temptation to presumption based on the repetition of Christ's words by Satan and the excised phrase from Ps 91:11 (Bentham, *Notable and Comfortable Exposition*).

88. Bentham concludes the same but relies on the analogy of faith rather than collation (Bentham, *Notable and Comfortable Exposition*).

89. Perkins, *Whole Works*, 3:392–96.

90. This preaching date is indicated on the title page of the published work. In the text itself, Perkins refers to "even 36 yeares and upward" that Christ had been patient with England, which is likely a reference to the time elapsed after Queen Elizabeth's ascension (Perkins, *Whole Works*, 3:368).

91. The first edition of this work was compiled and edited by Robert Hill, fellow at St. John's College and longtime acquaintance of Perkins. The executors of Perkins's will charged Thomas Pierson with revising and expanding it based on a more perfect copy of notes from the sermons. This final edition came out in 1606.

John's vision, 1:1–8 and 1:9–3:22, respectively.[92] He devotes the most space to the epistles to the seven churches, commands given to John to write. As he discusses these epistles, Perkins uses the analogy of faith, context, and collation in an effort to let Scripture interpret itself.[93] This will be demon-

92. This is precisely the division that Perkins's contemporary George Gifford makes (*Sermons Vpon the Whole Booke of the Reuelation. Set Forth by George Gyffard, Preacher of the Word at Mauldin in Essex* [London: T. Orwin for Thomas Man and Toby Cooke, 1596], 4–5).

93. A notable exception is Perkins's eschatology, in which post-Scripture events are identified and the beast and antichrist are associated with political and ecclesiastical Rome. This diversion must be understood in historical context. From her exploration of sixteenth-century Protestant commentaries on Revelation, Irena Backus concludes that the Reformed tradition did not see it "fundamentally as a book written for their own era. Only the papal Antichrist struck an immediate chord." In fact, "the sole common feature of all the commentaries is their unhesitating identification of the papacy as the apocalyptic adversary" (*Reformation Readings of the Apocalypse: Geneva, Zurich, and Wittenburg* [Oxford: Oxford University Press, 2000], 137–38). From Luther in 1530 to Jonathan Edwards, belligerence between Protestants and Roman Catholics was viewed as apocalyptic. It was out of this fertile ground that millenarianism was born, but after Perkins (Jeffrey Jue, "Puritan Millenarianism in Old and New England," in Coffey and Lim, *Cambridge Companion to Puritanism*, 261–62).

Luther followed Augustine in his understanding of eschatology but added a historicist approach. Calvin and the Reformed tradition developed eschatological optimism on top of this, for the Reformation, as an act of God, would surely triumph (Peter Toon, *Puritans, the Millennium and the Future of Israel: Puritan Eschatology 1600 to 1600* [London: James Clarke, 1970], 25). The historicist approach was not meant to be speculative or inconsistent with *sola Scriptura*; rather, for the Reformed tradition, the concept of mediate prophecy allowed for the application of Scripture to unfolding history (Beeke and Jones, *Puritan Theology*, 774–75).

As for Perkins himself, he rarely considered eschatological themes, but his views are accessible in his corpus. His *A Digest or Harmony of the Bookes of the Old and New Testament* reveals a historicist Augustinianism. He dates the binding and release of Satan to AD 295 and 1195 respectively, so the millennium is in the past. The two prophets in sackcloth preached in 395. The beast with seven heads persecuted the church and prophets in 495. In 695 another beast helped the first beast. The seals were opened in 795 and the four horsemen released in 895. Still to come, from Perkins's perspective, are the slaying of two prophets, the overcoming of the beast and whore of Babylon, the conquest over the dragon and death, the first resurrection, the last judgment, and the glory of the saints (Perkins, *Whole Works*, 2:736–27). Perkins discounts all dating of Christ's return and/or the end of the world in *A Fruitfull Dialogue Concerning the End of the World*. "Christian" responds to "Worldling" with regard to doomsday in 1588. Such claims are "flying tales" and "very lies," no more trustworthy than "Merlins drunken prophecies, or the tales of Robinhood." He says, "It is not possible for any to find out the time of the end of the world," and it would be unlawful if it were possible (Perkins, *Whole Works*, 3:467). After a catalogue of the harbingers of eschatological doom are enumerated, Perkins, or "Christian," lists seven signs that must come to pass before the end, the first six of which are complete or being completed: preaching of the gospel throughout the world, revealing of the antichrist (when Gregory declared himself universal bishop in 602), mass defection from the faith, corruption of manners, calamity, and exceeding hardness of heart. The seventh has yet to happen, the "conversion of the Jewes unto that religion which now they hate, as appeareth in the eleven to the Romans (Perkins, *Whole Works*, 3:470; see also 1:260–61). This last sign is of interest because it is absent in the earlier reformers. The view became a major competitor through the marginal notes of the Geneva Bible (Crawford Gribben, *The Puritan Millennium: Literature and Theology, 1550–1682*, rev. ed., Studies in Christian History

strated through examples from the preface, the vision of Christ, and the letters to the seven churches.

EXEGESIS OF THE PREFACE

Perkins sees potential Trinitarian and christological misunderstandings in Revelation's very first verse, to which he responds with the analogy of faith. That Jesus Christ is the author of this revelation does not exclude the other two persons of the Trinity. However, Christ, as the Second Person of the Trinity, does hold the special office of manifesting the will of God the Father to the church. The next phrase of Revelation 1:1 asserts this revelation was given to Christ by God. This does not mean that Christ is somehow less than God, lacking something. Rather, a distinction must be recognized between Christ as God and as mediator. As Christ is God, the Father gives him nothing. They are equal and hold everything mutually, with the exception of their personal properties. Yet, as mediator, Christ is God incarnate and is said to receive from his Father with respect to his humanity.[94]

Perkins defends this classic christological distinction from various passages of Scripture. Jesus himself claims that all power was given to him (Matt 28:18). Paul asserts that Christ was given the name above all names

---

and Thought [Milton Keynes, UK: Paternoster, 2008], 38). It is also significant because it indicates that the future is not totally bleak, which adds to the eschatological optimism that would later be picked up by millennialists.

Perkins fits with the bulk of Puritan eschatology in the sixteenth century and first three decades of the seventeenth. With anti-Catholicism, an Augustinian understanding of the millennium, and belief in an end-time conversion of the Jews, he did not go further than claiming that the end was near (Gribben, *Puritan Millennium*, 38). He uncomfortably straddles amillennial and premillennial positions, with his placement of the thousand-year binding of Satan in the past and his reference to a first resurrection in the future. This illustrates the danger of simplistic and anachronistic categories. Crawford Gribben warns that "there was a great deal of latitude both *between* and *within* apocalyptic discourse, and the contemporary distinctions between a-, pre- and postmillennialism simply do not account for the varieties of puritan belief" (*Puritan Millennium*, 29). For more on this topic, see Jeffrey K. Jue, *Heaven upon Earth: Joseph Mede (1586–1638) and the Legacy of Millenarianism*, International Archives of the History of Ideas (Dordrecht, Netherlands: Springer, 2006); Bryan W. Ball, *A Great Expectation: Eschatological Thought in English Protestantism to 1660*, Studies in the History of Christian Thought (Leiden: Brill, 1975); Richard Baukham, *Tudor Apocalypse: Sixteenth-Century Apocalypticism, Millenarianism and the English Reformation, from John Bale to John Foxe and Thomas Brightman* (Appleford, UK: Sutton Courtenay, 1978).

94. Gifford develops this same distinction between Christ as God and Christ as mediator (Gifford, *Sermons Vpon the Whole Booke of the Reuelation*, 5–6).

(Phil 2:9). Peter references Jesus receiving the promise of the Spirit and being made Lord and Christ (Acts 2:33, 36). Perkins then uses collation to defend the fact that Christ the mediator's receiving from the Father does not imply inferiority of Christ as God the Son. The point is that Perkins begins his exposition of Revelation with his scriptural hermeneutic, specifically the analogy of faith and collation.[95]

Revelation 1:3 promises blessing to its readers and hearers, and Perkins explains, via collation, that this is contingent on a certain frame of heart. He then lists the four heart qualities necessary for blessed reading and hearing: humility, honesty, belief, and hearing. Perkins cites James 4:6; Psalm 25:9; and Isaiah 57:15 as support for the argument that humble hearts are the exclusive receptors of grace. Similarly, the honest heart is referenced in Luke 8:15, which Perkins sees as one with the true purpose of living in no known sin. Hebrews 4:2 couples the reception of the word with faith. Finally, according to Psalm 40:6, blessed hearing must be true hearing. Having physical ears is not enough; the heart must also have ears. So Perkins qualifies the promise of Revelation 1:3 with other passages of Scripture.[96]

Perkins uses context to interpret the seven spirits of the next verse as a reference to the Holy Spirit. He notes that they are commonly taken as seven angels before God's throne. But this cannot be the referent, for grace and peace proceed from the seven in this passage. Further, this verse is a benediction, and if the seven spirits were angels, then angels would come before Christ. Identifying the seven spirits as the Third Person of the Trinity "is most agreeable to all the circumstances of the Text" and is warranted for two reasons. First, though the Spirit is one in substance, he is manifold, or seven, with regard to the gifts and operations that proceed

95. Perkins, *Whole Works*, 3:208–9. The commentary on Revelation by Francis Junius was published in English just three years before Perkins's sermon series. Junius's treatement of the text in general is quite brief in comparison, serving more as annotations, and he seems uninterested in the fine doctrinal qualification and expansion characteristic of Perkins (Franciscus Junius, *Apocalypsis: A Briefe and Learned Commentarie Vpon the Reuelation of Saint Iohn the Apostle and Euangelist, Applyed Vnto the History of the Catholicke and Christian Church. Written in Latine by M. Francis Iunius Doctor of Diuinitie, and Professor in the Vniuersitie of Heidelberge: And Translated into English for the Benefit of Those That Vnderstand Not the Latine.* [London: Richard Field for Robert Dexter, dwelling in Paules Church yard, at the signe of the brasen serpent, 1592], 1).

96. Perkins, *Whole Works*, 3:214.

from him. Second, the Spirit is seen in the form of seven lights in Revelation 4:5. Perkins provides a close reading of the immediate context as well as the larger context of the book to arrive at his interpretation.[97]

In the last verse of Revelation's preface, Christ claims to be the beginning and the end, a claim Perkins illuminates with other passages of Scripture. That Christ is the beginning first means he was before all things. He existed when no creatures existed. John 1:1 claims this for the Word, who is God the Son, the person of Christ. He is further called the beginning because all things were created by him. This is what Paul states in Colossians 1:16, that all things are from Christ. This verse also sheds light on Christ as the end of all things when Paul speaks of all things as created for him, that is to say, to serve his glory and result in his praise.[98] From beginning to end, his interpretation of John's preface leans on Scripture's ability to interpret itself.

EXEGESIS OF THE VISION OF CHRIST

Perkins continues his method as he exposits the vision of Christ himself. John says he saw "one like the son of man" in Revelation 1:13, which Perkins explains through context, collation, and the analogy of faith. Context rules out understanding the word "like" to indicate something other than Christ, perhaps an angel, for this "one" is previously said to be the first and last, once dead but now alive. The only possible referent is Christ. That said, neither is this a vision of Christ in his true manhood, for that would violate the analogy of faith. Christ is in heaven, seated at the right hand of the Father. When Stephen saw Christ, he saw his true humanity because at that point the Lord Jesus had ascended into heaven (Acts 7:55–56). Paul also

---

97. Perkins, *Whole Works*, 3:218. Junius offers a strikingly similar argument for the seven spirits representing God the Holy Spirit (Junius, *Apocalypsis*, 2). Another contemporary interpreter, John Napier, a Scottish mathematician who published a treatment of Revelation aimed at the Church of Rome and dating the apocalypse, affirms this understanding of the seven spirits (John Napier, *A Plaine Discouery of the Whole Reuelation of Saint Iohn Set Downe in Two Treatises: The One Searching and Prouing the True Interpretation Thereof: The Other Applying the Same Paraphrastically and Historically to the Text. Set Foorth by Iohn Napeir L. of Marchistoun Younger. Whereunto Are Annexed Certaine Oracles of Sibylla, Agreeing with the Reuelation and Other Places of Scripture* [Edinburgh: Robert Waldegraue, printer to the Kings Majestie, 1593], 72). See also Gifford for agreement in this interpretation (*Sermons Vpon the Whole Booke of the Reuelation*, 12–13).

98. Perkins, *Whole Works*, 3:233.

saw the Lord (1 Cor 9:5), but whether he saw his true manhood is unknown. In this case, John did not see Christ's true manhood but a resemblance of it. This interpretation is faithful to the context, the analogy of faith, and other passages in Scripture.[99]

Perkins brings other Scriptures to bear on the comparison of Christ's voice to the sound of many waters in Revelation 1:15. The sound of many waters first signifies the loudness and greatness of Christ's voice in that it is heard throughout the world through the ministry of the gospel, a promise testified to in both the Old and New Testaments. This great sound further signifies the power and efficacy of Christ's voice, the same voice that created the world (Heb 12:3) and called Lazarus out of the grave (John 11:43). One day, Christ will speak and all the dead will rise (John 5:28–29). Scripture attests to the power of Christ's voice, which Perkins uses to interpret the idea here in Revelation that it projects with the sound of many waters.[100]

Perkins similarly uses Scripture to make sense of Jesus' tongue as a sword. This sharp, two-edged sword is the doctrine of the law and the gospel. Hebrews 4:12 compares the word of God to a two-edged sword. Just as this kind of sword cuts and pierces deeply, so the law and gospel pierce the heart. The word of God also has a twofold effect as it operates differently on the reprobate and the elect.

For the reprobate, it brings eternal death (Isa 11:4). The word consumes the antichrist (2 Thess 2:8) and slays the dragon, the great enemy of the church (Isa 27:1). Perkins understands the judgment of the word to be threefold even in this life. Under its ministry, the wicked are shown their transgressions against the second table of the law, as seen in 1 Corinthians 14:24–25. Second, the word's judgment reveals the curse of the law as well as God's indignation and wrath against sin. This is the killing letter, per 2 Corinthians 3:6. Finally, the ministry of the word afflicts even the unregenerate conscience. This is clear in the cases of Felix and Belshazzar.

For the elect, the word also wounds, but through its wounding brings life instead of death. As God regenerates the heart and people are converted, the ministry of the word cuts away the old man. In John 15, Jesus calls this

99. Perkins, *Whole Works*, 3:246–47. Gifford shares Perkins's concern to emphasize the location of Christ in his manhood in heaven (Gifford, *Sermons Vpon the Whole Booke of the Reuelation*, 27).

100. Perkins, *Whole Works*, 3:250.

pruning. In Ephesians 6:17, the word is also called a sword in the hands of the elect, a defense against temptation. The sword is not an uncommon image in the Bible, and it often refers to God's word. Perkins returns to this reality as he interprets this vision of Christ with a sword protruding from his mouth.[101]

EXEGESIS OF THE EPISTLES

The majority of John's vision in Revelation 2–3 consists of Christ's command to write to the seven churches. Perkins consistently applies his scriptural hermeneutic to difficult verses within these epistles. In Christ's scolding of Ephesus (2:4), he remarks that the church left its first love. Perkins employs collation to qualify this with the doctrine that grace cannot be wholly and finally lost. He sets out to "shew the truth" of this doctrine "out of God's word." Matthew 16:18 teaches that the gates of hell will not prevail against the church, built on Peter's profession. Matthew 24:24 records Jesus claiming the impossibility of false prophets seducing the elect. In John 10:27–28, Jesus explicitly teaches that his sheep will never perish and no one can pluck them from the Father's hand. Paul in Romans 8 articulates the golden chain of salvation and argues that nothing can separate God's people from him. These and similar passages make it clear for Perkins that grace cannot finally be lost and that "losing one's first love" refers to decaying zeal and growing cold in good works.[102]

Perkins uses context to interpret Christ's comforting words to the church at Smyrna. John relays that their tribulation will last ten days. Some understand this to mean a long time, citing the stories of Jacob and the Israelites. Jacob complains to Laban that he had changed his wages ten times—that is, often (Gen 31:41). The Israelites are said to sin against the Lord ten times—that is, many times (Num 14:22). But such an interpretation does not fit this place, for here Christ purposes to comfort his people. Others claim the ten days represent ten years, appealing to the fact that

101. Perkins, *Whole Works*, 3:251–53. Napier organizes his commentary as discussion of the meaning of the text in a parallel column next to the text of Scripture. After each chapter, he then includes endnotes, which provide his exegesis. Upon consulting both of these, the similarities with Perkins in the interpretation of Rev 1:15–16 are obvious. This is true of the conclusions as well as the evidence (Napier, *Plaine Discouery of the Whole Reuelation*, 73–81).

102. Perkins, *Whole Works*, 3:269–70. Gifford concurs (*Sermons Vpon the Whole Booke of the Reuelation*, 46–47).

years and days are sometimes used interchangeably in Scripture. But there is no confirmation that Smyrna's affliction lasted ten years. Perkins opts for the understanding that ten days here refers to a short space of time, a limited amount of time, "because it is most suitable to all circumstances."[103] Perkins rules out other interpretations with context, using Scripture to interpret itself.

In the letter to Pergamum, Christ promises manna and a new name written in a white stone to those who overcome. Perkins uses collation to decipher this symbol-laden passage. Manna literally signifies the food God provided from heaven during Israel's wandering in the wilderness. In 1 Corinthians 10:3, Paul calls manna "spiritual food," as it represented Christ, the true spiritual food. Jesus himself claims to be bread come down from heaven (John 6:51). So the manna promised here in Revelation is Christ himself, the true food of eternal life. The new name written in the white stone is the son or daughter of God. Perkins cites 1 John 3:1 as explicit support for this. Further, as God gives this name, it is no mere title; it serves as proof of a new condition. God changed Abram's name to "Abraham" when he changed his estate. God changed Jacob's name to "Israel" when a change occurred. Likewise, God terms people "children of God" when he regenerates them. In the case of both the promised manna and the new name, Perkins uses collation to interpret the symbols.[104]

Perkins also uses the analogy of faith to limit the interpretation of Christ's message to Thyatira that he will give power over nations to the one who overcomes. He then explains the promise through collation. First, Perkins rejects the idea that Christ's sovereign power over the world is given to any creature. In fact, Christ's rule is incommunicable, as are his offices of prophet and priest. Power over nations is received by virtue of being united to Christ by faith, the process by which one enjoys all of his benefits. Ephesians 2:6 teaches the saints will be raised with Christ; 1 Corinthians 6:2 teaches they will judge the world with Christ. Therefore,

---

103. Perkins, *Whole Works*, 3:289. Junius also explains that the ten days are representative of a short time from the context (*Apocalypsis*, 7). Napier and Gifford conclude that they represent ten years (Napier, *Plaine Discouery of the Whole Reuelation*, 88; Gifford, *Sermons Vpon the Whole Booke of the Reuelation*, 60–61).

104. Perkins, *Whole Works*, 3:306–7. Junius comes to similar conclusions but does not leave evidence of collation (*Apocalypsis*, 8).

at least one way Christ's servants possess power through their union with him is by sharing in his glory in heaven. Perkins qualifies this phrase, which could easily be misread, with commonly held Christian beliefs and then interprets it with other passages of Scripture.[105]

Perkins then moves on to exegete the preface to Christ's epistle to Sardis. He continues to use both the analogy of faith and other biblical passages as he interprets Christ's claim to have the seven spirits of God. Again, the seven spirits are the Holy Spirit, which Perkins argued in his exposition of Revelation 1:4. The question now is what it means for Christ to have the Spirit differently from David, Peter, Paul, and other saints. Perkins answers with a distinction of how Christ has the Spirit according to his two natures. With regard to his divinity, Christ is the beginning of the Spirit, for the Spirit as the Third Person of the Trinity proceeds from the Father and the Son. According to his humanity, Christ has the Spirit in that the Spirit poured the perfection of all graces and gifts into him. In this sense, the difference in dispensation of the Spirit between Christ and the saints is the number and degree of graces and gifts. Christ in his manhood received them all in their perfection. Psalm 45:7 foretells this, and John 3:34 clearly teaches it by saying the Father gives the Son the Spirit without measure. So the analogy of faith and collation help Perkins make a needed distinction between Christ having the Spirit and Christians having the Spirit.[106]

In Christ's letter to the church at Philadelphia, he promises to write his new name on the one who overcomes. Perkins has already demonstrated that such naming indicates regeneration and includes sharing in Christ's glory. Here, he uses collation to extend the effects of this naming into this life. He defends the position that those who have Christ's new name must become new creatures in this life. Perkins argues from Paul's statement in 2 Corinthians 5:17 that anyone in Christ is a new creature and the new creation language in Galatians 6:15. In Ephesians 4:23–24, Paul exhorts believers to put off the old man and put on the new because mere knowledge and a profession of faith fall short. Perkins is clear: Christ only gives a new name to new creatures. Yet again, Perkins's exegesis illustrates his

105. Perkins, *Whole Works*, 3:325. Junius also cites Eph 2:6 and 1 Cor 6:2 as evidence that the power over nations comes through union with Christ (Junius, *Apocalypsis*, 10).

106. Perkins, *Whole Works*, 3:327–28.

persistence in bringing other Scripture to bear on his interpretation of individual passages.[107]

The last letter is addressed to the church of Laodicea, in which Christ claims to stand at the door and knock, promising to enter if anyone hears his voice and opens the door. Perkins uses collation and context to explain the meaning of Christ's knocking. The Laodiceans had barred Christ out by their sins, yet Christ pursues them, using means to enter for their good and to extend mercy. Similarly, the Lord sought Adam in the garden; Isaiah 65:1 also speaks of the Lord finding those who never seek him; and the parable of the lost sheep features Christ going after the stray. But how does Christ knock? What are the means he uses? The answer can be found in previous verses, where Christ threatens the church. These reproofs and rebukes are Christ's knocking. Perkins uses context and collation to interpret Christ's metaphor for both his pursuit of sinners and his extension of mercy. In this specific instance, as throughout his exposition of Revelation 1–3, Perkins uses Scripture to interpret Scripture, employing the various tools of his hermeneutic.

A CLOUD OF FAITHFUL WITNESSES: HEBREWS 11

Perkins preached through Hebrews 11 sometime after 1595. The sermons were later published by William Crashaw and Thomas Pierson at the request of Perkins's executors, who heard them preached and recorded them. He begins by asserting that two points must be known by every Christian concerning faith: the doctrine and the practice. He references his exposition of the Apostles' Creed as a summary of the whole doctrine of faith and intends his sermons on Hebrews 11 to provide the practice of faith. Hebrews 11 serves this purpose well, because in it "the practice of faith is most excellently and at large set down." He understands this chapter in light of Hebrews 10, where the author exhorts Christians to persevere in faith to the end and patiently suffer whatever befalls them due to their profession. Hebrews 11 is a continuation of this exhortation. Perkins claims "the whole chapter (as I take it) is nothing else in substance, but

107. Perkins, *Whole Works*, 3:354. Napier arrives at similar conclusions about the naming but leaves no evidence of collation (*Plaine Discouery of the Whole Reuelation*, 97).

one reason to urge the former exhortation to perseverance in faith; and the reason is drawn from the *excellency of* faith."[108]

In short, the chapter's argument offers an imperative to persevere because faith is excellent. Perkins breaks the chapter down into two parts: 11:1–3, which describes faith, and 11:4–40, which illustrates faith. The recollection of faithful Old Testament saints is made up of many parts: individual and collective attention that references antediluvian characters, patriarchs, and Israel's national history. I will draw from each of these textual divisions to argue Perkins's presentation of the practice of faith from Hebrews 11 required significant exegesis that depends on his threefold method to interpret Scripture with Scripture.[109]

EXEGESIS OF THE DESCRIPTION OF FAITH

In his description of faith in Hebrews 11:1–3, Perkins uses the analogy of faith to address the question of how Old Testament saints were saved. Those whom God saved under the old covenant put their faith in the coming Messiah and were therefore approved by God in the same way as new-covenant saints—namely, by double imputation. The sins of those who believe were laid on Christ and made his, whereas the holiness, obedience, and satisfaction of Christ was imputed to the saints. So it is for Christ's sake alone that God approves of those who are united to him. Perkins argues the story of Jacob and Esau illustrates this doctrine. Jacob put on Esau's garment and was therefore taken for his older brother and obtained Isaac's blessing. God's people are like Christ's younger brother. They have no right or claim to God's blessing of salvation on their own; we must be clothed in the righteousness of Christ. In this case, Perkins uses the analogy of faith to interpret Hebrews 11:2 and collation to illustrate the conclusion.[110]

---

108. Perkins, *Whole Works*, 3:1, emphasis original. Pagination starts over after Perkins's exposition of the Sermon on the Mount, which is the first work in volume 3.

109. Muller notes that Perkins largely followed Tomson's revision of the Geneva Bible but that he did not follow the marginal notes. He was exegetically and theologically independent. He did change the punctuation according to the logic of his argument ("William Perkins," 77–78).

110. Perkins, *Whole Works*, 3:5. Samuel Bird, an English contemporary of Perkins and a fellow interpreter of Heb 11, shares Perkins's hermeneutical tools but in this case does not address the salvation of Old Testament saints (*The Lectures of Samuel Bird of Ipswidge upon the 11. Chapter of the Epistle Vnto the Hebrewes, and Vpon the 38 Psalme* [Cambridge: Iohn Legate, Printer to the Vniversitie of Cambridge, 1580], 1–9).

EXEGESIS OF PREFLOOD EXEMPLARS

The writer of Hebrews begins the examples of faith with three faithful men before the flood: Abel, Enoch, and Noah. Perkins uses other passages of Scripture to explain two components of Abel's sacrifice (11:4). His sacrifice is said to be greater than Cain's, a fact to which God testifies. His sacrifice was better because he brought the best of his herd, as much as he could afford. This is confirmed by later commandments of the ceremonial law. God desired the Israelites' firstborn (Exod 34:19) and their firstfruits (Lev 23:10)—nothing with any blemish (Deut 15:21). Abel's offering met these criteria. The text further says God made clear that Abel's sacrifice was an acceptable act of worship. It does not speak to the mechanism of this approval, but Perkins proposes it was through fire from heaven consuming the sacrifice. Such commendation is seen in the cases of Aaron (Lev 9:24), Solomon (2 Chr 7:1), and Elijah (2 Kgs 18:28). These texts, according to Perkins, make his interpretation likely, but as Scripture does not explicitly say, it remains uncertain. Nonetheless, Perkins utilizes collation as he arrives at his interpretation of Abel's sacrifice.[111]

Enoch is said to have pleased God by faith (11:5), which Perkins argues must have its ground and warrant in God's word because faith and the word are inseparable. They are "relatives, and one depends upon the other: no *faith* , no *word*, to binde: no *word*, no *faith* to beleeve." So Enoch's faithful actions were directed by the word of God. Perkins cites other passages to support this point. First, 2 Timothy 3:16–17 speaks to the inspiration and sufficiency of Scripture. Perkins rhetorically asks, "How can the sufficiencie of Scripture be more sufficiently in words expressed?" He then refers to 1 Timothy 4:4–5, which asserts that Scripture sanctifies Christians' good works. If every action is sanctified by the word, then there must be direction for every action in the word. Through collation, Perkins arrives at the necessary coupling of faith and God's word and then applies this general truth to his interpretation of Enoch.[112]

---

111. Perkins, *Whole Works*, 3:17, 20. Bird uses collation extensively in understanding the nature of Abel's acceptable sacrifice yet concludes that faith was the difference, faith in the *protoeuengelion* (*Lectures of Samuel Bird*, 9–11).

112. Perkins, *Whole Works*, 3:28, emphasis original. Bird, producing a much shorter commentary, uses collation in the explanation of Enoch's being "taken up" (*Lectures of Samuel Bird*, 11–13).

Perkins makes use of the analogy of faith to arrive at the conclusion that Noah's righteousness in Hebrews 11:7 refers to Christ's righteousness by imputation. He parses the different types of righteousness that he deems commonly accepted. There is uncreated or absolute righteousness belonging to God alone and then the created righteousness of human beings and angels. But according to Perkins, this kind of created righteousness is twofold. First, it comes in the form of legal righteousness, spoken of in Scripture as perfect, civil, or inward. Second, Perkins mentions an evangelical righteousness that refers to the righteousness of Christ revealed in the gospel. Only this latter type of righteousness makes one righteous before God because it is based on the purity of the mediator's nature and both his active and passive obedience. How does one procure this evangelical righteousness? It must be exchanged for the sins of the saints by double imputation. Perkins points to 2 Corinthians 5:21 as the biblical warrant for one being justified by the righteousness of another. Perkins articulates the various levels of righteousness to show that it is only Christ's righteousness that could justify Noah.[113]

EXEGESIS OF THE PATRIARCHS' EXAMPLE

Hebrews 11:8 transitions from preflood men of faith to the patriarchs, beginning with Abraham and the land promised as an inheritance. Perkins uses the analogy of faith and other passages of Scripture to explain how Abraham inherited the land. He did not inherit it personally but rather sacramentally and in his posterity. According to Perkins, Abraham possessed Canaan sacramentally, or mystically, because it is a type of the heavenly promised land. This correlation between the physical land of Canaan and heaven is taken by Perkins as commonly held Christian doctrine, without need of defense. Abraham can also be said to have inherited the land because his descendants actually possessed it. According to Galatians 3:17, 430 years passed between the promise to Abraham and Israelites inhabiting the land. Perkins employs both the analogy of faith and collation to explain exactly how Abraham could be said to benefit from the promise of God.[114]

113. Perkins, *Whole Works*, 3:54–57. Bird does not discuss the specifics of the righteousness to which Noah was heir (*Lectures of Samuel Bird*, 18).

114. Perkins, *Whole Works*, 3:66. Bird does not address the question of how Abraham can be said to benefit from the promise of God (*Lectures of Samuel Bird*, 20–23).

The writer of Hebrews asserts that by faith Abraham and Sarah had innumerable descendants, like the stars of heaven and the sand of the seashore, two phrases Perkins interprets as figurative. There are two problems with reading the verse with bare literalism. First, the stars in heaven and the grains of sand on the seashore are more numerable than literal descendants; second, and crucially, Abraham and Sarah only had one child, Isaac. For these reasons, Perkins takes the verse figuratively and sees the comparisons as rhetorical flourish. This is common in Scripture. Perkins cites John 21:25, where the apostle claims that all the books in the world could not contain the words and deeds of Jesus in their entirety. Earlier in Scripture, Moses notes that the Canaanite cities had walls up to heaven (Deut 9:1). In the case of Abraham's descendants, the referent is both the nation of Israel and the spiritual children of God. This figural reading is made obvious through Perkins's common tool of collation.[115]

Perkins uses various Old and New Testament passages to account for Abraham's greatest test of faith, the sacrifice of Isaac. A legitimate question from the Genesis 22 narrative is how Abraham could offer up Isaac, given its seeming contradiction to both the law of nature and of God. The answer, for Perkins, comes in the special command of God. A hierarchy exists in the commands of God. For instance, the first commandment is to honor God and the fifth to honor parents, but when the two contradict, honoring God takes precedent. Jesus makes this clear when he tells his disciples they will have to hate their families for his sake. In the case of Abraham's sacrifice of Isaac, God's direct command trumps the general precept not to kill. Another example of this is Moses' bronze serpent. God forbids graven images, yet he commands Moses to make a brazen serpent as part of his relief plan for the coming judgment of Israel.[116] From these instances, Perkins concludes that all of God's commands include an implied caveat: "unlesse God command otherwise, for God is an absolute Lord, and so above his owne Lawes, hee is not bound unto them, but may dispense with them, and with us for the keeping of them at his will and

115. Perkins, *Whole Works*, 3:92. Bird assumes the two similes are figurative but does not give a defense (*Lectures of Samuel Bird*, 32).

116. Perkins, *Whole Works*, 3:110–11.

pleasure."[117] Collation aids Perkins in explaining this seemingly unjustifiable command.

Moving to an exposition of Isaac's faith, Perkins makes use of Genesis 27 and the analogy of faith to expound the blessing of Jacob and Esau in Hebrews 11:20. Isaac's blessing of Jacob is considered an act of faith, even though it was a mistake. To be sure, Isaac purposed to bless Esau despite the prophecy that he would serve his younger brother. But after he unwittingly blessed Jacob, he refused to reverse what he had done, even though Esau begged him to change course. This explanation comes from Perkins's attention to the details of the original Genesis account. The analogy of faith brings further clarity to the narrative. The counsel of God overrules the will of human beings. That Jacob received the blessing makes this apparent; his silly plan to trick his father worked. Throughout his discussion, Perkins employs both collation and the analogy of faith to explain why an unlikely event such as Isaac's blessing of Jacob is held up as an exemplary act of faith.[118]

A similar act of faith is referenced in Hebrews 11:21, where Jacob blesses Joseph's younger son over the elder. Perkins returns to the original account in Genesis 48 and uses collation to defend Jacob's action as an act of faith. In the Genesis narrative, Joseph brings Manasseh and Ephraim to Jacob for blessing, placing Manasseh, the elder, at his right hand and Ephraim at his left. Jacob proceeds to cross his hands and give Ephraim the principal blessing. Jacob's choice was not a show of favoritism or human prerogative but rather in accordance with the prompting of God. The context reveals Jacob did not know one child from the other. Further, later Israelite history confirms the birthright was indeed given to Ephraim, for his tribe grew to be far more populous—so much so that in Hosea the name Ephraim is given for the whole of Israel. Even more, out of Ephraim came captains and kings of Israel, such as Joshua (1 Chr 7:27) and Jeroboam (1 Kgs 11:26).

---

117. Perkins, *Whole Works*, 3:111. Bird does not reconcile the seeming contradiction between God's command to Abraham and the law of nature and of God, but rather focuses his attention almost entirely on applicational points (*Lectures of Samuel Bird*, 41–44).

118. Perkins, *Whole Works*, 3:123–25. Bird also explains this unlikely affirmation of faith with a close reading of the Genesis narrative. Like Perkins, he sees Isaac's faith demonstrated in his resolve to maintain Jacob's blessing after having been tricked (*Lectures of Samuel Bird*, 44–46).

Again, context and collation explain how a seemingly unlikely event may be included as an exemplary act of faith.[119]

EXEGESIS OF EXAMPLES FROM ISRAELITE NATIONAL HISTORY

Perkins reads Moses' accounting the reproach of Christ greater than the riches of Egypt in light of other passages of Scripture. It is not that Moses spurned wealth, comfort, and honor absolutely but that he chose the best of these. The New Testament celebrates the notion that being rewarded for the reproach of Christ is greater than anything the world has to offer. For example, in the Sermon on the Mount, Jesus promises blessedness to those who suffer for his sake. Later, 1 Peter 4:14 confirms this promise. Suffering for Christ humbles sufferers and makes them like Jesus, which is a foreshadowing of the transformation to be experienced in glory. Similarly, in 2 Corinthians 4:17, Paul argues the temporary affliction of this life brings eternal glory. In 2 Timothy 2:11–12, he goes on to say that those who suffer with Christ will also reign with him. Last, according to Paul, suffering for Christ is a sign of God's special love (Phil 1:29). For these reasons, each of them drawn from the New Testament, it becomes clear that the reproach of Christ in fact is greater than anything Egypt had to offer Moses.[120]

The author of Hebrews provides two examples of faith from the conquest of Canaan, both from the fall of Jericho. It might seem cruel that every living thing in Jericho was subjected to slaughter, with the exception of Rahab's household, but Perkins interprets this in light of other biblical passages. God commands the destruction of Jericho as part of his purpose to purge the land of the Canaanites (Deut 7:3). Despite this purpose, God commands the Israelites to offer peace to cities they come on (Deut 20:10). However, in Deuteronomy 20:17, he commands Israel to put to death all those who do not agree to the Lord's terms of peace. Perkins concludes that even though Jericho was given the chance to surrender,

119. Perkins, *Whole Works*, 3:128. Bird also concludes from the Genesis account that because Jacob was blind, his crossing his hands was at the prompting of God. However, he stops short of defending the claim from later Israelite history (*Lectures of Samuel Bird*, 47–49).

120. Perkins, *Whole Works*, 3:144. Bird also uses collation to demonstrate that Moses was not simply denying himself wealth, comfort, and honor but choosing the greater riches that come with the suffferings of Christ (*Lectures of Samuel Bird*, 62–65).

the people trusted in their high walls, a mistake that resulted in their doom. In this case, Perkins resolves a seemingly cruel command of God with collation.[121]

From Hebrews 11:32 until the end of the chapter, the examples of faith are briefly mentioned and handled together, allowing Perkins to provide a fuller picture through specificity. The writer of Hebrews provides a representative list of judges, kings, and prophets and then enumerates ten fruits of their faith (11:33–35). Perkins uses collation to explain these fruits of faith. For example, the last fruit is that women received their dead raised to life, and Perkins highlights two accounts: Elijah raising the son of the widow of Zarephath, and Elisha raising the Shunammite's son. Though Hebrews 11:35–38 does not reference any specific individuals, from context Perkins understands those listed to be the faithful during the time of the Maccabees until the coming of Christ. With the phrase "others also," Hebrews 11:35 clearly distinguishes what follows from the judges, kings, and prophets. Hebrews 11:39 then says that all the faithful people throughout the chapter had not received the promise of the Messiah, ruling out early Christian martyrs. Perkins remains faithful to his hermeneutical model by interpreting these rapid references according to context and collation.[122]

Perkins uses his scriptural hermeneutic throughout his exposition of Hebrews 11. All three of his interpretive tools are present: context, collation, and the analogy of faith. He makes sense of the whole chapter in relation to the writer's overall argument and in relation to chapters 10 and 12 specifically. In doing so, Perkins consistently uses Scripture to interpret itself as he walks through the individual references in Hebrews 11. In the few places where he does not implement his hermeneutic, it is because "the words" are "plaine and easie, and need no exposition."[123] Such is the case with Joseph's faith in 11:22 and the faith of the Israelites in 11:29. But when words, phrases, and ideas of Hebrews 11 do need exposition, Perkins overwhelmingly applies his stated interpretive method.

---

121. Perkins, *Whole Works*, 3:168. Bird includes a rather lengthy discussion of Jericho and Rahab but does not take up the question of the righteousness of the extermination of the city's inhabitants (*Lectures of Samuel Bird*, 71–84).

122. Perkins, *Whole Works*, 3:182, 184. Bird understands 11:35–38 as a general commendation of the faith of saints throughout the ages (*Lectures of Samuel Bird*, 113).

123. Perkins, *Whole Works*, 3:131.

JUDE

Perkins preached sixty-six sermons on Jude, which the executors of his estate commissioned Thomas Taylor to edit and publish. In *A Godly and Learned Exposition upon the Whole Epistle of Jude*, Perkins employs his hermeneutical method to interpret every verse. Context plays a prominent role as Perkins sees Jude making a singular and coherent argument throughout the short epistle. In his introductory remarks, Perkins claims that in general, Jude exhorts

> all Christians to constancie and perseverance in their profession of the Gospell. Secondly, to be aware and take heed of false teachers and deceivers which craftily creepe in among them. And thirdly, these deceivers are lively set out in their colours; and with them their destruction.[124]

How does he arrive at this broad interpretation? Perkins sees Jude as including a salutation (1–2) and conclusion (24–25), like most epistles. The body of the letter comes in the form of an exhortation. Jude 3–4 states the exhortation explicitly, "contend for the faith," and Jude 5–20 provides an answer to an implied objection that the seducers profess Christ, so there is no real danger. Perkins's answer can be summarized: "All such persons as give themselves libertie to sinne, shall be destroyed; But these seducers give themselves libertie to sinne; and therefore shall be destroyed."[125] The epistle's major premise is found in Jude 5–7, which offers three examples of destruction due to sin. The book's minor premise and conclusion is contained in Jude 8–19. The seducers' destruction is the result of their giving themselves liberty to sin; Perkins notes eighteen specific sins. In verses 20–23, Jude enumerates the means for maintenance of the faith

---

124. Perkins, *Whole Works*, 3:480. Richard Turnbull, a contemporary English commentator on Jude with Perkins, describes the overall message of exhortation in Jude in the same way in his preface to the reader. He also similarly includes an extensive chart outlining the argument of the book (*An Exposition Vpon the Canonical Epistle of S. Iames, Diuided into 28 Sermons or Lectures Made and Written by Richard Turnbul . . . ; Whereunto Is Annexed the Exposition of the Same Authour Vpon the Canonicall Epistle of Sainte Iude, with Foure Sermons Made Vpon the Fiftenth Psalme* (London: Iohn Windet, dwelling by Paules VVharfe, at the signe of the Crosse Keyes, 1592).

125. Perkins, *Whole Works*, 3:521.

before he pens a distinctly doxological conclusion.[126] This overall context is key to Perkins's understanding of the particulars. At the same time, also important are the tools of collation and the analogy of faith. A sampling of Perkins's interpretation from each major division will demonstrate his faithful implementation of his scriptural hermeneutic.

Jude's salutation addresses those called, sanctified, and preserved, all concepts Perkins explains with the analogy of faith and collation. The analogy of faith distinguishes between a general and special call. God's special call is effectual. Perkins draws attention to the details of this effectual call with other biblical passages. For example, 2 Timothy 1:9 shows the ground of this call is the free election of God. The means of the call, according to 2 Thessalonians 2:14, is the gospel.[127] Elsewhere in Scripture, Acts 13:48 teaches that "called" people are also predestined people. The effectual call brings a heart of flesh (Ezek 11:19), as was the case with Lydia (Acts 16:15), which makes it a powerful work of God alone (Rom 4:18; 2 Cor 4:6). Regarding sanctification, Perkins makes the common distinction between mortification and vivification. He also notes that the grace of God must appear in each of the seven human faculties. For example, sanctification of the mind includes knowing the things given by God in salvation (1 Cor 2:12), whereas sanctification of the affections entails treasuring Christ above all things (Phil 3:8). Perkins makes significant use of collation in his interpretation of perseverance. Initially, he cites 1 Peter 1:5 to show that it is God who preserves. Then he notes four grounds of perseverance, supporting each with collation: election (Rom 8:3), the promise of God (Jer 32:40), the

---

126. One of Perkins's English contemporaries divides the book of Jude up in much the same way, though he does not summarize the argument succinctly as such by explaining the relationship of the parts (Andrew Willet, *A Catholicon, That Is, A Generall Preservative or Remedie against the Pseudocatholike Religion Gathered out of the Catholike Epistle of S. Jude, Briefly Expounded, and Aptly, according to the Time, Applied to More Then Halfe an Hundreth of Popish Errours, and as Many Corruptions of Manners. With a Preface Seruing as a Preparatiue to the Catholicon, and a Dyet Prescribed After* [Cambridge: Iohn Legat, Printer to the Vniversitie of Cambridge. And are to be sold at the signe of the Crowne in Paules Churchyard, London, by Simon Waterson, 1602], 3).

127. Turnbull similarly uses the analogy of faith and collation. He distinguishes between the internal and external call of God and cites 2 Tim 1:9 and 2 Thess 2:14 in his exposition as well (Turnbull, *Exposition Vpon the Canonical Epistle*, 9).

office of Christ (John 10:28, 17), and the quality of grace (1 John 3:9). Perkins interprets all three steps of eternal life with Scripture.[128]

Perkins takes Jude's exhortation to contend for the faith as an opportunity to define "the faith" in significant detail, drawing twenty-one doctrines for belief and eleven imperatives for practice. Unsurprisingly, he arrives at these doctrines and imperatives via his dependence on collation. First, 2 Timothy 1:13 provides the exegetical warrant for Paul's distinction between the heads of faith and love in the doctrine of the gospel, which is "the faith." Perkins begins his list of doctrines with Scripture and then moves through the major categories: God, man, salvation, the church, resurrection, and final judgment. Perkins's primary doctrine is the inspiration of all Scripture, and his second is the sufficiency of Scripture, both of which he discerns from 2 Timothy 3:16. The practices of the faith that Perkins enumerates include repentance, worship, love of neighbor, and faithfulness. One example of how he draws the practices from Scripture is his ninth imperative of justice, mercy, and humility, all of which find their expression in Micah 6:8.[129] This sampling illustrates the way Perkins draws the Christian faith's doctrines and practices—thirty-two in all—from various passages of Scripture.

When discussing the destruction of those who give themselves liberty to sin, Jude mentions angels, a somewhat unusual move that Perkins explains by bringing other Scriptures to bear on the text. In the Bible, excellent things are often called "angelic." In Genesis 33, after being reconciled to Esau, Jacob describes his countenance as the face of an angel. Psalm 78:25 praises manna as angel's food. Paul, in 1 Corinthians 13:1, references the tongues of angels, signifying that if angels had tongues they would be most admirable. David, in Psalm 8:5, alludes to the creation of man as inferior to the angels. By pulling together these passages about angels, Perkins makes the point that angels are the most glorious, beautiful, and excellent

128. Perkins, *Whole Works*, 3:482–87. Turnbull simply distinguishes between internal and external sanctification and then emphasizes that God is behind perseverance (Turnbull, *Exposition Vpon the Canonical Epistle*, 11–14).

129. Perkins, *Whole Works*, 3:492, 511. Willet includes nothing like this breakdown of doctrines and practices that make up "the faith" in his comments on verse 3 (*Catholicon*, 13–14). Neither does Turnbull (*Exposition Vpon the Canonical Epistle*, 23–24).

creatures, yet even they are not exempt from punishment for sin. Thus, through collation, Perkins explains Jude's illustration of the fall of angels.[130]

Perkins goes back to Genesis 4 to explain "the way of Cain," the fourth sin of which the false teachers were guilty. In sum, the way of Cain entailed following the lusts of his own heart instead of the will of God. Cain's way includes seven degrees. First, Cain evidenced hypocrisy in his worship; he offered sacrifices but in unbelief. Second, Cain hated his brother because Abel's works were good. The third step of Cain's sin was murder, which he followed by lying to God. Fifth, Cain showed desperation in his complaint about his punishment. Sixth, he demonstrated false security and carelessness by not regarding his sin but instead building a city to preserve his name on earth, since it was not written in heaven. Finally, the way of Cain ends in profaneness, a total disregard for the worship of God among his descendants until Enoch. To interpret Jude's reference to Cain, Perkins returns to its source in Genesis 4.[131]

The tenth sin is incurable hypocrisy, for which Jude uses the picture of a fruitless tree, twice dead and plucked up. Perkins argues with a combination of collation and the analogy of faith that this double death is original sin and actual sin. He cites 1 John 2:19 against the idea that the second death mentioned here is spiritual death after regeneration. Those who fall away should be considered hypocrites. Romans 11:20 is sometimes used as evidence for the possibility of Christians losing their salvation. Perkins uses the analogy of faith to oppose such an interpretation by saying there are two kinds of planting: outward and inward. The distinction is true faith versus mere profession. In Jude's reference, his opponents have only the outward planting. Perkins uses both widely accepted doctrine and other verses to let Scripture make clear what could easily be misinterpreted.[132]

---

130. Perkins, *Whole Works*, 3:527. Willet does not attempt to explain Jude's reference to angels but similarly to Perkins concludes that the lesson is to take seriously God's judgment (*Catholicon*, 33–34). In his extensive treatment of the verse, neither does Turnbull, though he likewise sees the angels referenced as an example to motivate contending for the faith (*Exposition Vpon the Canonical Epistle*, 46–55).

131. Perkins, *Whole Works*, 3:549. Willet does not include such a sophisticated breakdown of Cain's sins, but he does recall Gen 4 and trace the "way of Cain" back to his hate and envy (*Catholicon*, 70). Similarly to Perkins, Turnbull also recounts Gen 4 and concludes that the way of Cain included five sins (*Exposition Vpon the Canonical Epistle*, 73–74).

132. Perkins, *Whole Works*, 3:560. Willet simply asserts that the reference is to hypocrites, assuming the doctrine of the saints' perseverance (*Catholicon*, 78). Turnbull understands twice

Perkins then employs collation to expound the meaning of restoration through fear, one of the means for maintaining the faith, which he terms "Christian severity." In the immediate context, Jude speaks of restoration through mercy and compassion, so the context shows that those who are subjected to Christian severity ought to first be shown gentleness in attempts at restoration. If gentler tactics fail, then salvation through fear is in order, the means of which are either civil or spiritual. According to Romans 13:4, the magistrate wields the sword so the wicked might fear. According to Perkins, however, the referent here is spiritual means, a fact made clear through the fact that Jude is addressing a church. Excommunication as laid out in Matthew 18:17 is a most severe censure, for in this case the whole church accounts the sinner unregenerate. We see this happen in 1 Corinthians 5:5, when an incestuous person is "delivered over to Satan." Perkins appeals to the teaching of Jesus and Paul and in so doing equates restoration by fear with excommunication.[133]

In his conclusion to his letter, Jude offers praise to "him who is able." Perkins explains this as the power of Christ, using collation to understand what this power consists of and the analogy of faith to grasp how Christ has it. According to Perkins, Christ's power can be split into two spheres: absolute and actual. Absolute power is his power to do even those things he will never do. Perkins gives two examples: when John the Baptist says God is able to raise up stones for Abraham's seed and when it is said that Jesus on the cross could have rescued himself by legions of angels. Christ's actual power, however, is the power by which he accomplishes his purposes. This may also be understood in parts: general and special. Christ's general actual power is his providential ordering of all reality, as spoken of in Psalm 115:3. His special actual power accompanies his grace, per Ephesians 1:19. In Jude, the context makes it clear that he is referring to this latter power. Passages such as Matthew 28:18 and Acts 2:36 teach that Christ's power was given to him in time, which would impinge his divinity if it were

---

dead as "altogether dead" and "unprofitable" and does not reference the issue of perseverance (*Exposition Vpon the Canonical Epistle*, 86–87).

133. Perkins, *Whole Works*, 3:587. For Willet, restoration through fear is a reference to preaching the law and threats of God's judgment, not specifically excommunication, though he does reference 1 Cor 5 as an example (*Catholicon*, 151). For Turnbull it is both threatening God's judgment and church discipline, specifically excommunication, as seen in 1 Cor 5 (*Exposition Vpon the Canonical Epistle*, 115).

not for the doctrine of the two natures of Christ handed down to Christians via the analogy of faith. As God, the Son cannot be said to receive power, but as man he can indeed be given power. His role as mediator required laying aside his power, subjecting himself to servanthood and even death. So again, in his resurrection and ascension, Christ received power. In his interpretation of Jude's concluding doxology, Perkins uses all three components of his scriptural hermeneutic.[134] This is characteristic of his handling of the whole epistle.

AN EXHORTATION TO REPENTANCE: ZEPHANIAH 2:1–2

In 1593, Perkins preached a series of sermons from Zephaniah 2. They were later published as *A Faithfull and Plaine Exposition upon the Two First Verses of The Second Chapter of Zephaniah*, also titled *A Powerful Exhortation to Repentance*.[135] William Crashaw, the editor and publisher, claims to have taken down Perkins's words himself, which were intended to stir up repentance. His exhortation is addressed to the nation of England, which he sees as having enjoyed abundant blessings from God but must repent of its sins to escape his impending judgment. Perkins uses the analogy of faith, context, and collation to allow Scripture to interpret Zephaniah 2:1–2, from which he urges his countrymen to repent.

Perkins begins by setting the passage in its context. In the first chapter, the prophet rebukes the Jews for their crimes of idolatry, fraud, and cruelty. In this second chapter, he exhorts them to repentance. In these first two verses, Zephaniah aims his exhortation at the obstinate and impenitent Jews; in the first verse, he is speaking to those less culpable. Perkins focuses on the former and expounds the text in five points. First, he focuses on the duty to be performed, which is to search. Second, he addresses the question of who is to be searched: "yourselves," which refers to the Jews, the

134. Perkins, *Whole Works*, 3:590–91. Willet's and Turnbull's explanation of "him who is able" centers on God the Father (Willet, *Catholicon*, 158–60; Turnbull, *Exposition Vpon the Canonical Epistle*, 117–18).

135. This date comes from multiple references to thirty-five years of gospel preaching and God's favor in England in the text, which are references to the reign of Elizabeth I, beginning in 1558 (Perkins, *Whole Works*, 3:421, 426). Also, in the dedicatory epistle, William Crashaw references Perkins's 1592 *Treatise of Repentance* and adds that that these sermons followed "shortly after."

third point. Fourth, the coming judgment of God provides the clear time limitation for repentance. Finally, the reason for repentance is implied in the previous point: the judgment of God.[136] Perkins draws each of these points from the text and walks through them, illustrating and applying each. Again, his interpretation is done with the typical tools of his scriptural hermeneutic.

Based on context, Perkins decides on the translation of "search." The term is commonly glossed as "gather," which Perkins acknowledges makes sense and is comprehended in the original. But he prefers "search" or "fan," which he sees as synonymous. The idea of "searching," "fanning," or "sifting" fits best because of the image of chaff being blown away at the end of the second verse. So, the command to "search yourselves" means "search, try, and fanne your selves, lest you be found like chaffe, and so flye away, and be consumed before the justice of God."[137] This task of searching is essential to the act of true repentance.

Perkins asserts that searching oneself must be done by the law, for it is the standard of holiness. He notes three rules for profitable searching by the law, using collation and the analogy of faith to expound on them. His first rule is important: every man from Adam has sinned in the sin of Adam. Perkins assumes this as an article of faith, but after articulating the implications of Adamic headship, he cites Romans 5:12 as his specific biblical warrant. Perkins's second rule is that in every natural man, the seeds of all sins exist. This accounts for the corruption of original sin, which Perkins again assumes as part of the analogy of faith. This corruption exists specifically in two parts: deprivation of all good inclination and proneness to all evil. The third rule is that human beings by nature are children of wrath and therefore enemies of God. Perkins cites Psalm 51:5 as support, but he appeals to the analogy of faith to explain what the curse of God consists of. He understands the curse to include bondage to Satan and the first and second deaths. Perkins also asserts the three rules for examining oneself by the law for repentance as part of the analogy of faith. Unsurprisingly, when he supports these rules with Scripture it is by simple collation.[138]

---

136. Perkins, *Whole Works*, 3:411.
137. Perkins, *Whole Works*, 3:411.
138. Perkins, *Whole Works*, 3:415–17.

Perkins answers the question of why Jews are not worthy to be called a beloved nation with context and collation. The context of Zephaniah 1 reveals that the Jews were guilty of three major sins: covetousness, cruelty, and deceit. These sins plagued even their princes, rulers, and priests—those who were supposed to be exemplary—and therefore made the nation and its rules all the more intolerable before God. Perkins points to the rest of Scripture to explain what it means for a nation to be unworthy. He particularly notes Israel's history and the fact that God blessed them above all others. This favor includes the covenant of grace, the oracles of God, and the promised land. This larger biblical context, coupled with the immediate context, explains the Jews' unworthiness as a nation.[139]

Perkins explains the metaphor of chaff passing away using the analogy of faith and collation. God is likened to a great husbandman, who sifts every person in the history of the world by separating his true followers from everyone else, the wheat from the chaff. Perkins asserts that God will do this definitively at the last judgment, a commonly held tenet of the Christian faith. He then explores the reality of this sifting as it takes place in the present world as well. On this point, Perkins draws from elsewhere in Scripture to argue for two "fans" used by God for this purpose: the preaching of the word and judgment. He cites Matthew 3:12, where John the Baptist identifies the preaching of the gospel as a fan that God uses to get rid of the chaff. However, when preaching does not bring repentance, judgment follows.[140] From particulars such as this to expounding the larger picture, Perkins uses his hermeneutic with its varying tools to interpret Zephaniah 2:1–2.

CONCLUSION

When wading through the spectrum of Perkins's sermons and commentaries, from those written in his own hand to those edited and published after his death, from serial lectures to his occasional and more public sermons, a consistent theme presents itself. Perkins used Scripture to interpret Scripture. In doing so, he relentlessly appeals to the analogy of faith, context, and collation as he explains individual texts. The implementation

139. Perkins, *Whole Works*, 3:419–20.

140. Perkins, *Whole Works*, 3:425.

of his scriptural hermeneutic formed the foundation for both the doctrines he emphasized and the uses he applied. After all, this threefold preaching method was the vehicle in which Perkins placed his hopes for further reformation. As it became clear that the desired reform would not come from the top down, preaching took on the primary role of transforming the superstitious, the ignorant, and the immoral populace into a godly people. The exposition of Scripture, with its interpretation and doctrine, directly combated popery, false beliefs, sheer ignorance, and other sinful practices. All of this appears in Perkins's plain preaching ministry. Biblical exposition remained central to the other genres in which Perkins worked as well, a point to which we now turn.

4

EXEGESIS IN PRACTICAL WORKS

For the Puritans, two commitments were nonnegotiable: the moral reformation of society, and piety at the personal and family levels. Both ignorant minds and sinful lifestyles needed to be remedied.[1] In an effort to bring every area of life into conformity with God's word, Perkins not only applied Scripture in preaching but also in numerous publications both on the Christian life and for the benefit of the clergy. I will consider these in order, arguing that Scripture and its interpretation according to the principles of *The Arte of Prophecying* played an integral role from beginning to end.

THE CHRISTIAN LIFE

Elizabethan England is normally regarded as a time of intellectual and cultural achievement, even as much of the population remained mired in various economic and social problems.[2] As the population grew 25 percent, the real value of wages declined 40 percent. The labor force swelled, which kept wages low, and food prices spiked because of greater demand.[3] The importation of precious metals from the New World caused inflation throughout Europe. Further, there were recurring years of famine throughout the 1590s.[4] In short, distress was widespread in both urban

1. Charles E. Hambrick-Stowe, "Practical Divinity and Spirituality," in Coffey and Lim, *Cambridge Companion to Puritanism*, 192.

2. For the achievements of Elizabeth I's reign, see John Guy, *Tudor England* (Oxford: Oxford University Press, 1988), 250–458; Susan Doran, *Queen Elizabeth I* (New York: New York University Press, 2003); David Michael Loades, *Elizabeth I* (London: Hambledon, 2003); Paul E. J. Hammer, *Elizabeth's Wars: War, Government, and Society in Tudor England, 1544–1604* (New York: Palgrave Macmillan, 2003).

3. Hindle, "Poverty and the Poor Laws," 301–15; Ian W. Archer, "Commerce and Consumption," in Doran and Jones, *Elizabethan World*, 411–26.

4. Patterson, *William Perkins*, 136; Paul Slack, *Poverty and Policy in Tudor and Stuart England* (London: Longman, 1988), 37–60; Guy, *Tudor England*, 403–7.

areas and the countryside.[5] The number of households below the level of subsistence reached 25 percent.[6]

Of course, some prospered during this time of increased commerce, but this was largely restricted to the few entrepreneurs and shrewd landowners. The textile industry expanded; lead, copper, and coal production enlarged; construction rose in isolated areas; and shipbuilding grew. It was the eve of the Industrial Revolution and the age of Western expansion.[7] Wise farmers began to breed increasing numbers of sheep for the growing wool market, which required fewer laborers and therefore put many out of work.[8] Large swaths of the population became transient, and whole families found themselves in vagrancy.[9] Such fluidity was unsettling enough to a society accustomed to fixed lifestyles and social categories, but add to this the increased level of crime, and one starts to see the volatility of the situation.[10]

In this setting, Perkins used Scripture to address people familiar with the brutality and banality of premodern life. He addressed them as individuals yet also as members of the human community, specifically in

5. Steve Hindle, *The State and Social Change in Tudor and Stuart England, c. 1550–1640* (Basingstoke, UK: Palgrave Macmillan, 2002), 38–50; Griffiths, "Tudor Troubles," 316–34.

6. Archer, "Commerce and Consumption," 415.

7. Ian W. Archer and F. Douglas Price, eds., *English Historical Documents, 1558–1603* (London: Routledge, 2011), 530–34; Joan Thirsk, *Economic Policy and Projects: The Development of a Consumer Society in Early Modern England* (Oxford: Clarendon, 1978), 45–77, 169; Patterson, *William Perkins*, 137; D. M. Palliser, *The Age of Elizabeth: England under the Later Tudors, 1547–1603*, 2nd ed. (London: Longman, 1992), 339–47; Muriel C. McClendon and Joseph P. Ward, "Urban Economies," in Doran and Jones, *Elizabethan World*, 427–38.

8. For change in English rural life, see R. W. Hoyle, "Rural Economies under Stress: 'A World So Altered,'" in Doran and Jones, *Elizabethan World*, 439–57; Mark Overton, *Agricultural Revolution in England: The Transformation of the Agrarian Economy, 1500–1850* (Cambridge: Cambridge University Press, 1996).

9. Marjorie K. McIntosh, *Poor Relief in England, 1350–1600* (Cambridge: Cambridge University Press, 2012), 141–85.

10. Paul Griffiths, *Lost Londons: Change, Crime, and Control in the Capital City, 1550–1660* (Cambridge: Cambridge University Press, 2008), 27–66, 98–178. See also Patterson, *William Perkins*, 138; Keith Wrightson, *Earthly Necessities: Economic Lives in Early Modern Britain* (New Haven, CT: Yale University Press, 2000), 132–81; Brodie Waddell, "Economic Immorality and Social Reformation in English Popular Preaching, 1585–1625," *Cultural and Social History* 5, no. 2 (2008): 165–82; Guy, *Tudor England*, 391–403; Jim Sharpe, "Social Strain and Social Dislocation, 1585–1603," in *The Reign of Elizabeth I: Court and Culture in the Last Decade*, ed. John Guy (Cambridge: Cambridge University Press, 1995), 192–211; Richard L. Greaves, *Society and Religion in Elizabethan England* (Minneapolis: University of Minnesota Press, 1981).

the arenas of family, church, and commonwealth.[11] God calls Christians regardless of their spheres of human existence—from the personal to the highest corporate level—to conform to his word. Given the harsh realities of life, this took on a profound urgency. The overlapping categories of piety—individual, family, church, and commonwealth—will serve as a path into Perkins's publications on the Christian life. At the foundation of all of life is faith, which is clear from his treatise on living well. At the personal level, Perkins addresses death, truly knowing Christ, the imagination, repentance, and controlling the tongue. He speaks to the family directly in his treatise on the household as well as to higher levels of society in his works on vocation and equity. Without exception, Perkins's arguments and principles pertaining to these various aspects of the Christian life are governed by Scripture.

HOW TO LIVE WELL

Perkins sees Habakkuk 2:4—"the just man shall live by his faith"—as the key to living the Christian life. To be saved by faith in Christ at death, one must live by faith in Christ before death. Perkins is interested in faith as the foundation of living well, especially when temporal things fail. He expounds this verse in his treatise *How to Live, and That Well: In All Estates and Time*, published in 1601. He first looks at the context of Habakkuk then closely at the verse itself. In Habakkuk 1, the prophet discusses with God why the Jews are oppressed by the Chaldeans, the enemies of God. In Habakkuk 2, God provides his answer—namely, the assurance that they will be delivered at the appointed time but not yet. The Lord then responds to the implied question of how the people are supposed to live in the meantime with the distinction, "the unjust man puffes up himself with vaine confidence, but the just man shall live by his faith."[12]

Perkins makes five points of explanation for the phrase, "the just man shall live by his faith." First, justice here is twofold: justice of the law and justice of the gospel. This distinction is stated as a truism, part of the rule of faith. Justice of the law is perfection, which has never been found

11. Patterson, *William Perkins*, 141; Hambrick-Stowe, "Practical Divinity and Spirituality," 198.

12. Perkins, *How to Liue*, 2; Perkins, *Whole Works*, 1:476.

in any person outside Adam, Eve, and Christ. The justice of the gospel is perfection of the sinner in Christ. So the just man in this case is the "one who turns to God, and by grace indeavours to please God, according to the whole law of God in his place and calling." Second, the life referenced here is also twofold: natural and eternal. The latter is proven by Paul's reference to this text in Romans 1 as support for God justifying sinners by faith. Related to this second point is a third: the faith recorded in this verse refers to justifying or saving faith, for one must live by the same faith that saves. This is why Paul, in Galatians 2:20, claims to live his life in the flesh by faith in the Son of God. Fourth, the construction of the words is "the just shall live by his faith," not "the just by faith shall live." According to Perkins, "by faith" modifies the words "shall live." He embraces this reading because Paul in Galatians 3:11–12 makes the distinction between living by faith and living by works, and only the former brings eternal life.[13] The last point Perkins considers is how a man should live by faith, and here he spends considerable time.

Perkins brings the whole of Scripture to bear on this concept of living by faith. This faith must be rightly conceived, and it must reign in the heart. The word of God alone is the foundation of a right conception of faith. Natural reason falls short in this regard. Perkins cites Ephesians 2:20 and Hebrews 11:3 in defense of this reality. But beyond knowledge of God's word, a right conception of faith requires one to trust that word. In Romans 1:5, Paul calls this trust "obedience that comes from faith." Moreover, this trust has six conditions, which Perkins deduces through collation: it must be absolute, sincere, inclusive of all Scripture, from an honest heart, stable, and constant. The reign of faith, then, is "when it beares rule & sway in the heart & life." It reigns by making one accept the calling of God and yield to his commands, which further confirms those who believe in their obedience. Further, this life of faith includes the spiritual and temporal life. Perkins cites numerous passages of Scripture to demonstrate that reconciliation, peace of conscience, joy of the Spirit, and newness of life all owe their existence to faith in the life of the believer. Similarly, the temporal life of calling, labor, and misery is led by faith. In every case, affliction reveals

13. Perkins, *How to Liue*, 3–6; Perkins, *Whole Works*, 1:476.

the reign of faith in the life of the Christian.[14] This treatise illustrates that Perkins used Scripture to interpret Scripture, according to the method outlined in *The Arte of Prophecying*, in an effort to expound on faith as the foundation of the Christian life.

HOW TO DIE WELL

Perkins's 1595 treatise, *A Salve for a Sick Man: Or, A Treatise Containing the Nature, Differences, and Kinds of Death: As Also the Right Manner of Dying Well*, is an exposition of Ecclesiastes 7:3.[15] Perkins uses Scripture to interpret its own words regarding death as a blessing from God. The context of this verse is important for understanding the counterintuitive idea that death is better than birth. In the first six chapters of Ecclesiastes, Solomon articulates the vanity of everything under heaven. Then, in Ecclesiastes 7, he transitions to rules of direction and comfort, that men might arm themselves against the misery of life rather than be dominated by despair. The first rule is that a good name is better than precious ointment; it is a gift of God that ministers to the heart more than the most precious salve can the senses. Some may object that this brings little comfort, given the reality that death is still the end. This objection leads to the second rule, which is the focus of this treatise: "the day of death is better than the day that one is born."[16]

Perkins proceeds with his exposition of the text by considering three points. First, he defines death as "a deprivation of life as a punishment ordained by God and imposed on man for his sinne." He references Romans 5:12 to further explain the punishment aspect of this definition. God is the executioner of this natural evil according to Isaiah 45:7, but humans are the procurers of it. The death referenced in this text is clearly the time of bodily death, when the body and soul are separated. Second, Perkins

14. Perkins, *How to Liue*, 17–52; Perkins, *Whole Works*, 1:477–81.

15. For a discussion of the commonality of death and the grief associated with it in Perkins's context, see David Cressy, *Birth, Marriage, and Death: Ritual, Religion, and Life-Cycle in Tudor and Stuart England* (Oxford: Oxford University Press, 1997), 379–95.

16. William Perkins, *A Salve for a Sicke Man, Or, A Treatise Containing the Nature, Differences, and Kindes of Death as Also the Right Manner of Dying Well. And It May Serue for Spirituall Instruction to 1. Mariners When They Goe to Sea. 2. Souldiers When They Goe to Battell. 3. Women When They Trauell of Child* (Cambridge: Iohn Legate, printer to the Vniversitie of Cambridge, 1595), 1–2; Perkins, *Whole Works*, 1:489.

explores how Solomon's assertion can be true by responding to six objections, bringing Scripture to bear on each through the analogy of faith, context, and collation. Third, the reason the day of death surpasses the day of birth is because the latter is one's entrance into the misery and woe of this life whereas the former ushers those in Christ into life eternal. Death brings freedom from all miseries that have their end in death, as taught by Romans 7:24; death doubles as the entrance into the presence of Christ, according to Philippians 1:23. On this foundational exegesis, Perkins builds his extensive application on preparation for death and one's disposition toward death.[17]

Perkins responds to several objections to his interpretation, which reveals his consistent hermeneutic. Some may object to the idea that the punishment of death does not come from God, given that Ezekiel 33:11 says God does not will the death of sinners. Perkins's response employs context and the analogy of faith. Ezekiel 33:10 makes clear that the address is not to all men but to God's people. Further, the Lord's words here are rhetorical in that there is an implied comparison. The Lord wills the conversion and repentance of a sinner rather than his destruction. God is just and ordains deserved punishment. The fact that he does not take pleasure or delight in the ruin of the wicked does not alter this.

A second objection, based on Genesis 2:17, argues that if God punished sin with death, Adam would have died when he sinned. Perkins responds by making the distinction between law and gospel. Every sentence of Scripture is one or the other. The sentence of law spoken of here must be understood in light of the covenant of grace made with Adam after the fall. With this in mind, Perkins says God's prohibition implies a bigger picture: "Thou shalt certainely dye whensoever thou eatest the forbidden fruit, except I doe further give thee meanes of deliverance from death, namely, the seede of the woman to bruise the serpents head."[18] Here is a clear example one passage of Scripture qualifying another.

Finally, in answering an objection about the body rotting in the grave, despite the soul's departure to Christ, Perkins appeals to the analogy of faith, particularly the believer's union with Christ. The whole person,

17. Perkins, *Salve for a Sicke Man*, 2–29; Perkins, *Whole Works*, 1:489–95.

18. Perkins, *Salve for a Sicke Man*, 4; Perkins, *Whole Works*, 1:489.

body and soul, are joined to Christ. This bond warrants the hope that the body will be raised to eternal glory at the final judgment.[19] By addressing the issue of death and dying well as a believer in Christ, Perkins exposits Scripture according his professed method.

THE TRUE MANNER OF KNOWING CHRIST CRUCIFIED

Perkins was concerned that knowledge of Christ was limited to mere mental assent for too many. He saw this shortcoming among common Protestants, many of whom made Christ the mere "patron of their sins," fleeing to him for refuge but refusing to mortify sin in their lives and follow the example of his passion. To address this perception, Perkins wrote his 1596 treatise, *A Declaration of the True Manner of Knowing Christ Crucified*, as an exhortation to more than head knowledge. While it is not an exposition of a single passage of Scripture, he begins by citing Isaiah 53:11; John 17:3; 1 Corinthians 2:2; Galatians 6:14; and Philippians 3:8 as the warrant for what follows.[20]

The proper knowledge of Christ crucified demanded by Scripture includes how one knows Christ and how Christ desires to be known. The first includes consideration of the cross, both knowledge of the historical event and application of that event to one's particular life and affections. The second involves knowledge of the merit, virtue, and example of Christ. The example of Christ is more than merely a pattern to imitate. It provides a remedy against vice, a motive for holiness, and a perspective on suffering. Further, it is out of this knowledge of the crucified Jesus that one finds proper knowledge of God, others, and self. While Perkins is doing something a bit different in this work from his normal expository enterprise, his exhortation remains saturated with Scripture.

19. Perkins, *Salve for a Sicke Man*, 24–26; Perkins, *Whole Works*, 1:494.

20. William Perkins, *A Declaration of the True Manner of Knowing Christ Crucified* (Cambridge: Iohn Legate, printer to the Vniversitie of Cambridge, 1596), 1, 27; Perkins, *Whole Works*, 1:626, 631.

MAN'S NATURAL IMAGINATIONS

A Treatise of Mans Imaginations began as sermons on Genesis 8:21. Perkins begins by "unfolding the text" as "preparation to the treatise."[21] In the beginning of the chapter, Moses recalls the drying of the floodwaters and Noah's sacrificing to God. God accepts the sacrifice in Genesis 8:21–22, and he makes decrees regarding the restoration of nature and his providential care over it. The promise not to curse the earth anymore on man's account comes first. Genesis 8:21 has three parts: the preface to the law, the law, and the reason for the law. The preface is the phrase, "and the Lord said in his heart." Perkins explains that God neither has a heart nor speaks as human beings do but that this is divine accommodation, an anthropomorphism, meaning simply that God determined this decree with himself. This demonstrates that God seeks to communicate in such a way that even the simpleminded may understand. The second part of the verse is the decree itself. The promise to curse the earth no more implies cursing in the past. Perkins explains this cursing with the analogy of faith and collation. God ordains and inflicts all curses, yet they are always justly deserved by sin. So in this instance, the destruction of the earth was a fruit of the wrath of God against the sin of man. Isaiah 45:7 offers another scriptural witness for God's creation of calamity.

The reason why God promises to curse the earth no more comprises the third part of the verse. The reason the Lord offers, that "the imagination of mans heart is evil even from his youth," seems counterintuitive, but the point is he will not continue to destroy the earth again and again. His justice is tempered by his mercy. In Perkins's general explanation of the verse, he uses his Scripture to interpret Scripture. This lays the foundation for a detailed explanation of man's natural evil thoughts, lack of good thoughts, and the way to reform them. Perkins succinctly articulates the meaning thusly: "the minde and understanding part of man is naturally so corrupt, that so soone as hee can use reason, he doth nothing but imagine that which is wicked, and against the Law of God." So everyone's natural thoughts are evil, and this extends to thoughts concerning God, neighbor, and self. The ubiquity of evil in the mind implies Perkins's second point:

21. Perkins, *Whole Works*, 2:456.

there is a total lack of good in the thoughts of man.[22] He then transitions into directions for reforming one's thoughts. This is not drawn directly from the text at hand, but as with the rest of the body of this treatise, its principles and arguments are drawn from Scripture.

THE PRACTICE OF REPENTANCE

In 1593, Perkins wrote *Two Treatises: 1. Of the Nature and Practice of Repentance. 2. Of the Combate of the Flesh and Spirit* for the purpose of fostering repentance among his countrymen. According to the preface, plague and pestilence had struck as judgments from God because people ignored the preaching of the word. If repentance did not follow, worse things could be expected. Perkins knew repentance could be understood in multiple ways. Taken generally, repentance is the whole of conversion, including contrition, faith, and new obedience—a substitute for regeneration. Taken particularly, repentance is the renovation of life and behavior. Perkins uses this latter meaning here.[23]

The first of Perkins's pair of treatises focuses on repentance. It is logically arranged with biblical support throughout. Perkins defines repentance as "a worke of grace, arising of a godly sorrow; whereby a man turns from all his sins unto God, and bringeth forth fruites [or] worthy amendment of life." The Spirit of God is the cause of repentance. The instrumental cause is the gospel, while the law and calamity are merely occasions for repentance. Under the term "repentance," Perkins includes mortification and newness of life; moreover, it is the duty of both natural and regenerate persons. The practice of repentance includes examination, confession, deprivation, and prayer. Perkins's comments regarding the examination of conscience are a potent example of collation. For each of the Ten Commandments, he provides a dozen or more Scripture

22. Perkins, *Whole Works*, 2:456–73.

23. William Perkins, *Two Treatises· I. Of the Nature and Practise of Repentance. II. Of the Combat of the Flesh and Spirit* (Cambridge: Iohn Legate printer to the Vniversitie of Cambridge. And are to be sold by Abraham Kitson at the signe of the Sunne in Paules Church-yard in London, 1593), To the Reader; Perkins, *Whole Works*, 1:454. Perkins explicitly makes this distinction between general and particular repentance here. The second edition of this work is virtually identical to the first. See William Perkins, *Two Treatises. I. Of the Nature and Practise of Repentance. II. Of the Combat of the Flesh and Spirit* (Cambridge: Iohn Legate, Printer to the Vniuersitie of Cambridge, 1600).

references in order to expand the ways the commandment is understood and applied. For example, he mentions many ways to break the eighth commandment's prohibition against stealing. One steals if one lives idly, according to 2 Thessalonians 3:11. According to Isaiah 1:13, giving or receiving bribes is also a breach of this commandment. Habakkuk 2:11 even includes rack-renting as an infraction in this regard. The list goes on. After discussing the practice of repentance, Perkins enumerates the motives of repentance. He highlights that the time for repentance is always present and afterward addresses specific cases of repentance.[24] Perkins's explanation of the various aspects of repentance fits naturally with his treatise on the combat between the flesh and the spirit, for true repentance incites conflict with one's flesh.

Perkins's second treatise is an exposition of Galatians 5:17, in which he employs all three tools of his hermeneutic. The crucial context of this verse is the whole of Galatians 5. In particular, 5:1–13 offers Paul's exhortation to the Galatians to maintain their Christian liberty. From there until the end of the chapter, he seeks to persuade them of other special duties, to serve by love, and to avoid contention and injury. Galatians 5:16 calls them to walk by the Spirit, which is the remedy for the aforementioned sins. The next verse, then, provides the reason walking by the Spirit is the remedy. Perkins comments, "The flesh & spirit are contrary; wherefore if yee walke according to the spirit, it will hinder the flesh; that it shall not carry you forward to doe injuries and live in contentions, as otherwise it would." To explain this verse, he highlights five points: there is combat between flesh and Spirit; the matter of the conflict is contrary lusting; the cause of the combat is that the Spirit and flesh are contrary; the subjects of the combat are the Galatians; and the effect is that neither good nor evil reigns supremely.[25]

Perkins claims the Spirit prevails over the flesh in this life and the next, but what about those for whom the flesh seems victorious? Perkins appeals to the analogy of faith to answer this question. It is clear from the overall witness of Scripture that some Christians are only such in name and show, while others are truly part of the body of Christ. If the former

24. Perkins, *Two Treatises*, 1, 8–70; Perkins, *Whole Works*, 1:455–68.

25. Perkins, *Two Treatises*, 71–93; Perkins, *Whole Works*, 1:469–73.

fall, they cannot be said to have extinguished the Spirit. Only the latter could be truly cut off, because it is impossible for the Spirit to conclusively fail. Finally, to explain the effect of the Spirit-flesh battle, Perkins brings Scripture from outside the context of Galatians. That the regenerate man cannot do the evil his flesh desires is attested to in 1 John 3:9. On the other side, Romans 7 provides forceful evidence that the regenerate man cannot do the good he is inclined toward. So the regenerate man awaits the glorified state when good will decisively reign.[26] Perkins's approach in these two treatises varies, but both draw heavily from Scripture, and the operative interpretive method is that Scripture interprets itself.

THE GOVERNMENT OF THE TONGUE

A Direction for the Government of the Tongue According to God's Word is the full title of Perkins's 1592 work on controlling the tongue. He penned the piece so that all Christians would follow the rules therein, quoting James 1:16 as his reason.[27] Like the title suggests, the rules for the holy usage of the tongue come from Scripture. Perkins honors this by citing specific biblical passages regarding the use of one's tongue for the glory of God and the good of neighbor. The prerequisites for the virtuous employment of the tongue are twofold: a pure heart, for Jesus says in Matthew 15:19 that out of the heart the mouth speaks; and a facility in the "language of Canaan," by which Perkins means frequent prayer.[28] The matter of speech concerns God, neighbor, or ourselves. Speech about God should not be in vain, according to the third commandment. Speech about neighbor should be considered beforehand, whether it be good or evil. Speech about oneself—both in praise and dispraise—should be minimal.

The manner of speech is Perkins's lengthiest engagement. Speech is to be gracious, truthful, reverent, modest, meek, and in accord with sobriety, urbanity, fidelity, and the care of the good name of others. In response to

26. Perkins, *Two Treatises*, 84–96; Perkins, *Whole Works*, 1:472–74.

27. William Perkins, *A Direction for the Governement of the Tongue, according to Gods Worde* (Edinburgh: Robert Waldegraue, printer to the Kings Maiestie, 1593), cap. XII; Perkins, *Whole Works*, 1:451. The second edition of this work is virtually identical to the first. See William Perkins, *A Direction for the Gouernment of the Tongue according to God's Word* (London: Iohn Legat printer to the Vniuersitie of Cambridge. And are to be sold in Pauls churchyard at the signe of the Crowne by Simon Waterson, 1603).

28. Perkins, *Direction for the Governement*, cap. I, XI; Perkins, *Whole Works*, 1:440, 450.

the objection that lying can be justified in some cases—for example, the case of Rahab and the midwives of Egypt saving spies—Perkins answers with a definitive "no." These individuals were commended for their faith, not their lying. What they did were excellent works of mercy, but the doers failed in the manner they performed them. Moreover, one must not let examples in Scripture overturn the rules clearly spelled out elsewhere.[29] While Perkins does not engage in significant exegesis in his discussion of ruling the tongue, his arguments are thoroughly biblical, and he sees them as eminently necessary given the common neglect of their implementation.

THE HOUSEHOLD

The subtitle of *Oeconomie: Or, Household-Government* is *A Short Survey of the Right Manner of Erecting and Ordering a Family, According to the Scriptures*. This provides an apt description of Perkins's work on marriage and family. Unsurprisingly, the phrase "according to the Scriptures" is key, for Perkins states up front that "the only rule for ordering the Familie, is the written Word of God." He stays true to this rule by appealing to "the expresse commandment of God" or "the custome and practice of holy men in their times" for virtually every point he argues. Perkins defines the family as "a natural and simple society of certain persons, having mutuall relation one to another, under the private government of one."[30] Perkins proceeds to explain the hierarchy of relationships within the family. The household, which owes God its regular worship, is founded on the marriage relationship. Perkins discusses the contract of marriage and marriage itself at length before enumerating the duties of the husband, wife, parent, child, master, servant, and head of household.[31] Beyond merely citing verses to

29. Perkins, *Direction for the Governement*, cap. V; Perkins, *Whole Works*, 1:443.

30. Perkins, *Whole Works*, 3:669. On the Christian household in Perkins's context, see Alexandra Walsham, "Holy Families: The Spiritualization of the Early Modern Household Revisited," in *Religion and Household*, ed. John Doran, Alexandra Walsham, and Charlotte Methuen, Studies in Church History 50 (Woodbridge, UK: Boydell, 2014), 122–60.

31. For family relationships in theory and practice in this era, see Helen Berry and Elizabeth A. Foyster, eds., *The Family in Early Modern England* (Cambridge: Cambridge University Press, 2007); S. D. Amussen, "Gender, Family and the Social Order, 1560–1726," in *Order and Disorder in Early Modern England*, ed. Anthony Fletcher and Joan Stevenson (Cambridge: Cambridge University Press, 1985), 196–217; J. A. Sharpe, *Early Modern England: A Social History, 1550–1760*, 2nd ed. (London: Arnold, 1997), 56–76.

support his various points, Perkins engages in several notable exegetical discussions.

Perkins responds to the Church of Rome's prohibition of clerical marriage and some of the biblical arguments used to support the position. One is the assertion that 1 Corinthians 7:5 demands clerical celibacy because it requires married couples to abstain from their physical relationship for fasting and prayer. Perkins objects from context that Paul here writes not of common and daily service to God but of the solemn and extraordinary exercise during times when prayer is needed acutely. So the text does not teach that abstinence is essential for effective prayer on a regular basis. Another Catholic argument for clerical celibacy comes from 1 Corinthians 7:32. Perkins objects, again from context but also the general teaching of Scripture, that carnality should not be attributed to all those who are married but only those married persons who have an inordinate care for worldly things. For Perkins, the married individual may certainly have a special regard for the things of God.[32]

In his lengthy discussion on incest, Perkins has to account for potentially problematic practices in the Old Testament. First, the sons of Adam and Eve must have married their sisters, given that they were the first family. From Perkins's perspective, this was a case of necessity, but more importantly, the relationships were sanctioned by special dispensation from God. The context of the early chapters of Genesis includes the creation mandate in 1:28. Of course, siblings provided the only option to fulfill this command, which means it must have been manifestly God's will. Second, Genesis 11:29 and 20:12 together indicate the possibility that Abraham's wife, Sarah, was also his sister. The relationship is difficult to decipher from the biblical witness, yet Perkins concludes that "God in those dayes tolerated many things, which not withstanding he did not altogether approve."[33] Perkins also accounts for polygamy by this appeal to progressive revelation, attested to by the entirety of Scripture and therefore part of the analogy of faith. Third, in Deuteronomy 25:5 Moses commands that the brother of a deceased man without issue should take his wife and

32. Perkins, *Whole Works*, 3:671–72.

33. Perkins, *Whole Works*, 3:675.

raise children unto him. Perkins argues this was a special law, peculiarly directed to the Israelites for the preservation of the family name.

Last, some object that the forbidden marriages in Leviticus 18 are part of the ceremonial law and therefore not binding. Perkins responds by looking at the context of the chapter. Consequences afflicted the Canaanites due to their forbidden practices well before Moses expressly forbade them. Perkins also brings the testimony of the prophets to bear from Ezekiel 22:10 and Amos 2:7. These count the prohibitions as moral rather than ceremonial. Further, Mark 6:18 and 1 Corinthians 5:1 provide New Testament evidence against such practices.[34] None of these examples warrant overturning the clear teaching of Scripture elsewhere. Perkins appeals to the analogy of faith, context, and collation to defend this overarching theme.

VOCATION

Perkins's extended treatment of calling is founded on exegesis of 1 Corinthians 7:20 and supported by Scripture throughout. *A Treatise of Vocations, or Callings of Men, with the Sorts and Kinds of Them, and the Right Use Thereof* was prepared for press by Perkins, according to the dedication letter by Thomas Pickering, and published in February of the year Perkins died. The critical context of 1 Corinthians 7:20 is 7:17–25, in which Paul handles two questions. First, must someone who is uncircumcised be circumcised when he becomes a Christian? Second, must a bondman leave his calling following his conversion to Christianity? Paul answers both the questions in 7:20. In essence, he says, "Let every man continue in that calling, wherein hee was called unto Christ: that is, wherein hee walked and lived when it pleased God by the ministry of the Gospel, to call him unto the profession of Christian religion."[35]

Perkins walks through three points of explanation for this command. First, he defines vocation as "a certain kinde of life, ordained and imposed on man by God, for the common good."[36] Second, he notes two kinds of calls: general and particular. The general call is the call to be a child of God, while

34. Perkins, *Whole Works*, 3:677–78.

35. William Perkins, *A Treatise of the Vocations, Or, Callings of Men, with the Sorts and Kinds of Them, and the Right vse Thereof* (London: Iohn Legat, printer to the Vniuersitie of Cambridge, 1603), 1; Perkins, *Whole Works*, 1:750.

36. Perkins, *Treatise of the Vocations*, 2; Perkins, *Whole Works*, 1:750.

the particular call is the personal call on one's life. Third, Perkins elucidates the holy and lawful use of particular callings. He highlights the virtue of constancy in executing the duties of one's personal call.[37] That said, "It is not the Apostles meaning to barre men to divert from this or that calling, but he gives them an item to keepe them from changing upon every light concert, and every suddaine occasion." The specifics of these points are backed up with Scripture. As Perkins claims, his three main points "are in some sort touched in the words of my text."[38]

EQUITY AND MODERATION

Epieikeia, or A Treatise of Christian Equity and Moderation was originally delivered as public lectures based on Philippians 4:5. Perkins understands this verse to be one of many exhortations in the chapter. In 4:1, Paul calls Christians to perseverance in faith and true religion; in 4:2–3, he commands them to mutual concord; in 4:4, Paul exhorts the Philippian believers to spiritual joy in the Lord. The "drift and scope" of the fourth exhortation in Philippians 4:5 is "to perswade the Philippians, and in them the whole Church, to the practice of *Equity*." Perkins sees two parts to the verse: "the exhortation" and "an excellent reason to enforce it."[39]

The exhortation is to both public and private moderation, as it is to "be knowne to all men." Perkins sees equity as a "Christian virtue" and "the marrow and strength of the common-weale."[40] In short, moderation is basic to the proper operation of society at every level. The careful navigation of law's extremity and mitigation is essential in public justice and public relationships.[41] Perkins draws from other passages of Scripture to describe the four principal duties of private equity. The first is bearing with others' natural infirmities. Proverbs 19:31 asserts that it is the glory of man to overlook infirmity, and Paul teaches in 1 Corinthians 13:7 that love suffers all things. Second, when Paul says love thinks no evil, he means to encourage the

37. Perkins, *Whole Works*, 1:773. Perkins mentions that men seem to like the callings of others better than their own and therefore move on every light occasion to alter their calling.

38. Perkins, *Whole Works*, 1:750, 775.

39. Perkins, *Whole Works*, 2:436, emphasis original.

40. Perkins, *Whole Works*, 2:436.

41. Perkins, *Whole Works*, 2:437–41. For an analysis of the debate over Perkins's social ethics and Perkins as a social reformer, see Patterson, *William Perkins*, 154–62.

practice of interpreting doubtful things in the best way possible (1 Cor 13:9). Third, moderation requires one not always insist on one's rights. An example of this is Jesus himself, when in Matthew 17:27 he pays the unnecessary toll. Finally, moderation demands the forgiveness of both private and personal wrongs. Otherwise, one cannot pray the Lord's Prayer, requesting forgiveness as one forgives.[42] Perkins derives the duties of equity from collation.

Perkins explains the motivation behind the exhortation from the phrase "the Lord is at hand." As an exhortation, the verse by definition includes an imperative and so demands application from its readers. God's moderation in dealing with humanity is an obvious motivator for the equitable duties demanded by this verse, but the text in this case provides more specific motivation. The statement that the Lord is at hand has two meanings, according to Perkins. It speaks of the last judgment as well as the present presence of God. Both are proper motivation, and Perkins concludes that "both senses are good, but we will cleave unto the latter." Therefore, it is "as if the holy Ghost had said; Use equity and moderation in your dealings, and remember who is at your elbow, stands by and lookes on, ready to judge you for it."[43] So Perkins's discourse on the weighty matter of equity, both public and private, is founded on exegesis, particularly using context and collation as tools.

CHRISTIAN MINISTRY

Perkins uses biblical exposition in his works composed for clergy, both in his treatise on pastoral calling and his pioneering efforts in casuistry. At the beginning of Elizabeth's reign, there was a need to fill all the ministerial positions. Many of the bishops resorted to mass ordinations with almost no quality control. After 1570, preparation of those entering the ministry steadily improved, though the infiltration of university graduates remained slow because appointments only occurred following the death or resignation of those with benefices. As the prophesyings were banned in the 1570s, university training became the best hope for ministerial improvement, one of the great Puritan initiatives. But university

42. Perkins, *Whole Works* 2:442–46.

43. Perkins, *Whole Works*, 2:447–52 (page 452 is misprinted as 425).

curriculum fell woefully short in its effort to prepare pastors.[44] For this reason, the writing, preaching, and teaching careers of men such as Perkins became essential. As Diarmaid MacCulloch notes, the reformation of the ministry was one of the great successes of the Elizabethan church. Through the efforts of senior clergy and pressure from laity, a "demoralized body of massing priests [turned] into a learned ministry capable of expounding the Protestant faith."[45] Unfortunately, the rise in educational standing and ministerial preparation was not matched by a corresponding improvement in economic position.[46]

William Crashaw, the author of the dedicatory epistle *The Calling of the Ministry*, notes how the pendulum swung away from the extreme dignity of the priest in the Catholic system to poverty, contempt, and general baseness. He further notes the difficulty for clergy to properly discharge their duties under the pathetic compensation structure. This was a circular problem because the dignity of the ministry was directly related to the duties of the ministry. Perkins himself was considered a model pastor by many, faithfully laboring in his duties, and thus his commentary on ministerial vocation proved to be highly valued. He offered an alternative to the disputes about polity that both worked within existing frameworks of the established church and resonated with the spiritual aspirations of his contemporaries. This did much to shift Puritan interests into personal and local piety.[47]

The foremost pastoral problem Perkins deals with is the issue of assurance. If salvation is of the Lord and according to his inscrutable predestination, then how can Christians know for sure whether God counts them among the elect? Answering this question is a significant theme across Perkins's writings, for he considered it the greatest case of conscience and even devoted whole works to it. Assurance became a frontline issue for two reasons. First-, second-, and third-generation Protestants were compelled to clarify the Reformers' doctrine of assurance in light of many who grew up in the church and took the grace of God for granted. The

44. Doran and Durston, *Princes, Pastors, and People*, 168–69.

45. MacCulloch, *Later Reformation in England*, 87–88.

46. Doran and Durston, *Princes, Pastors, and People*, 170.

47. Ian Breward, "William Perkins and the Ideal of the Ministry in the Elizabethan Church," *Reformed Theological Review* 24 (1965): 77.

Puritans, more than any other group, reacted against minimizing of sin and understanding mental assent as sufficient for salvation. Second, Puritans took sin and self-examination seriously, which often resulted in a lack of assurance.[48] For these reasons, assurance became a significant theme in Puritan ministries.

The ground of assurance in Perkins's theology and in the Puritan scheme in general is debated hotly. This debate often takes place amid larger questions concerning the relationship between Calvin and the Reformed tradition. Many scholars argue Perkins and his followers unhinged assurance from faith and made sanctification the primary ground of assurance.[49] Others have rightly countered this with a more nuanced alternative.[50] Whether faith is equated with assurance depends on the kind of assurance. Objective assurance, which consists of the belief that sins are pardonable because of Christ's finished work on the cross, is essential to faith. Subjective assurance, or full assurance, is the realization of Christ's sacrifice on one's behalf. One can lack this latter assurance or doubt one's salvation and still have saving faith.[51] In light of this, Perkins encourages personal striving because the covenant God works absolutely is most clearly seen in the impulses and actions of new life. Sanctification, then, becomes a test of justification. The covenant of grace is conditional, yet also all of grace, because God meets the conditions by gifting faith and working repentance. Therefore, according to Perkins, assurance is gained by looking at evidences of faith.[52] Joel Beeke summarizes this nicely: "One may know whether he is a child of God by examining the marks of saving

48. Beeke, "William Perkins and His Greatest Case," 264.

49. Kendall, *Calvin and English Calvinism*; Robert Letham, "Faith and Assurance in Early Calvinism: A Model of Continuity and Diversity," in *Later Calvinism: International Perspectives*, ed. W. Fred Graham, Sixteenth Century Essays & Studies 22 (Kirksville, MO: Sixteenth Century Journal Publishers, 1994), 355–84; R. N. Frost, *Richard Sibbes: God's Spreading Goodness* (Vancouver: Cor Deo, 2012); M. Charles Bell, *Calvin and Scottish Theology: The Doctrine of Assurance* (Edinburgh: Handsel, 1985); Michael P. Winship, "Weak Christians, Backsliders, and Carnal Gospelers: Assurance of Salvation and the Pastoral Origins of Puritan Practical Divinity in the 1580s," *CH* 70, no. 3 (September 2001): 462–81.

50. Beeke, *Assurance of Faith*; Schaefer, *Spiritual Brotherhood*; Shaw, "Drama in the Meeting House."

51. Beeke, "William Perkins," 268.

52. John von Rohr, "Covenant and Assurance in Early English Puritanism," *CH* 34, no. 2 (1965): 198–202.

grace in his life as they flow out of Christ and are ratified by the anointing of the Holy Spirit."[53]

Perkins was also an early Protestant proponent of casuistry.[54] He provided the "first extensive treatment of the subject by any Protestant in England" and "showed boldness and originality in writing about matters of conscience in his time."[55] Perkins's school of casuistry dominated until the end of the seventeenth century. William Ames, John Downham, and Joseph Hall were directly influenced by Perkins at Cambridge.[56] In fact, "several seventeenth century thinkers observed with pride that the

53. Beeke, "William Perkins," 277.

54. The topic of casuistry has garnered significant attention in recent scholarship. See John Mahoney, *The Making of Moral Theology: A Study of the Roman Catholic Tradition* (Oxford: Clarendon, 1987); Edmund Leites, ed., *Conscience and Casuistry in Early Modern Europe* (Cambridge: Cambridge University Press, 1988); Albert R. Jonsen and Stephen Toulmin, *The Abuse of Casuistry: A History of Moral Reasoning* (Berkeley: University of California Press, 1988); John Morrill, Paul Slack, and Daniel Woolf, eds., *Public Duty and Private Conscience in Seventeenth-Century England: Essays Presented to G. E. Aylmer* (Oxford: Clarendon, 1993); Randall C. Zachman, *The Assurance of Faith: Conscience in the Theology of Martin Luther and John Calvin* (Minneapolis: Fortress, 1993); James F. Keenan and Thomas A. Shannon, eds., *The Context of Casuistry* (Washington, DC: Georgetown University Press, 1995); Harold E. Braun and Edward Vallance, eds., *Contexts of Conscience in Early Modern Europe, 1500–1700* (Basingstoke, UK: Palgrave Macmillan, 2004); Braun and Vallance, eds., *The Renaissance Conscience* (Chichester, UK: Wiley-Blackwell, 2011).

55. Patterson, *William Perkins*, 92. See also D. G. Hart, *Calvinism: A History* (New Haven, CT: Yale University Press, 2013), 84, 169–70; Ian Breward, "William Perkins and the Origins of Puritan Casuistry," in *Faith and a Good Conscience: Papers Read at the Puritan and Reformed Studies Conference, 18th and 19th December, 1962* (Clonmel, Ireland: Clonmel Evangelical Bookroom, 1992), 8; George L. Mosse, *The Holy Pretence: A Study in Christianity and Reason of State from William Perkins to John Winthrop* (Oxford: Blackwell, 1957), 49; Thomas F. Merrill, *William Perkins, 1558–1602: English Puritanist* (Nieukoop, Netherlands: B. De Graaf, 1966), xi. For more discussions of Perkins's cases of conscience, see Kevin T. Kelly, *Conscience: Dictator or Guide? A Study in Seventeenth-Century English Protestant Moral Theology* (London: G. Chapman, 1967), 81–85; Ian Breward, introduction to Perkins, *Works of William Perkins*, 3:58–80; Breward, "William Perkins and the Origins of Reformed Casuistry"; Muller, "Covenant and Conscience"; McKim, *Ramism in William Perkins' Theology*, 96–102; Donald K. McKim, "William Perkins and the Christian Life: The Place of the Moral Law and Sanctification in Perkins' Theology," *Evangelical Quarterly* 59, no. 2 (April 1987): 125–37; Jonathan Long, "William Perkins: 'Apostle of Practical Divinity,'" *Churchman* 103, no. 1 (1989): 53–59; James F. Keenan, "William Perkins (1558–1602) and the Birth of British Casuistry," in Keenan and Shannon, *Context of Casuistry*, 105–30; Keenan, "Jesuit Casuistry or Jesuit Spirituality? The Roots of Seventeenth-Century British Practical Divinity," in *The Jesuits: Cultures, Sciences, and the Arts, 1540–1773*, ed. John W. O'Malley, et al. (Toronto: University of Toronto Press, 1999), 627–40; Keenan, "Was William Perkins' *Whole Treatise of Cases of Conscience* Casuistry? Hermeneutics and British Practical Divinity," in *Contexts of Conscience*; Winship, "Weak Christians, Backsliders."

56. Patterson, *William Perkins*, 111.

continent looked to England for definitive formulations in practical theology."[57] Catholic writers had traditionally dominated this field, and in the late sixteenth and seventeenth centuries they were particularly active in publishing on the related topics of moral theology, casuistry, and conscience. Dominicans in the universities of Spain and Portugal tended toward treating the moral issues in large treatises, drawing from natural law and Aristotelian philosophy. At the same time, the Jesuits, who were active in pastoring and educating throughout Europe, including England, were more inclined to apply theological principles to specific, everyday problems.[58]

The Reformers rejected medieval and Reformation-era Catholic casuistry outright because they believed it was built on a faulty theology of justification. Gone were the confessional and the sacrament of penance, major motivating factors of Catholic case divinity. But even the first-generation Reformers were concerned with conscience, so each of them gave detailed guidance on Christian duty. Perkins then collected and systematically arranged this material.[59] The time was ripe for such unique work. Tudor writing in general reveals a strong moralistic tone, for there was a lack of discipline in the ecclesiastical arrangement. Further, while English clergy engaged in the direction of conscience, Catholics criticized Protestants for their lack of casuistry.

But Perkins had theologically driven motivations as well. We already saw how Puritan soteriology sharpened the issue of assurance.[60] Beyond this, the Reformed doctrine of the third use of the law motivated Perkins and others to apply Scripture to the specifics of daily life.[61] Perkins wrote his cases of conscience "to refute the errors of Roman casuistry and use its valuable aspects for the strengthening of the Reformed faith so that it could be truly Catholic in its scope and depth."[62] Only the word of God was

---

57. Muller, "Covenant and Conscience," 309.

58. R. Po-chia Hsia, *The World of Catholic Renewal, 1540–1770*, 2nd ed. (Cambridge: Cambridge University Press, 2005), 10–60, 111–26; Patterson, *William Perkins*, 91.

59. Breward, "William Perkins and the Origins of Puritan Casuistry," 6–7.

60. Breward, "William Perkins and the Origins of Reformed Casuistry," 6–11.

61. Patterson, *William Perkins*, 93.

62. Breward, "William Perkins and the Origins of Reformed Casuistry," 12. Perkins's editor, Thomas Pickering, in the dedication of *Cases of Conscience*, identifies some of the shortcomings

binding on the conscience, so Perkins applied Scripture to the practical questions of life and interpreted it according to his biblical hermeneutic.

The rest of this chapter addresses Perkins's use and interpretation of Scripture in what can be categorized as his works written to equip pastors. The first work I will discuss is his treatise on the calling of the minister, where he unfolds the duties and dignity of gospel ministry. Second, I will explore Perkins's four publications that have assurance as their common theme. *A Discourse of Conscience* is the most academic of the four, in which Perkins defines conscience and stays primarily in a theoretical realm. Third, I will consider Perkins's case book of conscience, which is his most influential treatise. All of these writings were primarily written for pastors to aid them in their ministry, a ministry reliant on Scripture at every level.

THE CALLING OF THE MINISTRY

Perkins's *The Calling of the Ministry* is a collection of two treatises, both published posthumously in 1605. They originated as addresses at the University of Cambridge, presumably between 1584 and 1595, his tenure as a fellow at Christ's College. He discusses the duties and dignities of the ministry in both, from Job 33:23–24 and then Isaiah 6:5–9. The sum and substance of the first passage is that God uses means both to preserve sinners from falling and to help them rise again. Perkins arrives at this conclusion from the context. Job 32–33 is Elihu's conference with Job. Elihu was "a holy, noble, and wise young man," who in Job 33:1–7 prefaces his speech. In 33:8–13 he reproves Job's propositions, and in 33:14–24 he instructs Job in God's dealing with sinners. First, God preserves sinners through "admonitions in dreams and visions" and "scourges and chastisements." Second, in 33:23–24, Elihu asserts the "remedie and meanes" God uses to restore the fallen. The rest of the chapter, then, outlines the effect of this grace. The remedy and means, and the focus of Perkins here, is the minister, for whom there is found a five-point description in these verses: his titles, rareness, office, blessing from God, and commission and authority.[63] Perkins expands these points in the body of his treatise.

---

of Catholic case divinity and asserts that Perkins meets the need because his "grounds and principles" are "directly, or by just consequence out of the written word."

63. Perkins, *Whole Works*, 3:429–30.

Perkins draws from the whole witness of Scripture and the analogy of faith to explain the five descriptions found in these verses. The minister's titles are "messenger" or "angel" and "interpreter." Perkins uses collation to explain that the minister is sent from God to his church, drawing from the parallel designation in Malachi 2:7 and Revelation 2–3. He appeals to the analogy of faith to clarify the title of "interpreter of reconciliation" to the people of God, for God himself is the author, the Son the worker, the Spirit the ratifier, and the gospel the instrument. The true minister is rare, which is the plain meaning of the phrase "one in a thousand." This is because of contempt for ministers, the difficulties of the ministry, and the lack of preferment. Perkins illuminates these reasons with Jeremiah, Paul, and the maintenance of the Levites respectively. The office of the minister is "to declare unto man his righteousness"—namely, his lack of righteousness in himself and the offer of righteousness in Christ. This is seen clearly in Paul's preaching in the New Testament and Nathan's confrontation with David in the Old. God blesses the minister's labors by showing mercy to some. This is what is meant by the binding and loosing in John. Finally, the commission and authority given to the minister is to deliver the soul from hell and to redeem the penitent, who have been reconciled to God.[64] Perkins's hermeneutic, including the three tools of the analogy of faith, context, and collation, is operative as he exposits this Job passage.

From Isaiah 6:5–9, Perkins speaks to the minister's calling itself. The means of Isaiah's extraordinary confirmation in these verses comes through the context of the preceding verses. The confirmation itself consists of three parts: the effect of Isaiah's vision of the Lord, his consolation, and the renewing of his commission. The effect of his vision was fear, astonishment, and a direct result of the awareness of both his sin and the presence of God. The takeaway for ministers is that they must be broken over their sin and humbled in the consideration of their great function. Isaiah cries out about the pollution of his lips because, as a prophet, his mouth was to be used as the principal instrument of God's glory. According to Job 33:23, the minister is God's interpreter. Perkins explains, appealing to the analogy of faith, that when Isaiah saw the Lord, it was not the Lord in himself but a measure of his glory. Isaiah's consolation found its

64. Perkins, *Whole Works*, 3:430–38.

grounding in the Lord's forgiveness of his sins, the circumstance in which the angel touched his lips with a coal from the altar. The renovation of the prophet's commission consisted of God's inquiry, Isaiah's response, and God's command to go. Perkins explains God's inquiry is not for his own sake but ours. It is a clear teaching from Scripture that God is omniscient. Perkins further explains the Lord's reference to himself as "us" as a reference to his own plurality, similar to Genesis 1:26. The specific, Triune nature of God is clearly taught elsewhere in the canon, so it can be supplied in this case. It was not until God said "go and speak" that Isaiah began his prophetic ministry. Likewise, the apostles did not go into the world and preach the gospel until they were commissioned by Jesus. Therefore, the true minister must be called by the Lord and authorized to speak for him.[65] Here again, in his exposition of the minister's calling from Isaiah 6, Perkins employs all three aspects of his biblical hermeneutic.

EARLY WORK ON ASSURANCE

In 1589, Perkins compiled eight brief works under the title *A Treatise Tending Unto a Declaration, Whether a Man Be in the Estate of Damnation, or in the Estate of Grace: And if He Be in the First, How He May in Time Come Out of It: If in the Second, How He May Discerne It, and Persevere in the Same to the End.* This represents some of Perkins's earliest work and is loosely connected by his focus on assurance of salvation. The eight individual parts vary in length and genre, but all rely heavily on Scripture for their argumentation, even if this reliance is limited to the mere citing of biblical material.[66]

The first piece is *Certaine Propositions Declaring How Farre a Man May Goe in the Profession of the Gospel, and yet Be a Wicked man and a Reprobate.*[67] The

65. Perkins, *Whole Works*, 3:442–44, 448, 452, 457–59, 461.

66. William Perkins, *A Treatise Tending Vnto a Declaration Whether a Man Be in the Estate of Damnation or in the Estate of Grace and If He Be in the First, How He May in Time Come out of It: If in the Second, How He Maie Discerne It, and Perseuere in the Same to the End* (London: R. Robinson, for T. Gubbin, and I. Porter, 1590). The second edition will be referenced moving forward. While extremely close to the first edition, it was reviewed and corrected by Perkins himself. See William Perkins, *A Treatise Tending Vnto a Declaration, Whether a Man Be in the Estate of Damnation, or in the Estate of Grace and If He Be in the First, How He May in Time Come out of It: If in the Second, How He May Discerne It, and Perseuer in the Same to the End. Reuiewed and Corrected by the Author* (London: The Widdow Orwin, for Iohn Porter, and Iohn Legate, Cambridge, 1595).

67. Perkins, *Treatise Tending Vnto a Declaration*, 1; Perkins, *Whole Works*, 1:356. The unconscious hypocrite is seen as the "catch" of separating faith from assurance (Winship, "Weak

second is *The Estate of a Christian Man in this Life, which also Sheweth How Farre the Elect May Goe Beyond the Reprobate in Christianity, and that by Many Degrees*. These first two demonstrate precisely what the titles suggest, indicating what manifestations separate the reprobate from the elect. Third, Perkins includes *A Dialogue of the State of a Christian Man, Gathered Here and There Out of the Sweet and Savorie Writings of Master Tindall and Master Bradford*. Here, Eusebius explains to Timotheus how one may be sure of his salvation. The fourth treatise is *The Assertion*, which argues the reprobate may faithfully participate in all the religion of the Church of Rome. Fifth is Perkins's *A Dialogue Containing the Conflicts Betweene Sathan and a Christian*, where he provides insight into how the devil attacks Christians both strong and weak in the faith. The sixth and seventh treatises are *How a Man Should Apply Aright the Word of God to His Owne Soule* and *Consolations for the Troubled Consciences of Repentant Sinners*; both address the means by which Christians may attain assurance. The final treatise is *A Declaration of Certaine Spiritual Desertions, Serving to Terrifie All Drowsie Protestants, and to Comfort Them which Mourne for Their Sinnes*. The desertion referenced in the title refers to desertion by God.[68] Like in the previous works in this compilation, Perkins supports his principles with evidence from Scripture.

In Perkins's preface to the reader in *A Treatise Tending Unto a Declaration, Whether a Man Be in the Estate of Damnation, or in the Estate of Grace*, he brings coherence to the eight individual parts and grounds them in biblical exposition. He explains the rocky ground from the parable of the soils. The awful reality is that one may seem a Christian both to himself and the church but in reality be lost. Perkins considers three things from Luke 8:13: their faith, fruit of faith, and unsoundness. The faith of those who are rocky soil includes knowledge of and assent to God's word and the covenant of grace in Christ. But this consists of only a general familiarity, falling short of truly applying it to oneself. This is similarly testified to in John 2:24. The fruit that is born is referenced in the phrase, "They receive the word with joy." The fruit comes, but it is neither lasting nor substantial. These professors differ from true believers in that they are unsound. In

---

Christians, Backsliders," 472). The category of unconscious hypocrite is not original to Perkins but is clearly seen in Theodore Beza's theology (Shawn D. Wright, *Theodore Beza: The Man and the Myth* [Fearn, UK: Christian Focus, 2015], 141).

68. Perkins, *Treatise Tending Vnto a Declaration*, 18, 71, 112, 136, 147, 153, 166; Perkins, *Whole Works*, 1:362, 381, 396, 404, 408–9, 415.

other words, they do not continue to the end, for grace in them is scorched at the time of temptation. The similarity between temporary and true professors demands the hard work of personal heart examination. Perkins states that his purpose in writing was "to minister unto thee some help in this examining & observing of thine own heart."[69] The use of Scripture throughout the work and the revised edition's preface suggest Perkins's early conviction concerning the primacy of Scripture as well as a developing commitment to grounding his discourses in the context of exposition.

THE GREATEST CASE OF CONSCIENCE

In 1592, Perkins wrote *A Case of Conscience, the Greatest that Ever Was: How a Man May Know Whether He Be the Childe of God, or No* to address what he perceived as a widespread issue: doubt. He resolves the question with the word of God in the form of a dialogue for the benefit of the simpleminded and uneducated. At the end of this dialogue, he appends a lengthy discourse from the writings of Jerome Zanchius on the same question. This appendix defends the possibility of assurance through the testimony of the Spirit, Scripture, and predestination's effects, in that order. Zanchius also notes that God ordains the means as well as the end of salvation and is therefore confident in articulating the order of salvation, of which assurance is a part.[70] For Perkins's original contribution, he rewrites both 1 John and Psalm 15 as a dialogue.

Perkins follows the argumentation of 1 John verse by verse with precision. He sees the whole book as addressing assurance. From 1 John 2 he highlights that Christ is the ground of assurance and obedience is confirmation of the same. This latter theme is seen throughout the book; John describes it as walking in the light, loving the brothers, and laying down

69. Perkins, *Treatise Tending Vnto a Declaration*, To the Christian Reader; Perkins, *Whole Works*, 1:355.

70. William Perkins, *A Case of Conscience the Greatest That Euer Was; How a Man May Knowe Whether He Be the Child of God or No. Resolued by the Worde of God. Whereunto Is Added a Briefe Discourse, Taken out of Hier. Zanchius.* (London: Thomas Orwin, for Thomas Man and Iohn Porter, 1592), 39–83; Perkins, *Whole Works*, 1:429–38. The second edition of this work is virtually identical to the first. See William Perkins, *A Case of Conscience the Greatest That Euer Was; Hovv a Man May Know Whether He Be the Childe of God, or No. Resolued by the Word of God. Whereunto Is Added a Briefe Discourse, Taken out of Hier. Zanchius* (London: Printed by Adam Islip for Iohn Legat, Cambridge, 1595).

one's life. From 1 John 4, Perkins picks up the seal of the Spirit as another cause of assurance.

In a much shorter dialogue based on Psalm 15, Perkins lists seven practices that are marks of salvation. From both of these dialogues it is clear that obedience, or a changed life, is the only confirmation of salvation, which is wrought entirely by the Triune God. Perkins clearly distinguishes between the ground and evidence of assurance, giving primacy to the inner testimony of the Spirit.[71] In the end, Perkins's answer to the greatest case of conscience is entirely Scripture, expounded through a transformation of genre—namely, into the form of a dialogue.

A DISCOURSE OF CONSCIENCE

A Discourse of Conscience. Wherein Is Set Downe the Nature, Properties, and Differences Thereof: As Also the Way to Get and Keepe a Good Conscience is Perkins's doctrine of the conscience systematically laid out. He wrote the treatise in 1596 because he became convinced that sinning against conscience was extremely dangerous. While the work is not a consistent exposition of a single biblical text, it nonetheless remains biblical throughout. Perkins supports his argumentation with references, examples, and quotations from Scripture. He defines conscience as "part of the understanding in all reasonable creatures, determining of their particular actions either with them or against them."[72] The conscience has two duties. It bears witness or gives testimony, and it passes judgment. Conscience gives judgment because it is properly bound by the word of God. Human laws, oaths, and promises bind the conscience as well, if they are in accordance with God's word. The regenerate conscience, however, has two distinctive properties. The first is Christian liberty—that is, freedom from seeking justification by the moral law, the rigors of the law, and the ceremonial law. Christian freedom also consists of the licit use of things indifferent within the guidelines of Scripture. The other property is assurance of salvation. Perkins

71. Beeke, "William Perkins and His Greatest Case of Conscience," 269.

72. William Perkins, *A Discourse of Conscience Wherein Is Set Downe the Nature, Properties, and Differences Thereof: As Also the Way to Get and Keepe Good Conscience* (Cambridge: Iohn Legate, printer to the Vniversitie of Cambridge, 1596), 1; Perkins, *Whole Works*, 1:517. This is consistent with the definition of conscience among Puritans (J. I. Packer, "The Puritan Conscience," in *Faith and a Good Conscience*, 18).

argues that "an infallible certaintie of the pardon of sin and life everlasting" is possible.[73] He concludes with the individual's duty to obtain and keep a good conscience.[74] Again, all of these points are supported by Scripture, and there are multiple notable points of exegesis throughout his treatise.

Perkins anticipates objections to his claim that human laws are not intrinsically binding. He responds to them with careful exegesis of Scripture. One objection comes from Matthew 16:19. Here, Perkins explains that binding and loosing properly belongs to Christ, who holds the keys to heaven and hell, which is confirmed by Revelation 3:5. From the context of Matthew 26:18, Jesus is clearly not speaking to the making of laws but the forgiving of sins. This is even more clearly stated in John 20:23. Further, Matthew 23:4 condemns the scribes and Pharisees for burdening consciences with their traditions. Perkins appeals to context and uses collation to interpret this disputed text.[75]

Another objection comes from Acts 15:28–29. But Perkins says this does not stand because the apostles' rules here were given with a reservation of Christian liberty. Context shows the reason for the requirements is weak Jews. Further, it is the clear teaching of the analogy of faith that Christ abolished the ceremonial law and the apostles did not reestablish it. Further still, Paul himself was at this conference, and he clearly does not see the procedure as binding in his epistles. For instance, 1 Corinthians 8 identifies meat offered to idols as a thing indifferent.[76] So here again, Perkins employs context, collation, and the analogy of faith in order to make sense of this initially difficult verse.

Perkins responds similarly to objections to his claim that assurance is even a possibility for the believer. One objection comes from Job 9:20, 28. Perkins characteristically looks to the context first for interpretation. Bildad in Job 8 extols the justice of God. In 9:2, Job gives assent and then proceeds to magnify the justice of God. Here, at the end of the chapter,

---

73. Perkins, *Discourse of Conscience*, 6–83, 95–108; Perkins, *Whole Works*, 1:518–35, 538–40. This assurance is gained through various applications of the practical syllogism (Perkins, *Discourse of Conscience*, 137–39; Perkins, *Whole Works*, 1:547–48). For more on the practical syllogism, see Beeke, *Assurance of Faith*, 113–14.

74. Perkins, *Discourse of Conscience*, 156–69; Perkins, *Whole Works*, 1:551–53.

75. Perkins, *Discourse of Conscience*, 40–41; Perkins, *Whole Works*, 1:525–26.

76. Perkins, *Discourse of Conscience*, 41–45; Perkins, *Whole Works*, 1:526.

Job speaks not simply of himself in his own estate but himself as compared to God. In this case, the same despair would be true of even the elect angels.[77] Another objection comes from 1 Corinthians 4:3–4. Again, Perkins appeals to context, highlighting one of the major themes in the book: some among the Corinthians boldly had censured Paul and his ministry, but in 1 Corinthians 4 Paul defends himself by speaking of the excellency of his ministry, not his personal standing before God. Plus, in other places in Paul's corpus, such as 2 Timothy 4:8 and Romans 8:38, he readily evaluates his eternal estate.[78] In Perkins's technical work on conscience, he leans heavily on Scripture, and when interpreting difficult passages he characteristically relies on his methods of using Scripture to elucidate itself.

A GRAINE OF MUSTERD-SEEDE

In 1597, Perkins penned *A Graine of Musterd-Seede: Or, The Least Measure of Grace that Is or Can Be Effectual to Salvation* to speak into the Cambridge assurance debate.[79] The theme comes from Jesus' simile for the kingdom of heaven. Perkins defines the kingdom of heaven as "a certain state or condition, whereby we stand in the favour and love of God in and by Christ."[80] He asserts from the analogy of a mustard seed that the smallest measure of faith and repentance gains entrance into the kingdom. From this truth of Scripture, Perkins offers six conclusions, all of which build on one another.

Perkins supports his six conclusions with Scripture. The first is that the instant a man's conversion occurs, he is a child of God, even though at that moment he is more carnal than spiritual. The prodigal son is received by his father before he has a chance to confess. Nathan pronounces absolution of David's sin as he begins to repent and confess. Second, Perkins concludes the smallest measure of renewing grace carries with it promises for this life and the next. He quotes Isaiah 42:3, noting that even the smallest measure of the Spirit's gifts and graces will be cherished and accepted by

---

77. Perkins, *Discourse of Conscience*, 120–21; Perkins, *Whole Works*, 1:543. Here Perkins also appeals to the Hebrew, calling for "works" in 9:28 to be translated "sorrows."

78. Perkins, *Discourse of Conscience*, 123–24; Perkins, *Whole Works*, 1:543–44.

79. McKim, *Ramism in William Perkins' Theology*, 106.

80. William Perkins, *A Graine of Musterd-Seed, Or, The Least Measure of Grace That Is or Can Be Effectuall to Saluation* (London: Thomas Creed, for Raphe Iackson and Hugh Burwell, 1597), dedicatory epistle; Perkins, *Whole Works*, 1:636.

Christ. Third, an earnest and constant desire to be reconciled, to believe, and to repent, if sincere, is accepted by God for the things themselves. Matthew 5:5; John 7:37; and Revelation 21:6 all affirm that God accepts the will for the deed. Further, Romans 8:26 teaches that the desire of a good thing is accepted and taken by God for invoking his name. Groaning for a lively faith is to God a prayer made in lively faith. Paul identifies the groans as unspeakable because of their weakness. Perkins interprets the text this way because of its context. God knows the heart, even when there is a lack of understanding oneself. Fourth, grieving over the lack of any grace pertaining to salvation is grace in itself. Fifth, God accepts as true believers those who subject themselves to Christ, even if they are ignorant in many points of religion. The Samaritan woman, Rahab, and the apostles themselves illustrate this. Jesus told his disciples that the gates of hell would not prevail against the rock of their faith; he told them this before they knew of his death, resurrection, and reign from heaven. Finally, all the beginnings of grace addressed in conclusions one through five are counterfeit unless they increase. This caveat is clearly taught in the parable of the talents and Hosea's comparison of Ephraim's righteousness to the morning dew (6:4). Finally, Perkins concludes with a list of practices and meditations to help foster growth in faith.[81] The argumentation of this work is drawn from Jesus' analogy and supported in its particulars by Scripture interpreting itself.

CASES OF CONSCIENCE

Perkins was working on *The Whole Treatise of the Cases of Conscience* at the time of his death.[82] While he did not finish, he left 148 answers to questions concerning man considered by himself, in relation to God, and in relationship with fellow human beings. These three considerations are the topics of three books that make up his work on the conscience. The first book addresses salvation, assurance, and relief of a distressed conscience. The second touches on God, Scripture, and Christian religion, including many forms of outward worship. The third book applies the virtues of

81. Perkins, *Graine of Musterd-Seed*, 9–55; Perkins, *Whole Works*, 1:637–44. The list of meditations is not in the first edition.

82. McKim, *Ramism in William Perkins' Theology*, 98. For an in-depth treatment of conscience in Perkins's thought, see Markham, "William Perkins' Understanding."

prudence, clemency, temperance, liberality, and justice. According to his editor, Thomas Pickering, Perkins was particularly effective with case divinity because "his grounds and principles are drawn either directly, or by just consequence out of the written word."[83] This reliance on Scripture manifests itself in his grounding of the whole enterprise in the exegesis of Isaiah 50:4 as well as the biblical support for answers throughout.

Perkins interprets Isaiah 50:4 according to its context. This passage comes after the prophecy of the calling of the gentiles, which begins at Christ's death. In the previous verses of Isaiah 50, the prophecy details the rejection of the Jews in the days of Isaiah. Perkins states in reference to the whole chapter that "in this, and so in all other Prophecies of the like kinde, which treat of this point, Christ himselfe is brought in speaking in his owne person."[84] So in the preceding verses, it is Christ who disputes with Israel over its rejection. He was not the cause, but rather the people themselves were because of their sin. In 50:1, Christ through Isaiah reminds the Jews they cannot produce anything that testifies to his abandonment and appeals to their consciences because they indeed brought judgment on themselves. The next verse reminds them that God called them in great mercy and love, but they still would not obey. Isaiah 50:2–4 supplies the Lord's answer to the hypothetical charge that God cannot be expected to deliver because he does not have the same power he once did. But the text makes clear that the Lord has the power to ease and refresh the weary and afflicted. In light of these reflections, Perkins asserts a principal duty of Christ's prophetic office by alluding to the practices of Old Testament prophets.

Christ's prophetic office includes his ability to alleviate troubled consciences. Perkins concludes, "There is a certaine knowledge or doctrine revealed in the word of God, whereby the consciences of the weake may be rectified and pacified." He understands this as implied by the fact that Christ transferred the power to comfort distressed consciences to ministers of the gospel, just as he gave it to the prophets. This responsibility entails "a certaine and infallible doctrine propounded and taught in the Scriptures,

83. Perkins, *Whole Works*, 2:n.p. The quote comes from Pickering's dedicatory epistle to *The Whole Treatise of The Cases of Conscience*.

84. Perkins, *Whole Works*, 2:1.

whereby the conscience of men distressed may be quieted and releeved. And this doctrine is not attained unto by extraordinarie revelation, but must be drawen out of the written word of God."[85] Clearly, Perkins's interpretation of Isaiah 50:4 is the exegetical warrant for his endeavor to enumerate cases of conscience.

Perkins does more than ground his efforts in exegesis and cite Scripture as defense. He also uses his hermeneutic to explain certain difficult biblical texts. For example, to make sense of Jephthah sacrificing his daughter (Judg 11:39), Perkins carefully looks at the context. Jephthah cannot be said to have kept his vow by literally sacrificing his daughter, for this could not stand together with Scripture's commendation of his faith. Instead, Perkins argues Jephthah dedicated his daughter to God as a Nazirite. Thus, in Judges 11:37, she asks her father for leave to mourn her virginity. She does not mourn her life but her future estate, for singleness was considered a curse in Judea. This singleness also explains the agony of Jephthah, for not only was virginity a curse, but as his only child she provided his only hope for progeny. Further, Perkins claims the Hebrew for the daughters of Israel lamenting her annually would be better understood as them annually comforting her.[86] In this case, Perkins used a close reading of context to interpret this difficult text.

Perkins also uses context to interpret Luke 11:41. Here, Jesus confronts the Pharisees and accuses them of injustice and oppression. The remedy to these sins is the practice of charity that flows from a sincere heart and sanctifies one's resources. So the remedy is the giving of alms; the virtue is Christian liberality; and the fruit of obedience is salvation, assurance, restitution, and the purging of covetousness. Perkins is clear that generosity does not merit eternal life or cause any good thing God has promised, but it is the way one must walk to everlasting life. This fruit of generosity is a sign of God's mercy in Christ. As support, Perkins appeals to 1 Timothy 6:17–19 and the story of Zacchaeus. He also looks to Daniel 4:24 as an explanation of the verse in Luke.[87] In order to interpret Luke 11:41 and its exegetical ground for Christian liberality, Perkins makes use of context and collation.

85. Perkins, *Whole Works*, 2:1–2.

86. Perkins, *Whole Works*, 2:98.

87. Perkins, *Whole Works*, 2:143–47.

Perkins employs collation in his account of 1 Timothy 2:4, in which Paul speaks of God's desire that all will be saved. He says, "The Apostle is the best expounder of himself," and then quotes Acts 17:30, where Paul states that after Christ, God admonishes all men everywhere to repent. Just like in Acts, in 1 Timothy, Paul is saying that in this last age God desires all men to be saved. This is similarly supported by Paul's comments in 2 Corinthians 6:2; Colossians 1:16; and Romans 16:26. As for the universality of 1 Timothy 2:4, Perkins writes, "It must not be understood of all particulars, but of all kinds, sorts, conditions, and states of men" but in the same sense that Paul desires prayers for all people in 1 Timothy 2:1. Given the sin unto death in 1 John 5:16 and the accompanying prohibition on prayer, Paul cannot be urging supplication for every particular person but for all states of men. In this sense, God desires all to be saved.[88] Perkins interprets 1 Timothy 2:4 in light of various canonical passages.

Finally, Perkins utilizes the analogy of faith to account for the imprecatory psalms, particularly Psalm 109. Here David curses his enemies and even more directs his statements at particular people. Perkins asserts that all of the psalms were written for use by the church, but given the clear teaching of Jesus and the New Testament concerning loving one's enemies, praying imprecations against specific persons is out of bounds for the Christian. To account for the usefulness of such psalms despite this fact, Perkins says they must be used as "prophecies against the enemies of God, wherein the punishment of incurable men, that were enemies of God and his truth, is fore-told." David himself, on the other hand, as a prophet, had "an extraordinary spirit, or a pure zeal."[89] In the case of imprecatory psalms, Perkins uses the analogy of faith to rule out interpretive options.

CONCLUSION

In his practical works on the Christian life and ministry, Perkins expounded Scripture according to his hermeneutic as described in *The Arte of Prophecying*. He brought God's word to bear on all of life—at both the personal level and the varying spheres of human society. While preaching remains the pastor's primary responsibility, he must also apply biblical

88. Perkins, *Whole Works*, 2:23.

89. Perkins, *Whole Works*, 2:66.

truth to individual cases in order to help people in their struggle for assurance and aid in their pursuit of sanctification. This obligation caused Perkins to give considerable attention to conscience. In these initiatives, Perkins was thoroughly biblical, even as he used Scripture in different ways—from grounding whole works in exegesis to providing citations as warrant. When he did engage in interpretation, especially of difficult texts, he did so according to the analogy of faith, context, and collation, the three tenets of his scriptural hermeneutic. As Perkins was propelled by the herculean task of reforming the English populace and the conviction that Scripture was indeed the word of God, it should come as no surprise that the Bible took a central position in Perkins's practical works.

5

EXEGESIS IN THEOLOGICAL WORKS

Without a doubt, Perkins considered himself a biblical theologian, one who derived his theology from Scripture. Whether he was preaching, addressing practical matters, or writing polemics, the Bible made up Perkins's matter, and theology remained an ever-present extension. As a pastor, biblical scholar, and theologian, Perkins's disciplines and offices overlapped, a common occurrence in the sixteenth century. However, he also wrote some pointedly theological pieces as well. These fall into two categories: catechetical literature and works on soteriology. I will discuss these in turn and argue that in both instances Perkins implements his scriptural hermeneutic and its usual tools: the analogy of faith, context, and collation, each employed in an effort to have Scripture interpret itself.

CATECHISM

The Protestant Reformation's grand educational vision was the transformation of society through large-scale personal renovation. The roots and eventual growth of the Reformation significantly depended on successful education.[1] Gerald Strauss potently sums up this vision when he argues that the Reformation

> embarked on a conscious and, for its time, remarkably systematic endeavor to develop in the young new and better impulses, to implant inclinations in consonance with the reformers' religious and civic ideals, to fashion dispositions in which the Christian ideal

1. Fredrica Harris Thompsett, "Godly Instruction in Reformation England," in *A Faithful Church: Issues in the History of Catechesis*, ed. John H. Westerhoff and O. C. Edwards (Wilton, CT: Morehouse-Barlow, 1981), 175.

> of right thought and action could take root, and to shape personalities capable of turning the young into new men—into human elements of a Christian society that would live by evangelical principles.[2]

To accomplish this bold endeavor, Reformers aimed education at the population at large. Most of the time, this entailed preaching and catechism. These two disciplines went hand in hand, for "those who listened to sermons and read the Bible did so with faculties trained by catechisms."[3] In fact, catechism was essential so as not to preach over the people's heads.[4] Catechisms carried the burden of providing a theological infrastructure built from Scripture itself.

In England, Perkins's time "was an age of catechizing."[5] English Protestants produced almost 680 catechisms between 1530 and 1740.[6] The years 1536–1553 saw an ambitious, nationwide program of religious instruction for the young.[7] The "revolutionary intent" was "the construction of a vigorous program designed to nurture each Tudor citizen—individually and corporately—in knowledge, discipline, and love of God."[8] The 1570s to 1640s brought the victory of the question-and-answer catechetical format as well as an explosion in the production of catechisms. The Elizabethan authorities did not push for more catechisms but rather viewed the educational helps from the Edwardian and early Elizabethan

---

2. Gerald Strauss, *Luther's House of Learning: Indoctrination of the Young in the German Reformation* (Baltimore: Johns Hopkins University Press, 1978), 2.

3. Peter F. Jensen, "The Life of Faith in the Teaching of Elizabethan Protestants" (PhD diss., University of Oxford, 1979), 182.

4. Patrick Collinson, *The Religion of Protestants: The Church in English Society, 1559–1625* (New York: Oxford University Press, 1982), 234.

5. Collinson, *Religion of Protestants*, 232.

6. Ian Green, *The Christian's ABC: Catechisms and Catechizing in England c. 1530–1740* (New York: Oxford University Press, 1996), 51.

7. Philippa Tudor, "Religious Instruction for Children and Adolescents in the Early English Reformation," *Journal of Ecclesiastical History* 35, no. 3 (July 1984): 391–413.

8. Thompsett, "Godly Instruction in Reformation England," 175. See also Lynne Diane Durbin, "Education by Catechism: Development of the Sixteenth Century English Catechism" (PhD diss., Northwestern University, 1987), 269.

rules as adequate. The increase in number was instead due to the popular perception that such official documents needed supplement.[9]

Protestants looked to catechisms as manuals of belief, meant to instruct the ignorant, both young and old. There were five common benefits perceived by catechists. First, catechism provided the religious knowledge necessary for salvation. Second, it enabled deeper understanding of Scripture and what took place in church services. Third, it prepared individuals for robust participation in church life by framing their profession of faith, aiding in their understanding of sermons, and helping them to worthily participate in the Lord's Supper. Fourth, it enabled the catechized to distinguish between true and false doctrine. Fifth, it prompted Christian virtue and discouraged vice.[10] The technique was well adjusted to the oral, semiliterate era.[11] Further, given that English churches were purging themselves of wall paintings, statuary, priestly gestures, confession, religious drama, and other forms of popular religious instruction, catechisms became increasingly important.[12]

In the Reformed tradition, the Decalogue, the Apostles' Creed, and the Lord's Prayer served together as the traditional basis for catechisms.[13] The actual practice of catechizing included five operations or levels: teaching to remember answers, testing memory, explaining answers, testing how much individuals understood, and encouraging praxis. Perkins's expositions of the Apostles' Creed and the Lord's Prayer fit nicely within the two final levels of catechism: explanation and application. On the other hand, his general, elementary catechism, *The Foundation of Christian Religion, Gathered into Sixe Principles*, though it followed the question-and-answer format and shared significant doctrinal overlap, dramatically ignored the common catechetical structure. Perkins seems to have made "a deliberate attempt to bypass or short-circuit the conventional sequence in an effort to convey what [he] saw as essentials." Rather than trying to explain the

9. Green, *Christian's ABC*, 62–71. See also Margarita Patricia Hutchinson, "Social and Religious Change: The Case of the English Catechism, 1560–1640" (PhD diss., Stanford University, 1984), 101, 119–20.

10. Green, *Christian's ABC*, 26.

11. Collinson, *Religion of Protestants*, 233.

12. Green, *Christian's ABC*, 43; Hutchinson, "Social and Religious Change," 320.

13. Thomas F. Torrance, *The School of Faith: The Catechisms of the Reformed Church* (New York: Harper, 1959), xi; Durbin, "Education by Catechism," 272.

formulae to parishioners who already knew them but comprehended neither what they represent nor how they should be used, Perkins thought it better to start fresh by extracting the fundamentals out of these staple items and presenting the familiar in a new, memorable way. He largely succeeded in his initiative, as his catechism was used for a century and enjoyed over thirty editions.[14]

THE FOUNDATION OF CHRISTIAN RELIGION

In 1590, Perkins published *The Foundation of Christian Religion* with the purpose of instructing the ignorant, according to his prefatory epistle. He saw this short work as laying a foundation such that people could profitably hear sermons and participate in the sacraments. These activities were hindered, in Perkins's view, by a lack of application of those resources readily available—namely, the Ten Commandments, the Apostles' Creed, and the Lord's Prayer. Perkins highlights the need for his remedy with a list of twenty-nine false opinions in his dedicatory epistle. The most common theme by far is the individual's relationship to God and, more specifically, the details of salvation. Soteriology and its application were of paramount importance to Perkins, a point demonstrated by surveying his theological writings. In his particular context, distinguishing between the Protestant and Roman understandings of salvation could not be overemphasized. Therefore, it should come as no surprise that this catechism walks one through the process of attaining right standing before God.[15]

As the title suggests, Perkins draws six essential principles from the Christian faith. He organizes his work according to six responses to questions about God, man, Christ, receiving Christ's benefits, the ordinary means of grace, and the afterlife.[16] Perkins is careful to back up every phrase of each principle with explicit biblical warrant. In the second part of his work, he proceeds to explain the principles and in turn interprets the supporting passages through more detailed questions and answers.

14. Green, *Christian's ABC*, 93, 286–88.

15. William Perkins, *The Foundation of Christian Religion, Gathered into Sixe Principles. And It Is to Be Learned of Ignorant People, That They May Be Fit to Heare Sermons with Profit, and to Receiue the Lords Supper with Comfort* (London: Thomas Orwin for Iohn Porter, 1590). The list was later expanded to thirty-two. See Perkins, *Whole Works*, vol. 1.

16. Perkins, *Foundation of Christian Religion*, n.p.; Perkins, *Whole Works*, 1:1–3.

Perkins does not necessarily show the reader his exegesis, but he remains meticulously biblical. He does, however, briefly introduce doctrines and themes that appear and are exegetically supported throughout his works. It is worth enumerating these doctrines as an introduction to Perkins's theology.

Perkins was a Reformed catholic. He affirmed the Trinity and classical Christology. There is one God who is distinguished into three persons by their relations to one another.[17] The person of the Son became man; therefore the one person, Christ, has two natures, human and divine. Perkins emphasized the threefold office of Christ as mediator. As priest, Christ's satisfaction made atonement sufficient for all humanity, but his intercession extends only to the faithful, so not all are saved.[18] Christ's finished work is the only hope for human beings, who are all sinners in Adam and totally depraved. Perkins understands Adam as the head of all his progeny and original sin as the consequence of his infraction. The depravity of Adam and his offspring is complete, by which Perkins means it extends to the mind, conscience, will, affections, and body.[19] The benefits of Christ's sacrifice are appropriated by faith, which is preceded ordinarily by preparation, both of which are wrought by the Spirit. Perkins believed there were degrees of faith, a spectrum that began with mere desire to believe and ultimately grew into being fully persuaded of God's favor. According to Perkins, a primary avenue to full assurance is one's own sanctification. The means God uses to convey Christ and his benefits to his people are the preaching of the word and the two sacraments, which serve as signs,

---

17. Perkins, *Foundation of Christian Religion*, n.p.; Perkins, *Whole Works*, 1:3. Here Perkins affirms that the Father begets the Son, the Son is begotten of the Father, and the Spirit proceeds from the Father and the Son. All these relations are eternal.

18. Perkins, *Foundation of Christian Religion*, n.p.; Perkins, *Whole Works*, 1:4–5. Perkins does not use the language of hypostatic union in this instance, but he clearly articulates the doctrine. Neither does he tease out the sufficient/efficient distinction regarding the atonement, though he alludes to it.

19. Perkins, *Foundation of Christian Religion*, n.p.; Perkins, *Whole Works*, 1:4. Perkins does not develop a federal or covenant theology at this point, but his interaction with Rom 5 foreshadows it. He explains the propagation of sin with the illustration that "great personages by treason do not onely hurt themselves, but also staine their blood, and disgrace their posterity."

seals, and instruments.[20] All of these doctrines as well as the emphasis on salvation appear regularly in Perkins's corpus.[21]

THE LORD'S PRAYER

Perkins wrote *An Exposition of the Lords Prayer* "in the way of catechizing, serving for ignorant people."[22] In the dedication, he claims that the work "sets out the matter and true manner of invocation of God's holy name," and to this end he includes questions and answers pertaining to prayer in general. But in an advertisement to the reader, Perkins reveals a unique motivation for writing. He claims he would not have published his work, as he determined the Lord's Prayer to have been sufficiently treated, if he had not been misrepresented by a rogue publication of his original orations on the topic. Perkins desired to teach people the right meaning of the words they so often recite, for there can be no prayer or faith without knowledge.[23] This knowledge flows from his exposition of the text according to his stated interpretive method.

Perkins understands every part of the Lord's Prayer in the context of the whole. The body consists of six petitions, which Perkins explains individually and then expounds "wants to be bewailed" and the "graces to be desired" based on each. Perkins recites Scripture throughout this systematic organization. The first three petitions concern God—in particular, his glory and the means by which his glory is manifested and enlarged. The second three requests concern the petitioner—not absolutely, but that God might be glorified. Perkins connects the two because God's will is fulfilled by reliance on his providence for the daily needs of life, his mercy for the pardon of sin, and his power for resisting temptations.[24]

---

20. Perkins, *Foundation of Christian Religion*, n.p.; Perkins, *Whole Works*, 1:5–7.

21. It is worthy of note that Perkins's treatment of double predestination is restrained, even ambiguous in this work. He refrains from speaking of the immutable decrees of God and instead speaks of the godly going to heaven and unbelievers and reprobates to hell. Some thought it unwise to teach certain doctrine in full at an elementary level. Apparently Perkins was among this number (Green, *Christian's ABC*, 287).

22. William Perkins, *An Exposition of the Lords Prayer in the Way of Catechising Seruing for Ignorant People* (London: Robert Bourne and John Porter, 1592); Perkins, *Whole Works*, 1:323. This claim is printed on the title page of the work.

23. Perkins, *Exposition of the Lords Prayer*, dedicatory epistle and advertisement, 62; Perkins, *Whole Works*, 1:324–25, 334.

24. Perkins, *Exposition of the Lords Prayer*, 58, 103; Perkins, *Whole Works*, 1:333, 339.

Perkins begins his exposition with a definition of prayer drawn from collation: "To make prayer, is to put up our request to God according to his word from a contrite heart, in the name of Christ, with assurance to bee heard." That prayer is addressed to God comes from Romans 1:14. According to Romans 8:26, prayer is petitioning God from the heart, not mere lip service. Moreover, 1 John 5:14 teaches prayer must follow the rule of the will and word of God. It must also proceed from a contrite heart, per Psalm 51:17, and be offered in the name of Jesus, per John 14:14. Finally, according to Mark 11:24, faith is requisite to prayer. After identifiying the command to pray from Matthew 6:9, Perkins propounds a definition of prayer through collation.[25]

Perkins's explanation of "thy will be done" illustrates how his hermeneutic interprets individual petitions. First, the will of God is contained in the Bible, for in his word, God's will is revealed. This is taken as an undisputed article of faith. Second, Perkins sees three specific points of the will of God, which he draws from collation. From John 6:40, God wills for people to believe in Christ. Next, from 1 Thessalonians 4:3, God's will is the sanctification of body and soul. Then, from Romans 8:29 and Philippians 3:10, God wills the bearing of affliction in this life. Further, Romans 8:7 teaches the will of God is contrary to the wicked and corrupt will of man.[26] In this case and throughout his work on the Lord's Prayer, Perkins implements his hermeneutic of Scripture interpreting itself.

THE APOSTLES' CREED

In 1595, Perkins came as close as he ever would to a systematic theology with his *An Exposition of the Symbole or Creed of the Apostles: According to the Tenor of Scripture, and the Consent of the Orthodoxe Fathers of the Church*. At the start, Perkins defends his approach of treating Christian doctrine without a text of Scripture against those who claim that catechizing must follow the ordinary course of preaching. He claims that "in Catechizing the Minister hath his libertie to follow, or not to follow a certaine text of Scripture, as we do in the usuall course of preaching." Perkins sees warrant for this in the practice of the primitive church. For example, the author of

25. Perkins, *Exposition of the Lords Prayer*, 2–8; Perkins, *Whole Works*, 1:326–27.

26. Perkins, *Exposition of the Lords Prayer*, 62; Perkins, *Whole Works*, 1:337.

Hebrews summarizes the faith in principles of religion not drawn from a certain text of Scripture. But Perkins is intentional in his caveat that if ministers approach the catechism according to this method, they must "confirme the doctrine they teach with places of scripture afterward."[27] Perkins sees the exposition of Scripture as essential to preaching and biblical support as essential to catechism.

Scripture is also central given the nature of the Apostles' Creed: "It is a summe of things to bee believed concerning GOD and concerning the Church, gathered foorth of the Scriptures." In his dedicatory epistle, Perkins identifies the creed as "indeed the very pith and substance of Christian religion, taught by the Apostles, embraced by the ancient Fathers, sealed by the blood of Martyrs ... and hereupon hath been called the *rule of faith*, the *key of faith*."[28] At the same time, Perkins carefully distinguishes that the creed is a piece of "ecclesiastical writing," not "Divine" writing or the word of God. Describing the "scripture of God," Perkins asserts:

> not only the matter of them, but the whole disposition thereof, with the style and the phrase was set downe by the immediate inspiration of the holy Ghost. And the authority of these books is *divine*, that is, absolute and soveraigne: and they are of sufficient credit in and by themselves, needing not the testimony of any creature; not subject to the censure either of men or Angels; binding the consciences of all men at all times, and being the onely foundation of our faith, and the rule and canon of all truth.[29]

Perkins clearly applies verbal plenary inspiration, self-authentication, and total authority to Scripture. However, he intentionally does not extend these descriptors to the creed. Ecclesiastical writings may be called "the truth of God, so farre forth as their matter or substance is consenting with the written word of God." Their authority "doth not stand in the authoritie and pleasure of men and Councels, but in the consent which they have with the Scriptures."[30] So, the creed is subordinate to Scripture, even as

27. Perkins, *Exposition of the Symbole*, 1; Perkins, *Whole Works*, 1:121.
28. Perkins, *Exposition of the Symbole*, dedicatory epistle, 2; Perkins, *Whole Works*, 1:n.p., 121.
29. Perkins, *Exposition of the Symbole*, 3; Perkins, *Whole Works*, 1:122.
30. Perkins, *Exposition of the Symbole*, 3–4; Perkins, *Whole Works*, 1:122.

its consonance with it and its confession by the catholic church warrant its authority.

Perkins organizes his exposition according to the creed. It accounts for each person of the Trinity and the church. After articulating the classic orthodox doctrine of the Trinity, Perkins discusses God the Father as the omnipotent creator of all things. The Father's providence extends to Adam's fall and the covenant of grace, which is Perkins's segue into God the Son. After explaining the incarnation according to the classical interpretation of Chalcedon, Perkins spends over one-third of his work walking through the four Gospels' passion narratives. After a relatively brief treatment of God the Holy Spirit, Perkins addresses the church, specifically its properties and benefits. Perkins explains early on that for each article of the creed, he will explain the meaning, enumerate the consequent duties, and gather consolations. In large part, he remains true to this structure, which gives the work a sermonic feel. Within this organization and structure, Perkins does not limit himself to simply compounding biblical citations as warrant for doctrinal points. Instead, he engages in serious exposition of difficult texts of Scripture. In doing so, Perkins employs context, collation, and the analogy of faith, remaining consistent with his scriptural hermeneutic.

Context

Perkins's most extensive exegesis according to context is his lengthy treatment of Romans 9 within a larger discussion on predestination. According to his appraisal, Romans 9:6–23 describes the doctrine of God's eternal predestination. The first five verses of the chapter articulate Paul's grief concerning the Jews. In Romans 9:6 he begins to answer an assumed objection—namely, that the word of God is of no effect because of the failure of Israel. Paul's answer is that there has always been a distinction between those within and those outside the covenant, even among the Jews. He gives three examples to prove this point. First, not all descendants of Jacob are truly Israel. The second example, Isaac and Ishmael, demonstrates that not even all the descendants of Abraham are part of the covenant. Third, God unconditionally chose Jacob over Esau not because of anything they had done but according to his inscrutable will.[31]

---

31. Perkins, *Exposition of the Symbole*, 424–26; Perkins, *Whole Works*, 1:278–79.

At this point, Perkins responds to several objections. First, is it possible that the prerogatives mentioned in the text are only temporary or earthly blessings? Based on context, Perkins responds with a resounding no. If only temporal blessing were at stake, then Paul's examples do not address the charge. Clearly, Paul is grieved over the eternal consequences of the Jews' rejection of Christ. Further, the land of Canaan is a sign or figure of the covenant of grace. Romans 9, therefore, cannot be talking about mere earthly blessings. Second, some object by saying Jacob and Esau are references to their respective nations, which implies individuals and their eternal states are not addressed. Perkins, again looking at the context, argues that the text speaks of Jacob and Esau in their mother's womb. This is an impossibility for two nations. But even granting this interpretation based on Romans 9:12, the receiving of Israel and the rejection of Edom also proves God's eternal election and reprobation. In both responses, Perkins appeals to the verses' context.[32]

Perkins picks back up with his exposition of Romans 9:14–23, which consists of two objections raised and answered by Paul. The initial objection accuses God of injustice. But, Perkins says, God is just because he has absolute power and freedom of will, which applies even to the choosing and hardening of individuals. From beginning to end, salvation is of the Lord, which occasions the second objection. How can God hold people accountable if they are subject to his will? Paul's answer, according to Perkins, is a counterattack to the pride and presumption such an accusation reveals. God has the right and the power to predestine as Creator. Therefore, the righteousness of his will is not to be questioned. Ultimately, the exercise of God's mercy and justice is for his own glory.[33] In Perkins's thinking, Romans 9 is persuasive in proving predestination. As a result, he devotes significant space to letting the text speak for itself, interpreting each part by the context of the whole.

32. Perkins, *Exposition of the Symbole*, 426–28; Perkins, *Whole Works*, 1:279.

33. Perkins, *Exposition of the Symbole*, 428–30; Perkins, *Whole Works*, 1:280.

Collation

Perkins's interpretation of Genesis 1:26 and the image of God is peculiar but based on collation. It is unusual in that Perkins extends the image of God to angels. He defines the image of God as "nothing else but a conformitie of man unto God, whereby a man is holy as God is holy."[34] Support for this definition comes from Paul's exhortation to put on the new man in Ephesians 4:24, which consists of righteousness and holiness. Renewing God's image necessarily entails its original intent. Scripture does not speak of the image of God as something that consists in the substance of body, soul, or a person's faculties. Therefore, the image of God as conformity to God in righteousness and holiness extends to the creation of angels as well.

Perkins further argues that the image of God has two principal parts: wisdom and holiness. Having already defended the latter with the writings of Paul, he does the same for wisdom. Colossians 2:10 equates the image of the Creator with knowledge, which makes sense given the creation account. Adam, in his state of innocence, knew God, his will, and his wisdom concerning creation.[35] So in navigating the complex issue of man's creation in the image of God, Perkins appeals to where it is taught elsewhere in Scripture through collation.

Perkins also has a surprising interpretation of Genesis 3:15, which he arrives at by collation. This is the first revelation of the covenant of grace, "a compact made betweene God & man touching reconciliation and life everlasting by Christ." That Genesis 3:15 is the first allusion to the gospel is consistent with classical Christian interpretation; rather, what Perkins does with the "seed" is unexpected. The offspring of the woman includes Christ and all the elect, while the serpent's progeny consists of all the wicked. Romans 16:20 and 1 John 3:8 are cited as support. This division throughout human history is illustrated by Cain and Abel, the sons of God and daughters of men in Genesis 6:2, Isaac and Ishmael, Jacob and Esau, Jew and gentile. Perkins appeals to many places throughout the canon of Scripture to interpret this initial articulation of the covenant of grace.[36]

34. Perkins, *Exposition of the Symbole*, 81; Perkins, *Whole Works*, 1:150.

35. Perkins, *Exposition of the Symbole*, 81–82; Perkins, *Whole Works*, 1:150–51.

36. Perkins, *Exposition of the Symbole*, 118–20; Perkins, *Whole Works*, 1:164–65.

Perkins's interpretation of Jesus' reference to the separation of the sheep and goats in Matthew 25:32 offers another example of collation. Perkins cites the parable of the wheat and the tares in Matthew 13 to reinforce that this full and final separation will not be accomplished until the last day, the final judgment. This means it is the church's lot in this world to be troubled in many ways by the goats that live among them. As defense, Perkins alludes to Ezekiel 34:18, where goats muddy the water and trample the pasture. In this mixed arrangement, it is impossible to identify the goats definitively, but according to John 10:27, the sheep hear the shepherd's voice and follow him. Therefore, obedience is a distinguishing mark of sheep. To arrive at the meaning of the sheep and goats image, Perkins brings other Scripture to bear on the text.[37]

Walking in the Spirit is essential to Perkins's concept of the Christian life, which is manifested by the fruit of the Spirit. To illuminate the fruit of the Spirit (Gal 5:22–23), Perkins takes each of the nine characteristics in turn and interprets them according to other pertinent passages of Scripture. For example, joy is contrary to the nature of man, whose tendency is to envy the good of others. This is why Paul in Romans 12:15 commands Christians to rejoice with those who rejoice. Another example is that goodness is the readiness to do good and serve others. This is what Paul means in 1 Corinthians 9:22 when he claims to become all things to all men that he might save some. Perkins exercises collation for all of the fruits of the Spirit, letting Scripture interpret itself.[38]

Analogy of Faith

In his discussion of Christ's sacrifice as high priest, Perkins references Hebrews 7:17's comparison of Christ and Melchizedek. Using the analogy of faith, Perkins offers two reasons Christ is a priest according to the order of Melchizedek. First, both Melchizedek and Christ have the roles of king and priest. Second, neither has father or mother. Christ as he is God had no mother; as man, he had no father. In his interpretation of this

37. Perkins, *Exposition of the Symbole*, 383–84; Perkins, *Whole Works*, 1:263.

38. Perkins, *Exposition of the Symbole*, 412–18; Perkins, *Whole Works*, 1:274–76.

verse, Perkins simply utilizes the analogy of faith, particularly the offices of Christ and Chalcedonian Christology.[39]

Combination

Perkins understands God to have created the world and everything in it with his speech, by the power of his word. This is the plain meaning of Genesis 1's common construction "let there be." There are three ways Scripture speaks of God's word: substantial, verbal or written, and operative. Context reveals that the latter is the sense used here. While it is true the Father created through the Son, the Son is not meant here. Neither should one think of the words in this case as audible. Instead, this is a case of accommodation, in which the author describes God's powerful or operative word, spoken equally by all three persons of the Trinity. That God's pleasure, will, and appointment are all powerful and described as his "word" is confirmed by David in Psalm 33:6. This operative word is also reinforced by Jesus calling Lazarus from the grave (John 11:44) and Paul's comparison of salvation to the creation of light by God's command (2 Cor 4:6).[40] Perkins uses context and collation to explain this easily misunderstood phrase from Genesis 1.

Perkins uses all three tools of his hermeneutic in his interpretation of the fall in Genesis 3. Dissecting the story, he draws attention to the causes, time, greatness, and largeness of the fall. The outward cause is the devil, which he derives from context. Though the serpent is not explicitly identified, his fraud, seen in his slyly approaching Eve, implicates Satan. But the fall's inward cause was the will of Adam and Eve. This is supported by Solomon in Ecclesiastes 7:31, though an objection can be made that Adam could not will to sin if he were created good. Perkins appeals to a commonly accepted fact among theologians: Adam was created with the freedom to will either good or evil. Underneath this objection is an implication of God, a charge Perkins does not shy away from. God gave Adam grace in his ability to do good, but God withheld the grace of perseverance for his own just purposes.[41]

39. Perkins, *Exposition of the Symbole*, 262–63; Perkins, *Whole Works*, 1:218–19.

40. Perkins, *Exposition of the Symbole*, 57–59; Perkins, *Whole Works*, 1:142.

41. Perkins, *Exposition of the Symbole*, 105–7; Perkins, *Whole Works*, 1:160.

But though God was not a cause of the fall, "neither was it by any bare permission without his decree and will: for that is to make an idle providence: neither did it happen against the will of God; hee utterly nilling it." God decreed the fall, Perkins says, not as a sin against his commandment but as a way to execute his justice and mercy. Additionally, both the time and greatness of the fall are illuminated by context. Moses does not interpose anything between creation and the fall, so it was likely shortly after creation. Some say that simply eating the forbidden fruit was not a sufficient infraction to warrant its consequences. Perkins defends God's justice and enumerates the implications of the fall as such: unbelief, contempt of God, trying to be gods, unthankfulness, curiosity, blasphemy, murder, and discontentment. The largeness of the fall's consequences is clarified by Romans 5:12, where Paul claims death came to all men through Adam's sin. To interpret the fall, Perkins uses Scripture itself through context, collation, and the analogy of faith.[42]

In Matthew 1:21, when the angel reveals the name "Jesus," it is said he shall save his people from their sins, a statement Perkins interprets using collation and the analogy of faith. First, "his people" must mean the elect among both Jews and gentiles. This is attested to in Ephesians 5:23, where Paul claims that Christ is Savior of his body. Second, the analogy of faith rules out the possibility that Christ died to save all people, for if he made satisfaction for all, God could not justly condemn any. The determining factor in salvation cannot be the will of man accepting or rejecting Christ's sacrifice; otherwise God's will would be subject to another. So, by way of collation and the analogy of faith, Perkins limits the statement of Jesus' salvation of his people to the elect.[43]

Jesus' prayer in the garden of Gethsemane has a host of theological implications, and Perkins uses all of his hermeneutical tools to arrive at the passage's meaning. The analogy of faith, specifically the person-nature distinction of classical Christology, helps him navigate the fact that the Son of God is requesting of God what seems to be contrary to the will of God. To be sure, the person or subject of the incarnation is God the Son, but he prays through his manhood. The idea of the Son praying to

42. Perkins, *Exposition of the Symbole*, 108–11; Perkins, *Whole Works*, 1:161.

43. Perkins, *Exposition of the Symbole*, 124–25; Perkins, *Whole Works*, 1:167.

the Father should not be troubling, as though he were praying to himself, for the Son and Father are distinct persons. Further, Christ has two wills, since will is tethered to nature—and in this case, Jesus' human will was at variance with his divine will, though there remained no contradiction. In a similar case, when Paul desired to preach in Asia and Bithynia but was hindered by the Spirit, Paul's will did not contradict the will of God but was at variance with it. The context—namely, the anguish of the cross and the coming wrath of God—explains the cause of Christ's prayer. Perkins uses context, collation, and the analogy of faith to interpret Jesus' garden prayer. At the same time, he upholds the true divinity and humanity of Christ while protecting consistency within the Godhead.[44]

Perkins follows a similar line of interpretive reasoning to explain Matthew 27:46, where Jesus questions God's forsaking of him. How could Christ, who is God himself, be forsaken by God? Reflecting on this question is powerful. Context shows Jesus, clearly identified as the Son, addressing God. Perkins argues that Christ is crying out to God the Father according to a common rule he gathers from other passages. As a general rule, when a text compares God to the Son or Spirit, it is using "God" to refer to the Father. Further, Perkins employs the person-nature distinction to conclude that Christ's manhood was forsaken, not his divinity. Here again, Perkins uses context, collation, and the analogy of faith to interpret a text with wide-reaching theological consequences.[45]

Perkins entreats Reformed Christology, part of the analogy of faith in his conception, to explain some of the unusual aspects of Christ's post-resurrection appearances. The first is Jesus suddenly being taken from the two disciples' sight after the post-Emmaus meal together. What this cannot mean, in Perkins's estimation, is that the body of Jesus became spiritual and disappeared. Instead, Perkins offers a couple of alternatives, which he draws from collation. Jesus could have held their eyes like he did when he first met them on the road, or he could have departed with great speed enabled by his glorified body. A second appearance occurred in the upper room, where the doors were shut. Again, Jesus could not have passed through the door or wall, which would be against the nature of bodies.

---

44. Perkins, *Exposition of the Symbole*, 185–90; Perkins, *Whole Works*, 1:189–91.

45. Perkins, *Exposition of the Symbole*, 243–44; Perkins, *Whole Works*, 1:211.

Instead, according to Perkins, he likely altered the substance of the door so he could pass through, just like he thickened water in order to walk on it. Perkins's christological conception limited his interpretative options in the case of these postresurrection appearances, and collation provided alternative possibilities.[46]

In interpreting passages of Scripture that would seem to teach the universality of redemption, Perkins has a patterned approach. First, he denies universalism based on the analogy of faith, and then he explains the reference in light of Scripture. For example, in 1 Timothy 2:4, the word "all" cannot mean all particular persons, or else God's will would be done and all would be saved. Rather, the referent is all kinds of men. Perkins supports this interpretation with the opening of 1 Timothy, where Paul exhorts Timothy to pray for all men. This does not mean every individual human, and neither does Paul teach that God will save every individual human. Similarly, Romans 11:32 would seem to argue that God purposes to have mercy on all, but this cannot be the case per the analogy of faith. "All" in this case must be understood as all those who are to be saved, including both Jews and gentiles. Galatians 3:22 speaks of this same reality. In the cases of John 3:16 and John 6:15, "world" cannot mean every particular person in the world. In these instances, "world" refers to the elect among Jews and gentiles. The context of these verses is Jesus' effort to overthrow the Jewish conceit of believing God did not love the gentiles. Perkins cites Romans 11:12–15 and 2 Corinthians 5:18 as defining the term "world" for the New Testament. In all of these incidents, Perkins limits the interpretive options with the analogy of faith and then explains the verses through collation.[47]

So far, we have explored Perkins's catechetical literature. His catechism proper and his works on the Lord's Prayer and the Apostles' Creed all give a foundational role to Scripture as interpreted according to the analogy of faith, context, and collation. In short, even in this theological genre of catechism, Perkins uses Scripture to interpret itself as his method of exegesis.

---

46. Perkins, *Exposition of the Symbole*, 316–19; Perkins, *Whole Works*, 1:239. The historical context for these postresurrection narrative explanations is the Lutheran and Reformed debate over Christ's presence in the Lord's Supper.

47. Perkins, *Exposition of the Symbole*, 471–75; Perkins, *Whole Works*, 1:296–97.

This will prove true of his theological works on soteriology as well, from the pastoral works to the more scholarly.

GOD'S SOVEREIGNTY IN SALVATION

The theological issue most widely discussed in late sixteenth-century England was salvation. The topic consumed university scholars, clergy, and government officials, causing division between Protestants and the Church of Rome and reverberating throughout different theological camps. Perkins emerges as the foremost English writer on the subject, for "his was a remarkably clear, coherent, and biblically centered view, and he put it at the heart of his evangelical message."[48] He engaged in national and international discussions from almost the beginning of his career. From his *Golden Chaine* in 1590 to two treatises on grace and predestination in the late 1590s, Perkins wrote often about salvation.

Throughout the sixteenth and seventeenth centuries, the Reformed tradition as a whole wrestled with the theological locus of salvation. Richard Muller has demonstrated that development took place generationally both during and preceding the period of Reformed Orthodoxy. Calvin, Bullinger, Vermigli, and Musculus developed the first codification. Among them, there was "no disagreement over the necessity of grounding the concept of salvation by grace alone in the eternal and unalterable will of God," despite their differences on the order of the decrees, double predestination, and how the fall fits into the counsel of God. Theologically, the rest of the sixteenth century elaborated the positions and resolved tensions posited by Calvin and his contemporaries. With Beza, Ursinus, and Zanchi, one observes a move toward more explicit scholastic theology, but it was not until Polanus and Perkins that a fully formulated system emerged. However, it is essential to recognize that this development was not one of the substance of theology.[49]

In addition to being hotly debated around the Christian world at large, the issue of predestination caused major controversy locally in Cambridge. The doctrine had early proponents in England, such as Tyndale, Frith, and

48. Patterson, *William Perkins*, 64.

49. Muller, *Christ and the Decree*, 69, 74, 125. In this work, Muller is speaking directly in the "Calvin vs. the Calvinists" debate. See my introduction.

Barnes.[50] By the 1570s, it was well-established, and by the 1590s predestination dominated the scene.[51] On several occasions, however, a kind of proto-Arminianism bubbled up in Cambridge, which provided the circumstances for Perkins to enter the discussion.[52]

In the late 1570s, Peter Baro, the Lady Margaret's Professor of Divinity, publicly expressed his views, arguing for free will and against the immutable decree of God.[53] This implied humans might cooperate or refuse to cooperate in their salvation. Baro quarreled with Laurence Chaderton in 1581, again showing his hand. This was quickly followed up by a treatise on providence. Baro was cautious but clearly differed from the establishment, moving the discussion from the mind of God to individuals with their sin and merit.[54] However, the strife spread beyond Baro. In 1584, Samuel Harsnett, fellow of Pembroke College, preached a sermon at Paul's Cross on Ezekiel 33:11. Harsnett's agenda showed, as he deliberately and provocatively attempted to make predestination seem absurd.[55] This context provided the backdrop of Perkins's education as well as his academic and pastoral career. It also induced the young leader to write his internationally significant *Golden Chaine*.

In 1595, William Barret, the chaplain of Caius College, attacked the predestinarian consensus in a highly contentious sermon at Great St. Mary's. Even more, he accused Calvin in particular of arrogance and criticized others from the Reformed tradition for being Calvinists.[56] Barret

50. Carl R. Trueman, *Luther's Legacy: Salvation and English Reformers, 1525–1556* (Oxford: Clarendon, 1994); Wallace, *Puritans and Predestination*, 6; Bryan D. Spinks, *Two Faces of Elizabethan Anglican Theology: Sacraments and Salvation in the Thought of William Perkins and Richard Hooker* (Lanham, MD: Scarecrow, 1999), 41.

51. Shaw, "William Perkins and the New Pelagians," 272.

52. The idea of a "Calvinist consensus" during this period is contested. Those who are persuaded that it was a reality include Patterson, *William Perkins*; Shaw, "William Perkins and the New Pelagians"; Wallace, *Puritans and Predestination*; Nicholas Tyacke, *Anti-Calvinists: The Rise of English Arminianism, c. 1590–1640* (New York: Clarendon, 1987); Hoyle, *Reformation and Religious Identity*; Collinson, *Religion of Protestants*. A representative of the contrary is Peter White, *Predestination, Policy and Polemic: Conflict and Consensus in the English Church from the Reformation to the Civil War* (Cambridge: Cambridge University Press, 1992).

53. Patterson, *William Perkins*, 70.

54. Hoyle, *Reformation and Religious Identity*, 47–49.

55. Patterson, *William Perkins*, 71; Hoyle, *Reformation and Religious Identity*, 68.

56. Porter, *Reformation and Reaction*, 277–363; Lake, *Moderate Puritans and the Elizabethan Church*, 201–42.

intended to offend, basically accusing the Church of England of being led astray by a foreign, mistaken "Calvinist" party. The university authorities were determined to respond with severity, so Barret was forced to read a retraction prepared for him in the same pulpit. This action did not satisfy many; some were even willing to embellish the very definitions of orthodoxy to cast Barret as a heretic.[57] William Whitaker, Regius Professor of Divinity, submitted the Lambeth Articles to Archbishop John Whitgift, who approved them with minor revisions. These additions to the Thirty-Nine Articles aimed at definitively settling the Cambridge dispute by making them explicitly teach double predestination, a hope dashed by the queen's eventual aborting of the effort.[58]

Still at Cambridge, Baro kept a low profile for a number of years, perhaps because many perceived him as Barret's theological predecessor. Of course Baro disagreed with the Calvinistic Lambeth Articles, a fact he had to explain himself on more than one occasion. He expressed his views publicly again in 1596, accusing the Lambeth Articles of making God the author of evil and the work of Christ redundant. As an alternative, he taught conditional election based on God's foreknowledge.[59] While Perkins was not directly or officially involved, the blatant insubordination of Barret and Baro indirectly assaulted his views. The whole affair of the mid-1590s provided the context of Perkins's later treatises on predestination. Perkins, compelled by the turmoil in Cambridge, wrote on the topic of salvation academically and with precision but not to the exclusion of Scripture.[60]

57. Hoyle, *Reformation and Religious Identity*, 73–75.

58. Porter, *Reformation and Reaction*, 364–71; Lake, *Moderate Puritans and the Elizabethan Church*, 218–26.

59. Hoyle, *Reformation and Religious Identity*, 80–81.

60. The lack of characters such as Baro and Barret at Oxford allowed the university, while thoroughly Protestant, to be less rigid, insistent, and precise (C. M. Dent, *Protestant Reformers in Elizabethan Oxford*, Oxford Theological Monographs [Oxford: Oxford University Press, 1983], 238).

A GOLDEN CHAINE

Perkins wrote *A Golden Chaine: Or, The Description of Theologie* in Latin and published it in 1590.[61] The subtitle and opening of the work has led many to believe it is a kind of systematic theology. He defines theology as "the science of living blessedly for ever," a blessedness that arises out of knowing God, which Perkins couples with knowledge of the self.[62] He then divides his discussion between God and his works. In the treatment of the latter, it becomes readily apparent Perkins intends to write a pastoral soteriology, not a systematic theology.[63]

Affixed to the beginning of *A Golden Chaine* is a chart, with its descending bubbles that outline the outworking of God's predestination, a decree ordered before creation and the fall. This infamous chart has resulted in an unfair caricature of Perkins as a scholastic theologian who could not possibly back up his abhorrent system with Scripture. When actually reading his work, one quickly finds that Perkins had biblical warrant for his supralapsarian logic. He cites Ephesians 1:4, 11 and Romans 9:21 as support for God's decree, which he defines as "that by which God in himselfe, hath necessarily, and yet freely, from al eternity determined al things." The decree as it concerns humanity is predestination, its execution by means of creation, fall, and either redemption or damnation. For predestination, Perkins offers 1 Thessalonians 5:9 and Romans 9:13, 22.[64] Predestination manifests itself in the twin decrees of election and reprobation. For Perkins, the doctrine of election, "God's decree, whereby on his owne free will, he hath ordained certain men to salvation, to the praise of the glorie of his

61. William Perkins, *Armilla Aurea, Id Est, Miranda Series Causarum et Salutis & Damnationis Iuxta Verbum Dei Eius Synopsin Continet Annexa Tabula* (Cantabridgiae: Ex officina Iohannis Legatt, 1590). The work was quickly expanded in a second edition and translated. This expanded edition is used here. See Perkins, *Armilla Aurea Id Est, Theologiae Descriptio*; William Perkins, *A Golden Chaine, or the Description of Theologie Containing the Order of the Causes of Saluation and Damnation, according to Gods Woord. A View of the Order Wherof, Is to Be Seene in the Table Annexed. Written in Latine by William Perkins, and Translated by an Other. Hereunto Is Adioyned the Order Which M. Theodore Beza Vsed in Comforting Troubled Consciences* (London: Edward Alde, and are to be sold by Edward White at the little north doore of S. Paules Church at the signe of the Gunne, 1591).

62. Perkins, *Armilla Aurea*, 1; Perkins, *Whole Works*, 1:11.

63. Muller, "Perkins' A Golden Chaine." For negative assessments of *A Golden Chaine* as a cold, hardened predestinarian system, see Wallace, *Puritans and Predestination*, 56–61; White, *Predestination, Policy and Polemic*, 98.

64. Perkins, *Armilla Aurea*, 16, 19–20; Perkins, *Whole Works*, 1:15–16.

grace," is found clearly in Ephesians 1:4–6; Revelation 20:12; and 2 Timothy 2:10. The foundation of election is Jesus Christ, the means are the covenant of grace, and its execution is accomplished through the degrees of effectual call, justification, sanctification, and glorification.[65] The decree of election receives vastly more attention than its counterpart, the decree of reprobation.[66]

Reprobation, also according to the free and just purpose of God's will, is the part of predestination whereby God "determined to reject certaine men unto eternall destruction, and miserie, and that to the praise of his justice." But the foundation of its execution is the fall of Adam. As Perkins asserts, he does not "set downe any absolute decree of damnation, as though we should thinke that any were condemned by the mere and alone will of God, without any causes inherent in such as are to be condemned."[67] Perkins defends this doctrine with Romans 9:21 and 1 Peter 2:4, 8. Further, he asserts that Cain and Abel, Ishmael and Isaac, and Esau and Jacob serve as types for humanity, some elected, others rejected. Again, Perkins distinguishes between God's decree and the means of its execution, considering the purpose of God separately from subordinate middle causes. The controlling theme of the treatise is that predestination is for God's glory, to the praise of his mercy and justice.[68]

Perkins sets his contribution in the context of four current views of predestination in his preface. The first he terms "Pelagian" because it makes predestination dependent on man. In this scheme, election and reprobation are according to God's foreknowledge of either faith or rejection of his grace. The second view is held by the Lutherans, who believe God offers grace to everyone and, foreseeing that all will reject, purposes to have mercy on some. Perkins labels Rome as semi-Pelagian. This view holds

65. Perkins, *Armilla Aurea*, 44–45; Perkins, *Whole Works*, 1:24. Perkins's emphasis on holy living and Christian practice, even in such an intensely theological work, earned him the label of "father of pietism" from Heinrich Heppe (Muller, *Christ and the Decree*, 131). See also F. Ernest Stoeffler, *The Rise of Evangelical Pietism* (Leiden: Brill, 1965), 55; Hoyle, *Reformation and Religious Identity*, 65; Muller, "Perkins' A Golden Chaine," 80.

66. Reprobation takes up less than 4 of the treatise's 103 pages in Perkins's collected works edition.

67. Perkins, *Armilla Aurea*, 329; Perkins, *Whole Works*, 1:105. Regarding reprobation, Perkins maintains his supralapsarian logic but refrains from making reprobation fully coordinate with election. No one is condemned but for sin (Muller, *Christ and the Decree*, 170–71).

68. Perkins, *Armilla Aurea*, 329–37; Perkins, *Whole Works*, 104–7.

that predestination is based partly on mercy but also on foreseen preparations and meritorious works. Last is Perkins's own position. He claims,

> the cause of the execution of Gods predestination, is his mercy in Christ, in them which are saved; and in them which perish, the fall and corruption of man: yet so, as that the decree and eternal counsel of God, concerning them both, hath not any cause besides his will and pleasure.[69]

The theological context of predestination is further evidence of Perkins's intention of addressing salvation throughout *A Golden Chaine*.

Collation

Throughout his work, Perkins scarcely writes a paragraph without referencing Scripture, though he also does significant exegesis according to the method articulated in *The Arte of Prophecying*. Perkins's careful exegesis relies heavily on collation. As he discusses original sin, Perkins cites Romans 1:19–20 to show that whatever remains of the image of God, it serves only to remove humanity of its excuse before God's judgment. Perkins uses collation to conclude humanity cannot discern the knowledge of God because of ignorance, impotency, vanity, and an inclination inherited from Adam only to evil thoughts. For example, 1 Corinthians 2:14 teaches that the mind is ignorant or deprived of knowledge concerning sincere worship or eternal happiness. Luke 24:45 and 2 Corinthians 3:5 prove the mind is impotent, unable to understand spiritual things even when they are taught. The mind is vain, counting falsehood as truth and truth as falsehood. This reality is asserted in Ephesians 4:17; 1 Corinthians 1:2; and Proverbs 14:12. Finally, the mind is naturally inclined to conceive and devise only evil, from Genesis 6:5 and Jeremiah 4:22. Here, Perkins extensively employs collation to explain why people are unable to respond properly to the knowledge of God available to them.[70]

Perkins then uses collation to explain the four degrees of sin found in James 1:14–15. The first is temptation. Satan allures people to sin by offering it to the mind, as in the case of Judas (John 13:2). Temptation can also come

---

69. Perkins, *Whole Works*, 1:n.p.

70. Perkins, *Armilla Aurea*, 31–37; Perkins, *Whole Works*, 1:20.

upon occasion of some external object perceived by the senses, as referenced in Job 31:1. The second degree is conception, which Psalm 7:14 speaks of in terms of consent and resolution to commit sin. After the actual committing of the sin comes the fourth degree, the perfection of sin. By perfection, Perkins means reaping the consequence of sin, which is death and damnation. This is seen in the case of Pharaoh, who presumptuously sins to the point that he is hardened. Such presumptuous sin is also referenced in Psalm 19:13. Here again, Perkins uses collation to arrive at the meaning of presumption. Numbers 15:30 reveals presumption as sins committed in contempt of God. Another form of presumption is assuming God's mercy when doing evil. This second form is condemned in Ecclesiastes 8:11 and Romans 2:4. These are but two examples of Perkins using Scripture to illuminate itself in his discussion of sin.[71]

In Perkins's rather lengthy response to the Church of Rome's view on salvation, he refutes the concept of a second justification by works. In this refutation, he cites Deuteronomy 27:26 and uses other passages to show that not even the works of the regenerate are righteous according to legal justice. Perkins appeals to the example of David, who in Psalm 143:2 does not want even his best works to fall under God's judgment for his justification. Job 9:3 and Daniel 9:18 are further evidence of how short even the works of the regenerate fall. When it comes to justification, Perkins is adamant that works merit nothing, whether before or after regeneration. He defends this with Scripture, interpreted with itself by collation.[72]

Combination

Perkins does not exclusively rely on collation to interpret Scripture in his *Golden Chaine*. Also in his discussion of second justification, Perkins cites Galatians 5:2–4, arguing that justification by works in any sense overturns the foundation of the faith. He interprets these verses according to context and collation. The context of Galatians reveals that Paul's opponents mingled the merit of Christ with works of the law. So Paul belabors the point: not just external works of the law but all moral works are excluded from justification. Thus, in Romans 4:5, Paul speaks of Abraham's belief—not

71. Perkins, *Armilla Aurea*, 38–42; Perkins, *Whole Works*, 1:22–23.

72. Perkins, *Armilla Aurea*, 318–22; Perkins, *Whole Works*, 1:102.

his postregeneration works—as that which resulted in imputed faith. Ephesians 2:10 also excludes good deeds from justification. So here, in further defense against meritorious works of any kind, Perkins understands Scripture according to itself through context and collation.[73]

Perkins also combines the analogy of faith with collation. While arguing that Christ is the foundation of election, Perkins interprets Hebrews 2:17 and demonstrates Jesus was a man in every way, except for sin. Perkins appeals to the analogy of faith in order to assert that Christ's human nature included body and soul, with everything that comes with them. Using collation, Perkins shows that Christ in his humanity was subject to human infirmities. Matthew 4:1 proves he was tempted; Hebrews 5:7 proves he feared; Mark 3:5 proves he experienced anger; and Matthew 26:39 proves he briefly forgot his office in response to great agony. For further understanding of Christ's human infirmities, Perkins again brings the analogy of faith to bear. These infirmities affected Christ's human nature only, were common to all men, and were assumed not by necessity but willfully as part of his humiliation. Human infirmity is not natural to prefallen man, and Christ was without sin. Therefore, Christ's human infirmities were not experienced as a consequence but for his people. Elucidating the complexities of Christ's human nature, Perkins relies on Scripture as it is understood according to other passages and shared theology.[74]

Another example of Perkins combining the analogy of faith with collation is his treatment of apostasy, specifically the sin against the Holy Spirit referenced in Matthew 12:32. This sin is so called not because it is done against the divine person of the Spirit, for this would be an infraction concerning the whole Godhead. Rather, this sin is done against the immediate action of the Spirit. It must involve obstinate malice against the Spirit. Peter's denials out of fear and Paul's persecution out of ignorance were not apostasy. According to Hebrews 10:29, the object of apostasy is both the majesty of God and the Mediator. Moreover, according to Hebrews 6:5–6, the sin against the Spirit can only be committed by one who has been enlightened and tasted the good gift of God. However, the elect by definition cannot commit this sin. With these clarifying passages in mind

73. Perkins, *Armilla Aurea*, 319–20; Perkins, *Whole Works*, 1:102.

74. Perkins, *Armilla Aurea*, 49–51; Perkins, *Whole Works*, 1:25.

as well as the analogy of faith, Perkins offers his definition: "the sin against the holy Ghost, is a voluntarie, and obstinate deniall of, and blasphemie against the Sonne of God, or that truth which was before acknowledged concerning him, and so consequently, an universall defection from God and his true Church."[75]

Perkins's most extensive exegesis comes via his exposition of the Ten Commandments, which falls within his discussion of the covenant. His treatment of the Decalogue accounts for nearly half of the treatise, as Perkins walks through each commandment's "resolution," "affirmative part," and "negative part." He lets Scripture interpret itself through various applications of the analogy of faith, context, and collation. In each case, Perkins arrives at the commands and prohibitions through collation. This will be illustrated with one example from each table.

Perkins explains the first commandment, the prohibition against other gods, through context, collation, and the analogy of faith. God reminds his people that he is Jehovah who delivered them from Egypt. Perkins appeals to context to support his conclusion that this is a preface to the first commandment only and not all of the commands. Commandments two through four, which comprise the rest of the first table, include their own reasons for obedience. God's employment of the name "Jehovah," the first reason for obedience, signifies several things that Perkins mines through collation. Revelation 1:8 teaches God is eternal; Exodus 6:1 and Romans 4:17 show he mightily accomplishes what he promises. So, the very fact that God is Jehovah provides a reason for the command. A second reason lies in the claim, "thy God." In these words, the covenant of grace is found. Perkins cites Jeremiah 31:33 to explain the covenant between the Lord and his people as it pertains to the remission of sins and eternal life. The exodus serves as a type for deliverance from the kingdom of darkness (1 Cor 10:1–2; Col 1:13). The other gods, or strange gods, are not therefore gods by nature; Philippians 3:19 and 2 Corinthians 4:4 lend further support for this. These false gods, God forbids "before my face." Noting the anthropomorphism and appealing to the analogy of faith, Perkins asserts this reference to God's face is figurative for his presence, which, being everywhere, provides the third reason for obedience. God's people are always in his presence, so

75. Perkins, *Armilla Aurea*, 334–36; Perkins, *Whole Works*, 1:106–7.

rejecting him in his very presence is a heinous crime. As he exegetes the first commandment, Perkins remains true to his hermeneutic.[76]

Perkins's exposition of the tenth commandment, against covetousness, utilizes both context and collation. In order to specify what it means to covet, Perkins distinguishes between three movements of the heart. First is Satan's suggestion of sin, which the mind does not receive, and therefore no sin is committed. A clear example of this is the temptation of Christ in Matthew 4. Second is the more permanent sinful thought that stirs an inward joy. This is covetousness. The third motion of the heart is a matter of the will offering its full assent to sin, which is what the five former commandments speak to. Lust preceding consent is revealed as sin by the law according to Romans 7:7. The objects of wicked desire are simply items that belong to one's neighbor. But Perkins notes all desire is not wrong—only evil concupiscence, according to Colossians 3:5 and Galatians 5:17. Examples of proper objects of desire include the necessities of life and the Spirit. Perkins's explanation of the tenth commandment remains consistent with his method of using Scripture to interpret itself.[77]

Before leaving Perkins's biblical interpretation in *Golden Chaine*, it is important to note how he brings theological precision regarding the two natures and one person of Christ to bear on the text of Scripture. There are two keys to understanding what Perkins is doing. First, the Son of God added a second nature to himself; therefore, the divine Son is the subject of the incarnation. Second, in this union there is a communication of properties, in which there is a true and real predication. This means things concerning one of Christ's natures are to be attributed to his person. As one approaches Scripture, this has major implications. For example, some texts speak of Christ according to his divine nature. John 8:50 is an example of this, as Jesus claims to be Yahweh. Other texts must be understood in light of his human nature only. An example of this is found in Acts 20:28's reference to Christ purchasing the church with his blood. Perkins brings the analogy of faith's Chalcedonian Christology with him as he exposits

76. Perkins, *Armilla Aurea*, 75–80; Perkins, *Whole Works*, 1:32–33.

77. Perkins, *Armilla Aurea*, 203–6; Perkins, *Whole Works*, 1:69.

particular texts.[78] This careful effort to interpret Scripture according to itself is apparent throughout *A Golden Chaine*'s theological formulation.

A TREATISE OF GOD'S FREE-GRACE, AND MANS FREE-WILL

Perkins wrote *A Treatise of God's Free-Grace, and Mans Free-Will* no earlier than 1598 and first published it in 1601.[79] He discusses the topic in the context of an exposition of Matthew 23:37–38, for in these verses, both the will of God and the will of human beings are referenced with regard to salvation. Perkins begins by looking to the context of Matthew 23, the whole of which is a sermon by Jesus to the Jews of Jerusalem. Jesus reproves the scribes and Pharisees in Matthew 23:1–36 and follows this by an invective against the city of Jerusalem's rebellion, foretelling its destruction as a consequence for sin. Perkins spends the majority of his time on the manner of Jerusalem's rebellion, which he unpacks by looking at the will of God, the will of man, the harmony of the two, and the love and patience of God's will.[80]

Within his treatment of God's will, Perkins relies on the analogy of faith and context to interpret Christ's words, "I would." He leans on the analogy of faith to assert Christ's two natures and therefore his two wills. In this instance, Christ's divine will is the referent, which is clear from the context. Jesus speaks of gathering the Jews by the ministry of the prophets, which took place throughout Israel's history and began long before the incarnation. The divine will is the will of the Godhead, including the Father and Spirit, because will is tied to nature. This leads Perkins to make a distinction concerning the will of God.[81]

Perkins uses collation to distinguish between the will of God's good pleasure and his signifying will, arguing that the latter is the will of God in Matthew 23:37. God's good pleasure is the decree of predestination according to Ephesians 1:5. God's will is also entirely sovereign, for Romans 9:16

78. Perkins, *Armilla Aurea*, 49–51; Perkins, *Whole Works*, 1:25–26.

79. In at least three instances, Perkins references forty years of the grace of God to England, which are references to the reign of Elizabeth I, beginning in 1558 (William Perkins, *A Treatise of Gods Free Grace, and Mans Free Will* [Cambridge: Iohn Legat, printer to the Vniuersitie of Cambridge. And are to be sold at the signe of the Crowne in Pauls churchybard by Simon Waterson, 1601], 4, 46, 159; Perkins, *Whole Works*, 1:720, 726, 743).

80. Perkins, *Treatise of Gods Free Grace*, 1–13; Perkins, *Whole Works*, 1:720–22.

81. Perkins, *Treatise of Gods Free Grace*, 23; Perkins, *Whole Works*, 1:723.

asserts he has mercy on whomever he will. It is the cause of all things, even as it remains often hidden from humanity's perspective. Isaiah 46:10 teaches that this will of God cannot be thwarted; therefore, it cannot be the referent in Matthew 23:37. Instead, in this sermon, Jesus speaks of the signifying will of God, which Perkins defines as "when he revealeth some part and portion of his pleasure, so far forth as it serves for the good of his creature, & the manifestation of his justice or mercy." He goes on, "This signifying will is not indeed the will of God properly, as the will of his good pleasure is, for it is the effect thereof: yet may it truly be so tearmed."[82] This will is propounded clearly in Scripture. This is why Paul says in Romans 12:2 that Christians are to prove what is the good will of God. God's commands, his word, comprise his signifying will.

At times, an apparent contrariety exists between God's decree and his revealed will. For instance, in Genesis 22, God tells Abraham to offer his son Isaac as a sacrifice; however, his decree is to spare Isaac. This seems to be a contradiction because the purpose of the command—to test Abraham—remained concealed. But Abraham's trial and Isaac's continuance are both consonant ends. Among other passages, Perkins appeals to God's message to Nineveh through Jonah. The declaration seems to be an unequivocal promise of impending destruction, while the exception clause is concealed. Instead, God's decree is the repentance of Nineveh, and his declaration proves to be a means to that end. In Matthew 23, God's signifying will is the gathering of Jerusalem's inhabitants through the ministry of the word.[83]

Perkins employs collation again when explaining the bondage of man's will in the state of corruption. He claims that "though the liberty of nature remains, yet liberty of grace, that is, to will wel, is lost, extinguished, abolished by the fall of Adam." There is no power or aptness in man to will what is truly good. Perkins defends this with a litany of references: Ezekiel 36:26; John 6:44; Romans 8:7; 1 Corinthians 2:14; and Ephesians 2:4. Not only is the human will impotent when it comes to doing good, but it is so prone to

82. Perkins, *Treatise of Gods Free Grace*, 33; Perkins, *Whole Works*, 1:724. Perkins addresses this distinction of will his discussion of tropes in *The Arte of Prophecying* (*Prophetica*, cap. V; *Whole Works*, 2:657).

83. Perkins, *Treatise of Gods Free Grace*, 33–42; Perkins, *Whole Works*, 1:725–26. Perkins addresses the concept of threats and promises being conditional in his discussion of tropes in *The Arte of Prophecying* (*Prophetica*, cap. V; *Whole Works*, 2:657).

evil that it can do nothing but sin. For this level of human bondage, Perkins cites Jeremiah 17:9; Romans 6:20; and 2 Timothy 2:26. Furthermore, the good human beings do is ascribed wholly to God in Scripture, most notably in John 1:13; 15:5; and Ephesians 2:10. The will of man is bound, and Perkins uses a range of biblical passages to prove it.[84]

Perkins concludes his treatise by briefly accounting for the desolation spoken of in Matthew 23:38 via collation and context. The destruction is both perpetual and terrible. Perkins draws its perpetual nature from Luke 21:24–25, which foretells of Jerusalem being trampled underfoot until the time of the gentiles is fulfilled. One finds evidence for the fulfillment of this prophecy in the frustrated attempts to reconstruct the city and temple under Emperor Julian—not to mention the failed Crusades centuries later. Perkins recounts the horrifying siege of Jerusalem and its aftermath at the hand of Vespasian (AD 70) as the initial fulfillment of the desolation mentioned here. Perkins finds warrant for this in the context of Matthew 23:37–38. For example, in Matthew 24:34, Jesus provides a very particular time for the fulfillment of this prophecy—that is, before the passing of his hearers' generation. This most terrible destruction by Rome fits perfectly, within the compass of forty years.[85] In this treatise, Perkins utilizes all of the tools of his scriptural hermeneutic even as he grounds his discussion in the exegesis of a particular passage.

TREATISE ON PREDESTINATION

Perkins wrote *A Christian and Plaine Treatise of the Manner and Order of Predestination, and of the Largenesse of Gods Grace* in Latin and published it in 1598 to speak into the Cambridge predestination controversy. This was an academic debate that drew international attention. For these reasons, Perkins offers what could be considered his most scholarly treatise. Here, we find Perkins using calculated precision, scholastic distinctions, and appeals to a variety of authors, from Aristotle and other philosophers to patristic, medieval, Reformation, and contemporary sources. Scripture, of course, assumes a central role. In his epistle to the reader, Perkins asserts, "The doctrine of Predestination and Gods grace is to be founded upon the

84. Perkins, *Treatise of Gods Free Grace*, 68, 70–77; Perkins, *Whole Works*, 1:729–31.

85. Perkins, *Treatise of Gods Free Grace*, 176–84; Perkins, *Whole Works*, 1:745–46.

written word of God, and not upon the judgements of men." Perkins also articulates foundational points from common reason coupled with the light of nature, with which the doctrine of predestination must agree. He goes on to clearly subordinate the witness of all ancients, doctors, and schoolmen to the authority of Scripture but purposes to utilize them because it is "necessary, that there should be had an example of consent and concord in that doctrine, which is expounded in the holy books, and is propagated to all posterity." Further, Perkins's alternate title on the first page of text indicates that the order of predestination here propounded is "as neere as the Author could collect it out of the Scriptures."[86]

Though Perkins asserts the authority of Scripture and claims reliance on it at the outset, his treatise neither is founded on exegesis of a particular passage nor explicitly references Scripture as much as his other theological works. Perkins claims the supreme end of predestination is the manifestation of God's glory, and its general means are creation and the fall. Election showcases his mercy, whereas reprobation reveals his justice. These twin doctrines both have two acts. In election, God's first act is his purpose to bestow love and favor on particular men and women. The second act is the means—namely, redemption through Christ. Reprobation also has two acts. God purposes to forsake certain men and women; second, he ordains punishment for some, the destruction due their sin. This double act in reprobation is key for Perkins because it allows God total sovereignty and protects him from moral culpability. Perkins's supralapsarianism accounts for the first act, while damnation is God's just response to sin.[87] This constructive account is relatively short compared to Perkins's defense of it against four contrary charges and his critique of conditional election, in which he highlights the doctrine's eleven errors.[88] All of this is not to say Perkins does not rely on Scripture. His overall arguments are not unique to this treatise within his corpus, and biblical and exegetical support can be observed in his earlier work on similar subjects as well as in his sermons

86. William Perkins, *De Praedestinationis Modo et Ordine et de Amplitudine Gratiae Diuinae Christiana & Perspicua Disceptatio* (Cantabridgiae: Ex officina Iohannis Legat, 1598), *ad lectorum*, 1; Perkins, *Whole Works*, 2:605–6.

87. Perkins, *De Praedestinationis Modo*, 1–28; Perkins, *Whole Works*, 2:606–11. So Perkins distinctly considers ends from means in the counsel of God, though they are not separate (Muller, *Christ and the Decree*, 165).

88. Perkins, *De Praedestinationis Modo*, 28–159; Perkins, *Whole Works*, 2:611–40.

and commentaries. Yet even here, explicit Scripture references appear with frequency, and when he delves into exegesis, he operates according to the rules of his traditional hermeneutical method.

Perkins defends the double act of God in election with his exegesis of Romans 8:29–30, using context and collation. He sees a clear distinction between the decree and its execution. God's decree is his foreknowledge and predestination, whereas the means are calling, justification, and glorification. A similar distinction is made in 1 Peter 1:2. Foreknowledge should not be taken as foreseeing future faith, for those God foreknew he predestined to be like Christ—that is, just. Scripture is clear that righteousness is received by faith, so it cannot be that God foreknows men will believe and then after predestines them to believe. Rather, God foreknows who will believe because he decreed that they should. Further, "to know" often means to embrace or approve. Two examples of this are Psalm 1:6 and Matthew 7:23. Scripture also teaches that the prescience and purpose of God are one and the same, as in 2 Timothy 2:19 and Romans 11:2–5.[89] So Perkins defends his position with a close reading of the text and brings interpretive insights from other passages of Scripture.

In Perkins's defense of his own position, he interprets several biblical passages in harmony with a limited view of the atonement's efficacy. First, in 2 Corinthians 5:19, when Paul says that in Christ God was reconciling the world unto himself, the word "world" should be taken to mean all nations, rather than all human beings. This and other passages must be interpreted in light of Romans 11:12, 15, where Paul explains the reconciling of the world is the reconciliation of the gentiles after the casting away of the Jews. Everyone will not be saved, but some from every nation will indeed be saved. Second, 1 Timothy 2:4 seems to teach that God wants every human being to be saved, but Perkins uses collation to show this cannot be true. He appeals initially to other Pauline statements, including Acts 17:30; Romans 16:25; Colossians 1:26–27; and 2 Corinthians 6:2, which teach that God's will to save does not extend to all the descendants of Adam. Perkins then extends his references to 1 Peter 1:20 and John 12:32, concluding that "God willeth that all should be saved: but that God willeth, and that he hath always willed that all men in all ages should be saved, I utterly deny." The word "all" can be taken distributively, which would indicate every

89. Perkins, *De Praedestinationis Modo*, 6–9; Perkins, *Whole Works*, 2:607.

particular person. This, for instance, is Paul's intention in 2 Thessalonians 1:3 when he joins "everyone" with "all." It can also be understood collectively, which refers to anyone, not everyone. In this sense, Matthew 9:35 speaks of Jesus healing every disease. In much the same way, God's will that all men be saved extends to some of every estate or condition.[90] In interpreting both of these passages, Perkins relies heavily on collation.

Perkins also appeals to the analogy of faith and collation in his handling of conditional election's error of making the human will determinative in salvation, specifically through his interpretation of Matthew 23:37. Here, Christ is said to have willed the salvation of the Jews in Jerusalem, but as an act of his revealed will rather than the will of his good pleasure. This distinction is clear from the whole of Scripture. God calls all in common unto salvation through the preaching of the word of God, but he does not effectually enable all to meet the conditions of salvation; he does not grant to all repentance and faith. Acts 7:51 provides another instance of Jews resisting the external ministry of the word, not the inward and effectual operation of the Spirit.[91] Within this learned treatise on predestination, Perkins does exegesis in his constructive theology, in its defense, and in his offensive against conditional election. In doing so, he utilizes context, collation, and the analogy of faith to allow Scripture to interpret itself.

CONCLUSION

Scripture serves as the source and norm of Perkins's expressly theological works. Whether writing for the purpose of theological instruction in his catechetical works or entering the world of sophisticated theological debate in the university setting, Perkins grounds his theology in Scripture. But he does not build his theology on prooftexting or vague appeals to biblical teaching; rather, he engages in rigorous exegesis, interpreting Scripture according to Scripture itself. Yes, he appeals to patristic, medieval, and contemporary authorities. Yes, he remains consistently within the Reformed tradition. Yes, he has educational goals in view. Yes, he writes in the heated environment of 1590s Cambridge. Nonetheless, Perkins relentlessly uses Scripture to interpret itself by making use of the analogy of faith, context, and collation.

90. Perkins, *De Praedestinationis Modo*, 75–77, 79–82; Perkins, *Whole Works*, 2:622–23.

91. Perkins, *De Praedestinationis Modo*, 147–48; Perkins, *Whole Works*, 2:638.

6

EXEGESIS IN POLEMICAL WORKS

POLEMICS AGAINST THE CHURCH OF ROME

When Perkins wielded his pen against Rome, the Protestant Elizabethan settlement was not entirely settled. With the revolving door of Tudor monarchs, the Church of England oscillated between Catholicism and Protestantism or some mixture of both. Contemporaries not privy to the final outcome would have been very much aware of the precarious position of England's national church. Just how Protestant were the English people? This is a question left for the historiography of the English Reformation. Once asked, this question implies another: Was the Reformation "from above" or "from below"?[1] Ultimately this is a false dichotomy. For England to adopt Protestantism officially, both monarch and Parliament had to be involved. But for Protestantism to really succeed, it had to be accepted by the people. It seems clear the change did not definitively take place until late in Elizabeth's reign.[2] For Perkins, then, it was not at all certain until late in his life that his people would turn from Rome. The uncertainty of his country's allegiance drove Perkins to oppose Catholicism with Scripture.

1. The work done on this question is vast. A. G. Dickens, *The English Reformation*, 2nd ed. (University Park, PA: Pennsylvania State University Press, 2005), represents the "from above" camp. For revisionist interpretations, see Eamon Duffy, *Saints, Sacrilege and Sedition: Religion and Conflict in the Tudor Reformations* (London: Bloomsbury, 2012); Christopher Haigh, *English Reformations: Religion, Politics, and Society under the Tudors* (Oxford: Oxford University Press, 1993); and G. W Bernard, *The King's Reformation: Henry VIII and the Remaking of the English Church* (New Haven, CT: Yale University Press, 2005). Postrevisionist mediation includes Alec Ryrie, *The Gospel and Henry VIII: Evangelicals in the Early English Reformation* (Cambridge: Cambridge University Press, 2003), and Ethan H. Shagan, *Popular Politics and the English Reformation* (Cambridge: Cambridge University Press, 2003).

2. Doran and Durston, *Princes, Pastors, and People*. Some historians argue that Protestantism was never accepted by a significant number of English men and women (Christopher Haigh, "The Church of England, the Catholics and the People," in *The Impact of the English Reformation, 1500-1640*, ed. Peter Marshall [London: Arnold, 1997], 249).

The Catholic threat Perkins and his contemporaries felt from within and without was more than mere perception. That Catholic voices rather than Catholic beliefs were stamped out during Edward's reign is illustrated by both the ease of Mary's reversals and the number of her supporters.[3] The consolidation of Catholics under Mary encouraged unity and outspokenness among Rome's sympathizers under Elizabeth.[4] Mary's bishops courageously took a stand against Elizabeth's settlement, which cost them their careers and freedom.[5] At this point, what happened to the Catholic community in England is debated. Did it die and, with the advent of the missionary priests, return as something distinct in the late 1570s and 1580s? Or did it live on, adapting to the reality of disestablishment? At heart, this is a question about the continuity or discontinuity of the recusant Catholic community of Elizabethan England and its medieval antecedents.[6] Evidence suggests the Catholic community continued and Marian priests functioned as pioneers in sustaining the officially proscribed religion. They found patronage among the conservative laity, especially the gentry. The missionaries, then, brought new confidence to the Catholic community and aided in its expansion.[7] That said, Catholicism's continuity or discontinuity is irrelevant for the purposes of this book. The significant fact is this: adherents of the old faith existed and became increasingly active throughout the second half of the sixteenth century.

---

3. Duffy, *Saints, Sacrilege and Sedition*, 220–21.

4. Lucy E. C. Wooding, *Rethinking Catholicism in Reformation England* (New York: Oxford University Press, 2000), 269.

5. Peter Marshall, *Reformation England, 1480–1642* (London: Arnold, 2003), 170.

6. For discontinuity proponents, see John Bossy, *The English Catholic Community, 1570–1850* (New York: Oxford University Press, 1976), 4, 11; and J. C. H. Aveling, *The Handle and the Axe: The Catholic Recusants in England from Reformation to Emancipation* (London: Blond and Briggs, 1976), 21. For the continuity perspective, see Alexandra Walsham, *Catholic Reformation in Protestant Britain* (Aldershot, UK: Ashgate, 2014), 173; Christopher Haigh, "The Continuity of Catholicism in the English Reformation," in *The English Reformation Revised*, ed. Christopher Haigh (Cambridge: Cambridge University Press, 1987), 178; J. J. Scarisbrick, *The Reformation and the English People* (Oxford: Blackwell, 1984), 142. Marshall provides a nice synthesis and balance (*Reformation England*, 176–78). For a history of research and bibliography on this topic, see Walsham, *Catholic Reformation in Protestant Britain*, 4–27.

7. Scarisbrick, *Reformation of the English People*, 142–45. For Catholic patronage among the gentry, see Michael C. Questier, *Catholicism and Community in Early Modern England: Politics, Aristocratic Patronage and Religion, c. 1550–1640*, Cambridge Studies in Early Modern British History (Cambridge: Cambridge University Press, 2006).

The Elizabethan settlement only temporarily silenced the Marian theological establishment. Key leaders were imprisoned, while others were scattered.[8] By 1563, Catholics were forbidden to participate in Church of England services by papal decree.[9] Over one hundred Oxford University men fled the country during Elizabeth's first decade. They sought to wait on Providence and train good leaders, expecting England to return to the Catholic fold. Among these men was William Allen, who founded the English College of Douai in 1568.[10] Similar seminaries appeared in Rome and other strategic locations, quickly becoming the training ground for missionary priests. The first of these missionaries returned to England in 1574.[11] The more significant date, however, is 1580, the commencement of the Jesuit mission to England and the arrival of Edmund Campion and Robert Parsons. Campion became the movement's first martyr; Parsons led the English missionary enterprise into the seventeenth century. With the influx of Catholic missionaries in the 1580s, it became a truism among English Protestants that Jesuits favored the use of force and Catholicism increasingly became viewed as treason.[12]

Sanction of violence for the Catholic cause in England was not new. Mary Stuart was the hope of Catholic plots for the duration of her almost-twenty-year imprisonment. The first was the Northern Rebellion of 1569, which sought to free Mary. Pius V, in an attempt to aid the uprising, issued the bull *Regnans in Excelsis*, excommunicating Elizabeth in 1570.[13] However, the 1580s saw the height of the Catholic schemes. John Somerville's assassination attempt and the Throckmorton Plot both took place in 1583. The Parry Plot came to light in 1585. The Babington Plot the following year, of which Mary Queen of Scots was aware, culminated in her execution in

---

8. Duffy, *Saints, Sacrilege and Sedition*, 209.

9. Marshall, *Reformation England*, 171.

10. Bossy, *English Catholic Community*, 12–13.

11. Kenneth L. Campbell, *The Intellectual Struggle of the English Papists in the Seventeenth Century: The Catholic Dilemma* (Lewiston, NY: E. Mellen, 1986), 12.

12. Walsham, *Catholic Reformation in Protestant Britain*, 315–20; Marshall, *Reformation England*, 178; Duffy, *Saints, Sacrilege and Sedition*, 12.

13. Campbell, *Intellectual Struggle*, 8. Campbell here points out that such episodes obscure the fact that the vast majority of English Catholics at home and abroad were loyal to their queen. Further, many loyalist Catholics attacked the Jesuits and missionary enterprise ferociously (Arnold Pritchard, *Catholic Loyalism in Elizabethan England* [Chapel Hill: University of North Carolina Press, 1979], 175).

1587. War with Spain began in 1585, and the climax of this conflict in 1588 brought very real threats posed by the Spanish Armada—so much so that England's victory could only be interpreted by contemporary Protestants as divine intervention.[14] Though English Catholics divided over the Archpriest Controversy, they nonetheless entered the seventeenth century as an active community of nonconformity.[15]

For Perkins, the Protestant future of his beloved England remained uncertain. Various and widespread Catholic communities existed, posing a real threat to the progress of reformation. This was the impetus behind Perkins's polemical urgency. To be sure, one can observe an apologetic edge throughout Perkins's preaching and writing, but *A Reformed Catholike* and *A Warning against the Idolatry of the Last Times* pick up this initiative directly. As we will see, Perkins takes aim at Roman Catholicism's vestiges of superstition and the dark arts, a foe related in Perkins's mind.

A REFORMED CATHOLIKE

A Reformed Catholike—written in 1597, according to the dedicatory letter—was given quite the lengthy subtitle: *A Declaration Shewing How Neere We May Come to the Present Church of Rome in Sundrie Points of Religion: And Wherein Wee Must for ever Depart from Them*. This provides the overall strategy of Perkins's polemic. He writes because of the creeping sentiment that Protestants should reconcile with Rome. Perkins rejects this notion because he sees the Church of Rome as another religion, as different as darkness from light. As proof, its variance on the essence of Christ's work grounds his apologetic in his exegesis of Revelation 18:4.[16] He interprets Babylon as Rome, arguing for this reading as the Holy Spirit's intent. He draws out the doctrine that all who will be saved must depart from the Church of Rome.

The vast majority of *A Reformed Catholike* applies this doctrine, showing the manner and measure of separation. He articulates twenty-one

14. Marshall, *Reformation England*, 179.

15. Campbell, *Intellectual Struggle*, 24; Bossy, *English Catholic Community*, 42–46; Marshall, *Reformation England*, 182–83.

16. "And I heard another voice from heaven, saying, Goe out of her my people, that ye be not partakers of her sinnes, and receive not of her plagues" (William Perkins, *A Reformed Catholike, Or, A Declaration Shewing How Neere We May Come to the Present Church of Rome in Sundrie Points of Religion* [London: J. Legat, 1597], 1; Perkins, *Whole Works*, 1:556).

points of religion and shows how close one may come to Rome and still be a Christian and just how far one must dissent.[17] Perkins follows the pattern of consent, dissent, reasons, and then objections throughout the work.[18] The reasons portion is where most of his biblical work occurs. He finishes the piece with further exposition of Revelation 18:4 and appends an advertisement to Roman Catholics in which he demonstrates that the religion of Trent is against the grounds of orthodoxy, specifically the Apostles' Creed, the Ten Commandments, the Lord's Prayer, and the institution of the two sacraments.

Perkins's stated purpose in his letter to the reader is threefold: to show that the Church of England and the Church of Rome differ in substance, to win over those in the Roman Church, and to educate common Protestants. While a polemical treatise, *A Reformed Catholike* is an exposition of Revelation 18:4 and an application of the doctrines therein. Perkins interprets the verse according to its context. Revelation 17 describes the whore of Babylon, and her destruction is the topic of the next chapter. Revelation 18:4 is "a caveat serving to forewarne all the people of God, that they may escape the judgement which shall befall the whore." It has two parts, first the command to "come out" and second the reasons for the command, which Perkins enumerates briefly at the end of the treatise. The greater part of the treatise provides the application of the first doctrine: "That all those who will be saved, must depart and separate themselves from the faith and religion of the present Church of Rome."[19] For Perkins, this doctrine of separation is clearly in the text.

Perkins argues that the Babylon spoken of in this passage was not the Babylon of Assyria, nor was it Egypt, but "mystical" Babylon. He explains, "Whereof Babylon of Assyria was a type and figure; and that is Rome, which is without question here to be understood." The whore of Babylon is "the state or regiment of a people that are inhabitants of Rome and appertaine

17. The twenty-one points of theology are free will, original sin, assurance, justification, merit, satisfaction, traditions, vows, images, real presence of Christ in the supper, Mass, fasting, perfection, worship of saints, intercession of saints, implicit faith, purgatory, papal supremacy, sacraments, faith, and repentance.

18. For Perkins's use of patristic sources in his "reasons," see David M. Barbee, "A Reformed Catholike: William Perkins' Use of the Church Fathers" (PhD diss., University of Pennsylvania, 2013).

19. Perkins, *Reformed Catholike*, 1, 9; Perkins, *Whole Works*, 1:556–57.

thereto." Perkins demonstrates that "this may be proved by the interpretation of the holy Ghost," again appealing to context. In the final verse of Revelation 17, the whore is said to be a city that reigns over the kings of the earth. In the apostle John's time, Rome fit such a description by itself. Further, Revelation 17:7 speaks of the whore sitting on a beast with seven heads and ten horns, the seven heads being seven hills according to 17:9. So, according to Perkins, the whore is a city set on seven hills, which is an unmistakable description of Rome. He denies the claim that she is symbolic for all wicked men because the text demands a particular place. Why? Because 17:2 says the whore is opposed to the kings of the earth, with whom she commits fornication. As already pointed out, she is described as a city that sits on seven hills and rules the earthly kings. Neither can there be two Romes; "Ecclesiastical Rome in respect of state, princely dominion, and crueltie in persecuting the Saints of God; is all one with the heathenish Empire: the See of the Bishop being turned into the Emperours court, as all histories do manifest." Even more, the fornication referenced in 17:2 and 18:3 alludes to participation in the whore's spiritual idolatry. It was not the policy of pagan Rome to force its religion and idolatry on foreign subjects, while it is very much one of the endeavors of the Church of Rome. Last, the ten kings symbolized by the ten horns leave the whore desolate and naked; though once under the authority of the pope, they are now withdrawing themselves. Perkins provides the kings of Bohemia, Denmark, Germany, England, and Scotland as examples. He concludes his interpretation with an appeal to patristic and medieval authorities.[20]

Perkins appeals to context in his exegesis and grounds his figural interpretation in the text. From his interpretation of "go out of her," he briefly draws four more doctrines. First, the true church of God is and has been in the Church of Rome. Second, the Church of Rome is not a true church, even though members of the people of God reside in it. Third, humanity is divided into two groups, those who are part of Babylon and those who are God's people. Fourth, God provides special care for his children, in this case warning them to depart before the coming judgment. Perkins's polemical purpose continues to be apparent. This is also true of his explanation

---

20. Perkins, *Reformed Catholike*, 2–3, 5–7; Perkins, *Whole Works*, 1:556–57. See chapter 3, where I deal with this exceptional exegesis in the context of the book of Revelation.

for the command. The people of God are to go out of the Church of Rome and avoid seven principal sins: atheism, idolatry, adultery, magic, perjury, reversing God's commands, and lying.[21]

Within this larger polemical paradigm drawn from Revelation 18:4, Perkins does noteworthy exegesis while defending his positions on how far Protestants may consent with Rome and where they must depart from Rome. His reasons are drawn primarily from Scripture, though he often offers as supplemental evidence the judgment of the ancient church, in which he brings the witness of medieval and patristic writers to his side. He discusses difficult texts with disputed interpretations, which is to be expected, given the nature of the work as polemic. Often, he addresses the Church of Rome's favorite passages, an absolute must if his arguments are to be persuasive. His approach remains faithful to his understanding that Scripture interprets itself, utilizing the methods of context, collation, and the analogy of faith. Perkins's exegesis within eight doctrinal points will be highlighted in the following.

First, in his discussion of free will, he defends the position that salvation is wholly of God and that human beings do not will it even in part. He looks at Philippians 2:12–13, in which Paul commands his audience to work out their salvation. However, this does not mean they have the power to do this in themselves. Therefore, Paul adds that it is God who works. Perkins highlights this immediate context in his interpretation, concluding that natural free will is excluded in spiritual things. God gives the power to will spiritual good, but this is an act of grace. Perkins brings 1 Corinthians 15:10 to bear as a parallel. Here, Paul claims to have labored in the faith yet immediately follows this statement with the clarification that it was not him but God's grace in him. Through the use of context and collation, Perkins concludes that "though there bee not in mans conversion a natural co-operation of his will with Gods spirit, yet is there a supernaturall co-operation by grace, inabling man when his is to be converted, to will his conversion."[22]

Second, Perkins defends the fact that original sin remains in the believer after regeneration and baptism; he argues against Rome's appeal

21. Perkins, *Reformed Catholike*, 328–33, 335–44; Perkins, *Whole Works*, 1:616–19.

22. Perkins, *Reformed Catholike*, 22–24; Perkins, *Whole Works*, 1:560.

to Romans 7:17 by appealing to the verse's context. Here, Paul claims that it is no longer he himself who does what he does not want to do but rather the sin that dwells in him. Rome asserts that Paul is not speaking of original sin, because original sin comes from sin and is the occasion for sin. Perkins responds, "By the circumstances of the Text, it is sinne properly: for in the words following, Saint Paul saith, that this sin dwelling in him, made him to doe the evil which he hated." Further, in Romans 7:24 Paul cries out to be "delivered from this body of death." Again, Perkins concludes from context that Paul speaks of original sin, for original sin causes one to sin and entangles the individual in punishment and misery as a consequence.[23]

Third, Perkins gives significant attention to the nuances of justification. He defends imputation over infusion based on 2 Corinthians 5:21 and Romans 5:19. The former verse says Christ was made sin so that sinners might be made the righteousness of God. There is a clear parallel between how Christ was made sin and how sinners are made righteous. Christ was made sin by imputation; therefore, sinners are made righteous by imputation. If, on the other hand, sinners are justified by an infusion of righteousness, then Christ was made sin by the infusion of sin, "which to say, is blasphemy" and contrary to the analogy of faith. For example, Romans 5:19 compares the first and second Adam. One made many sinners; the other made many righteous. Again, there is a parallel here. The first Adam's guilt, which is more than the natural propagation of corruption, was imputed to all his posterity, just as Christ's obedience is imputed to his spiritual posterity.[24] This interpretation, consistent with the Protestant doctrine of imputation, is necessitated by Perkins's understanding of the clear teaching of Scripture, the analogy of faith.

Perkins also defends justification by faith alone as an essential difference between the Protestant church of England and the Church of Rome. Roman Catholics often employed Luke 7:47 as support, because Jesus supposedly grants the sinful woman who washed his feet forgiveness on account of her love. On the contrary, appealing to the analogy of faith, Perkins argues the woman's love was not the cause of her pardon but a manifestation of the pardon she had already been granted. Perkins pulls

23. Perkins, *Reformed Catholike*, 30–31; Perkins, *Whole Works*, 1:561.

24. Perkins, *Reformed Catholike*, 68–69; Perkins, *Whole Works*, 1:568.

in 1 John 3:14 as a parallel example. Here, love for the brethren is a sign of being transferred from death to life. It is specifically not the cause. Rome also occasionally cited Galatians 5:6 to support its claim that justification is by faith and love together. Perkins's defense again includes the analogy of faith. Scripture is clear, according to Perkins, that "the property of true faith, is to apprehend and receive something unto it selfe." On the other hand, love is "of another nature." It "doth not receive in, but as it were give out of itselfe in all the duties of the first and second table towards God and man." Yet, love always accompanies faith, "as a fruite and unseparable companion thereof."[25] In Perkins's view, this text does not speak of justification but of putting faith into practice, which requires love.

Perkins further distinguishes between the Church of England and the Church of Rome on the requirement of good works. Rome argued that Romans 3:28 excluded not all works but only ceremonial and moral ones, those that precede faith. Perkins responds that Paul excludes all works of the law—without exception. He argues this from context, for in Romans 3:24 Paul explicitly states that "we are justified freely by his grace." Also, in Romans 3:27 Paul asserts that justification by faith excludes all boasting. This exclusion is paralleled in Ephesians 2:8–9. Therefore, Perkins concludes from context and collation that justification in Romans 3:28 is "merely passive" and that the sinner does "nothing on his part, whereby God should accept him to everlasting life."[26]

Rome also argued from Psalm 7:8, in which David requests to be judged according to his righteousness, that it is possible for sinners to be justified by their righteousness. Perkins responds by explaining two kinds of righteousness. There is righteousness of a person, which is one's standing before God, and there is righteousness of a cause or action, which is determined to be good by God. This distinction is necessitated by the overall teaching of Scripture. That David here is speaking only of the second kind of righteousness is clear from context, for he was being falsely charged with having sought the kingdom. Similarly, in Psalm 106:30–31, Phineas's killing of Zimri and Cosbie was imputed to him for righteousness. This could not be a satisfaction of the law but rather a statement of God's acceptance of

25. Perkins, *Reformed Catholike*, 84–85; Perkins, *Whole Works*, 1:571.

26. Perkins, *Reformed Catholike*, 93; Perkins, *Whole Works*, 1:573.

his actions. Similarly, in his interpretation of Psalm 7:8, Perkins uses the analogy of faith, context, and collation to let Scripture interpret itself.[27]

Fourth, on the topic of merit, Rome argued that works are meritorious by covenant, because God promised to reward them. Catholics appealed to Revelation 2:10; 3:4; and 2 Timothy 4:8. In the first Revelation passage, the crown of life is promised to those who are faithful unto death. Perkins's response consists of the analogy of faith. In Scripture, God sets forth two covenants: legal and evangelical. In the legal covenant, eternal life is promised to works, for that is the condition of the law. In the evangelical covenant, however, everlasting life is promised to the worker based on the person and merit of Christ. So, in Revelation 2:10, the promise is not made to fidelity but to the faithful person. Faithfulness, says Perkins, "is but a token that he is in Christ: for the merit of whose obedience GOD promiseth the crowne of life."[28] He cites Revelation 22:12 as an example of the same. Here, Christ promises to give to the worker according to his works, not to the work or for the work. Perkins concludes,

> And thus the bond of all other promises of the Gospel, in which God willingly binds himself to reward our workes, doth not directly concerne us, but hath respect to the person and obedience of Christ, for whose sake alone God binds himselfe as debter to us, and gives us recompense or reward, according to the measure of our faith testified by our workes.[29]

Perkins uses this same line of biblical reasoning to respond to similar objections from Revelation 3:4 and 2 Timothy 4:8.

Fifth, Perkins uses Exodus 20:4, the second commandment, to deny the validity of images in worship. Some in the Church of Rome claimed the second commandment forbade images of false gods. But, according to Perkins, it is clear from collating other Scripture that the prohibition refers to images of the one true God. He writes, "Thus much the holy Ghost, who is the best expounder of himself, teacheth most plainly," and then references Deuteronomy 4:15–16 and Isaiah 40:18, 20. Some also claim the

27. Perkins, *Reformed Catholike*, 96–97; Perkins, *Whole Works*, 1:573.

28. Perkins, *Reformed Catholike*, 113; Perkins, *Whole Works*, 1:576.

29. Perkins, *Reformed Catholike*, 113; Perkins, *Whole Works*, 1:576.

second commandment refers to idols. For this objection, Perkins simply appeals to context—namely, the first commandment. Idols are forbidden by the first commandment, so a prohibition against making idols in the second commandment would confound the two.[30]

Sixth, in his discussion of the real presence of Christ in the Lord's Supper, Perkins argues that the difference between the Church of England and Rome is not the presence of Christ but the manner of his presence. The doctrine of transubstantiation "overturnes sundry articles of faith," most significantly the true humanity of Christ.[31] This is a clear appeal to the analogy of faith. So when Jesus, in John 6:55, asserts his flesh is meat and his blood is drink, it must be understood spiritually. The eating and drinking is to be done by faith, not with the mouth. This is precisely what Jesus argues in this context, specifically that to believe in him, to eat his flesh, and to drink his blood are all one and the same. John 6:53 supports this, since no one before the first advent of Christ could have been saved according to Rome's reading. "This is my body" must be interpreted figuratively. It cannot be interpreted according to the proper meaning of the words because they contradict the analogy of faith. However, when Scripture speaks of sacraments, it is common to give the sign the name of the thing signified. Perkins cites Genesis 17:10–11; Exodus 12:11; 1 Corinthians 5:7; 10:4; and Luke 22:20 in support of this claim. Further, at the time of the Last Supper's institution, when the words were spoken, Jesus had not yet been crucified, so neither of the elements could have been received in a bodily manner.[32] In his *Arte of Prophecying*, Perkins identifies these required figurative interpretations as tropes—specifically, as a sacramental metonymy.[33]

Perkins denies the sacrifice of Mass based on a plain reading of Hebrews 9:15–26; 10:10. The distinction between the bloody and unbloody offering of Christ's sacrifice is foreign to the text. One of Rome's objections came from Genesis 14:18, where Melchizedek gives Abraham bread and wine as a sacrifice. Jesus, a priest after the order of Melchizedek, offers himself in

30. Perkins, *Reformed Catholike*, 173–74; Perkins, *Whole Works*, 1:588.

31. Perkins, *Reformed Catholike*, 183; Perkins, *Whole Works*, 1:590. Catholic missionaries used wonders wrought by sacraments as heavenly testimonies to the truth of their religion (Walsham, *Catholic Reformation in Protestant Britain*, 31).

32. Perkins, *Reformed Catholike*, 196–99; Perkins, *Whole Works*, 1:592.

33. Perkins, *Prophetica*, cap. V; Perkins, *Whole Works*, 2:656.

sacrifice to God in the form of bread and wine. Perkins responds to this by showing that Melchizedek was a type of Christ in several ways but not in regard to his sacrificing. He was a king and priest; a prince of peace and righteousness; had neither father nor mother; and blessed Abraham as his superior. This final resemblance—the blessing of Abraham—was the demonstration of Melchizedek's priesthood, not a sacrifice. The bread and wine given to Abraham were merely for refreshment. Another of Rome's objections was based on the paschal lamb. They claimed this lamb functioned as both a sacrament and a sacrifice. Perkins agrees it was a sacrament but not a sacrifice. He defends this conclusion through collation. For example, Mark 14:12 refers to a "sacrifice" that simply means "kill." Genesis 31:54 and 1 Samuel 9:12 provide similar evidence.[34]

Perkins answers two more objections to his denial of Mass, which are founded on Malachi 1:11 and Hebrews 13:10. The Malachi passage, according to some, refers to clean sacrifice in the New Testament—namely, the Mass. Perkins argues the referent is a spiritual sacrifice—that is, a clean sacrifice of prayer from the gentiles (1 Tim 2:8). The Hebrews passage references an altar; this enabled the Church of Rome to conclude there must also have been a real sacrifice. Yet from context, Perkins demonstrates it is a spiritual altar. The text contrasts Christ's sacrifice with the material tabernacle, a fact that becomes obvious from the following two verses.[35]

Seventh, based on Matthew 19:21, the Church of Rome concluded that forsaking all brought one a greater reward in heaven. This interpretation manifests a belief in the possibility of perfection and works of supererogation. Such an interpretation goes against the analogy of faith—and based on context and collation, Perkins's interpretation is different. Like a strict Pharisee, the young man in Matthew 19:21 tried to earn his salvation. But Jesus' command reveals the corruption of the man's heart. Therefore, "the words alleadged are a commandement of trial not to all, but special to him," similar to the Lord's command to Abraham to sacrifice Isaac.[36]

Eighth, Perkins equates the pope with the antichrist as an argument against his supremacy. This comparison was common among the Protestant

34. Perkins, *Reformed Catholike*, 213–16; Perkins, *Whole Works*, 1:595.
35. Perkins, *Reformed Catholike*, 216–17; Perkins, *Whole Works*, 1:596.
36. Perkins, *Reformed Catholike*, 240–41; Perkins, *Whole Works*, 1:600.

Reformers and in Elizabethan England. Perkins grounds the assertion in his interpretation of 2 Thessalonians 2:3–4: "The man of sin (which is that Antichrist) shall exalt himselfe above all that is called God." He comments on the verse, "The Popes supremacie was judged by the sentences of Scripture, & condemned long before it was manifest in the world: the spirit of prophesie fore-seeing and fore-telling the state of things to come."[37] According to Perkins, the restraining force referenced in 2 Thessalonians 2:6 was the Roman emperor. As the Roman Empire decayed, the See of Rome flourished. These are the two beasts spoken of in Revelation 13.[38] In this instance, Perkins's interpretation stays close to the text—and, given its prophetic nature, he takes the liberty to identify what the text foretold.[39] In this, his most significant work of polemical theology against the Church of Rome, Perkins utilizes Scripture and employs context, collation, and the analogy of faith to interpret Scripture with itself.

A WARNING AGAINST THE IDOLATRY OF THE LAST TIMES

In *A Warning against the Idolatry of the Last Times*, published in 1601, Perkins criticizes the Church of Rome and pushes his countrymen to further reformation. In his dedicatory letter, Perkins indicates that he wrote this work no earlier than 1598. He references God's blessing on England in bestowing the gospel under a gracious queen for more than forty years, a clear allusion to Elizabeth I. He continues to say England owes God its thankfulness, which it has failed to give. The response must be "to repent of our unthankefulnesse, to imbrace the Gospel more than we have done, and to walke worthy of it in holinesse of life."[40] In his preface to the reader, he expands this to four causes for writing. First, he seeks to convince the Church of Rome of its idolatry. Consequently, he will refute those who claim Protestants and the Church of Rome differ in circumstances but not

37. Perkins, *Reformed Catholike*, 288–90; Perkins, *Whole Works*, 1:609. The translation of the verse is Perkins's.

38. Perkins, *Whole Works*, 1:609.

39. For Perkins's discussion of prophetical history of the church, see Perkins, *Prophetica*, cap. III; Perkins, *Whole Works*, 2:648.

40. William Perkins, *A Warning against the Idolatrie of the Last Times and an Instruction Touching Religious, or Diuine Worship* (Cambridge: Printed by Iohn Legat, printer to the Vniuersitie of Cambridge. And are to be sold at the signe of the Crowne in Pauls Churchyard by Simon Waterson, 1601), dedicatory epistle; Perkins, *Whole Works*, 1:670.

in substance.[41] Second, he seeks to convince recusants of Rome's idolatry. Third, he wants to foster further animosity toward Rome's religion. Fourth and finally, he desires to educate the general populace with regard to the true worship of God, that they might worship not with empty externals but with understanding.[42] To these ends, Perkins turns to Scripture, specifically 1 John 5:21.

The apostle writes in 1 John 5:21: "Babes, keepe your selves from Idols." From the exposition of these words, Perkins draws his treatise on idolatry and true worship. He begins by looking at the book's context. John's intent is "to set down markes and tokens, whereby men may know whether they be the children of God or no." Perkins then moves to the immediate context. Here, at the end of his letter, John is answering the objection that a child of God may fall away and lose his assurance. This implies that there is no assurance of salvation except for the present. In 1 John 5:18–20, John answers the objection negatively. Perkins summarizes, "The effect of the answer is, that hee which is borne of God so preserves himselfe by grace, that he cannot be drawne by Sathan to commit the sinne that is to death." Then in 1 John 5:21, he provides the rule for how children of God should preserve themselves: "hold fast the true and spiritual worship of God: and for this cause avoide all things that may withdraw your hearts from God, especially take heede of idols." John's use of "babes," or "my little children," shows his tender love and care, making the command more palatable to his audience. From this negative command, Perkins explains what an idol is and how one avoids them. Then, from its positive counterpart, he elucidates what true worship of God looks like. This move from the negative to the positive is not simply a convenient platform; it is demanded by the text. Perkins understands "the propertie of a divine law, in forbidding any thing to command the contrarie."[43] The following is a brief summary of Perkins's argument and examples of how he uses Scripture along the way.

Perkins explains the command in two ways: by defining what an idol is and by discussing how to keep from them. Idols are images either of

41. This was the primary purpose in Perkins's writing of *A Reformed Catholike*.

42. The self-definition of English Protestants was directly linked to how they perceived their relationship to Rome (Walsham, *Catholic Reformation in Protestant Britain*, 23).

43. Perkins, *Warning against the Idolatrie*, 1–2, 88–90, 105; Perkins, *Whole Works*, 1:672, 694, 698.

false gods or the one true God. The golden calf incident in Israel's history is an illustration of the latter. The context of Exodus 34:5, Aaron's statement about the holy day of Jehovah, makes this apparent. According to Perkins, there are three kinds of idols. The first is when God is conceived differently than he has revealed himself in his word. In 1 John 2:13, John says that he who denies the Son does not have the Father. The second happens when God is worshiped differently from he has revealed in his word. The second commandment rules out any images used in the worship of God. Third, idols are made when God's properties or actions are given to creatures. This happens, for example, when God's divinity is attributed to Mary and the pope. Saints, sacraments, works, and the Eucharist are all examples of this in the Church of Rome. What belongs to God is most frequently given to creatures through worship. This includes praying to angels and saints, swearing by anything other than God, pilgrimaging to holy places, and using the crucifix. Here, Perkins uses ample biblical evidence on the subject.[44]

Second, Perkins discusses how to avoid idols. To eschew idolatry, one must avoid making idols, having idols, the religious use of idols, and even the users of idols. The two lawful uses of images are appointed by God, such as the cherubim on the mercy seat, and the common use in society, such as images on coins, which Jesus himself acknowledges. With respect to the users of idols, both their deceits and their fellowship must be avoided. Rome uses five deceits to excuse this practice, all of which must be shunned. First, it claims to use images of God, saints, and angels but not to worship idols. Second, it claims not to worship the actual images but the God they point to. Third, it claims it only worships God and merely gives honor to angels, saints, and images with its service. Fourth, it claims its prayers to saints, its veneration of images, and its relics are confirmed by miracles. Fifth and finally, it claims it is only heathen idolatry that Scripture condemns. Perkins spends considerable time demonstrating the excuses of Rome as deceit.

But not only should their deceits be avoided but fellowship with idolaters should be spurned, too. Sharing the same faith with them and joining in the exercise of their religion is wrong. Some appeal to 2 Kings 5:18,

44. Perkins, *Warning against the Idolatrie*, 2–54; Perkins, *Whole Works*, 1:672–85.

where Naaman prays to God in the temple of an idol. Perkins explains from context that the prayer was one of confession, an appeal for mercy. In civil society, one may have dealings of necessity in day-to-day life. Paul does not forbid the Corinthians from interacting with the idolatrous of the world but with a brother who is an idolater. However, one must not enter into marriage or "leagues of mutual aide & protection" with idolaters. Malachi 2:11 condemns intermarriage as an abomination, and 2 Chronicles 19:2 forbids helping the wicked in their pursuits.[45] Perkins's guidelines for avoiding idolatry are clearly saturated with Scripture.

Perkins expounds the positive command to truly worship God by providing a definition of true worship. He does so in six points. The first is the foundation of worship, which is knowledge of God and ourselves. Second, the rule of worship is worship governed by Scripture, which is basically an articulation of the regulative principle. Third, the end of worship must be the glory of God. Fourth, worship must be conducted by acceptable persons—that is, those who have been turned to God by the Spirit. Fifth, worship must be directed to the Son. Sixth and last, worship of God must be incommunicable, voluntary, and sincere.[46] In short, true worship must be governed by Scripture from beginning to end.

According to Perkins, worship is either principal or less principal. Principal worship is a work of God in us, making us holy and good, restoring his image in us. It is worship in spirit and truth, according to John 4:24. It is love out of a pure heart, good conscience, and authentic faith, according to 2 Timothy 1:5. Principal worship begins in this life and continues into eternity. It pleases God in itself. It includes subjection to God and cleaving to him through love and confidence, which is manifested through humility, patience, prayer, and thanksgiving.[47]

On the other hand, less principal worship is outward worship. It is worship with the body, which is called adoration. In contrast to principal worship, it is not pleasing to God in itself but by reason of inward worship.

---

45. Perkins, *Warning against the Idolatrie*, 54–84; Perkins, *Whole Works*, 1:685–93. At this point Perkins gives the same interpretation of Babylon being the Church of Rome in Rev 17–18 as he did in *A Reformed Catholike* (Perkins, *Works*, 1:556–57). He goes on to give four further reasons why the Church of Rome is idolatrous (*Warning against the Idolatrie*, 94–105; *Whole Works*, 1:695–98).

46. Perkins, *Warning against the Idolatrie*, 105–23; Perkins, *Whole Works*, 1:698–702.

47. Perkins, *Warning against the Idolatrie*, 123–41; Perkins, *Whole Works*, 1:702–6.

This less principal worship consists of worship in the church, worship in the home, and personal worship. The church service includes preaching, fellowship or mercy to those in need, the Lord's Supper, and public prayer. Household worship involves instruction and prayer. Personal worship involves the private reading of Scripture and prayer. That Scripture is central to all three levels of external worship is consistent with Perkins's overall emphasis on the word.[48]

The interpretation of Scripture drives both the overall argument and the particulars of *A Warning against the Idolatry of the Last Times*. This is true of both this treatise and *A Reformed Catholike*. Perkins writes polemically against the Church of Rome elsewhere, but the only other focused polemical work is *The Problem of the Forged Catholicism*. Here, Perkins distinguishes between reliable and unreliable patristic texts then goes through Rome's doctrines, showing that they are not catholic. There is no exegesis because he is responding in a specialized way with a specific goal—namely, to prove patristic witness sides with the Protestant Reformation and the Reformed church specifically.[49]

Perkins also writes polemically against the dark arts of witchcraft and astrology. In this endeavor, he primarily uses the interpretation of Scripture according to the method articulated in *The Arte of Prophecying*. Even his anti–dark arts writings are exegetical.

THE DAMNED ART OF WITCHCRAFT

Related to the religion of Rome, at least in the minds of many Protestants, was magic.[50] Protestants saw Rome's Mass as ecclesiastically sanctioned magic, state-sponsored superstition. The idea of priest as conjurer extended to other sacraments and rituals as well.[51] Moreover, many Protestants dismissed the role of saints, images, and relics in Roman

---

48. Perkins, *Warning against the Idolatrie*, 141–81; Perkins, *Whole Works*, 1:706–16.

49. Perkins, *Whole Works*, 2:485–602.

50. This was certainly true in England (J. A. Sharpe, *Witchcraft in Early Modern England* [New York: Longman, 2001], 16). For an extensive bibliography on magic and witchcraft in late medieval and early modern Europe, see David J. Collins, ed., *The Cambridge History of Magic and Witchcraft in the West: From Antiquity to the Present* (New York: Cambridge University Press, 2015), 719–42.

51. Helen Parish, "Magic and Priestcraft," in Collins, *Cambridge History of Magic*, 394.

devotion as superstitious.[52] Outside the religion of Rome was common magic, learned magic, and diabolical magic. Perkins dismissed all three as witchcraft. Though rarely labeled as magic, common magic included simple rituals intended to control natural and spiritual phenomena such as illness, prosperity, or love. It was also prevalent across stratified society. Practitioners were labeled "cunning folk" or "wise men" and "wise women." They did not invoke demons openly, but opponents such as Perkins regularly accused them of relying on demonic forces.[53] Though the designation is modern, "learned magic" strove toward intellectual and moral legitimacy throughout the early modern period. The so-called discipline included ritual magic, image magic, divination, alchemy, and astral magic. Practitioners tended to be literate and educated, scientists in a day when magic and science could not be distinguished. Most forms were socially acceptable, though ritual magic concerned itself with the conjuring of spirits, which opponents such as Perkins considered necromancy.[54] Perkins's opposition to common and much of learned magic illustrates the broader diabolization of magic, which is central to the discussion of early modern understandings of witchcraft.

Diabolic magic, or witchcraft, arose in the fifteenth century, but it can be traced back to the patristic era. The idea of superstitious arts stemming from association with demons is seen as early as Augustine. This pact with the devil influenced the emerging perception of witchcraft in the fifteenth century. Many Christian authorities believed it both defined magic and epitomized its evil. As such, witch hunting and executions subsisted on the conviction that witches were sworn agents of the devil in a campaign against Christian society.[55]

Until about 1400, witchcraft existed as an elite art, primarily among clergy. Generally, this group was literate and benefited from the twelfth-century renewal of learning that came with the Crusades, which included

52. Parish, "Magic and Priestcraft," 404; P. G. Maxwell-Stuart, *Witchcraft in Europe and the New World, 1400–1800* (New York: Palgrave, 2001), 47.

53. Catherine Rider, "Common Magic," in Collins, *Cambridge History of Magic*, 303–21.

54. David J. Collins, "Learned Magic," in Collins, *Cambridge History of Magic*, 333–48.

55. Michael D. Bailey, "Diabolic Magic," in *Cambridge History of Magic*, 361–62; Christina Larner, *Witchcraft and Religion: The Politics of Popular Belief*, ed. Alan Macfarlane (New York: Blackwell, 1984), 3; Keith Thomas, *Religion and the Decline of Magic* (New York: Scribner, 1971), 438.

learned magic. Richard Kieckhefer memorably identifies this as the "clerical underworld."[56] But by the fifteenth century, the witch became a common stereotype. The notorious publication *Malleus Maleficarum*, released in 1486 by two Dominicans in the Holy Roman Empire, furthered this stereotype. The work consists of three main parts: the theoretical reality of witchcraft, the practice of and cures for witchcraft, and the methods for exterminating witchcraft through judicial prosecution.[57] It includes infamous excesses, such as the incubus, succubus, Witch's Sabbath, and torture. However, it was not until the late sixteenth and early seventeenth centuries that Europe's witch hunting reached its height. The Reformation produced no substantial change in demonology or conceptions of diabolical witchcraft.[58] In fact, Luther reinforced the direct involvement of the devil, and Calvin buttressed the role and power of Satan and the concept of the pact.[59] It is along this trajectory that we find Perkins.

England is representative of Europe with regard to witchcraft. Its low-intensity witch trials, absence of bizarre elements, and isolated accusations are the historical norm. It was the German experience of excess that was unique.[60] Before the mid-sixteenth century, it is difficult to know what witchcraft and witchcraft trials looked like in England. There was no real English contribution to demonology, and witchcraft only appreciably featured in recourse to cunning folk. In fact, witchcraft remained legal until 1542, but the prohibition was not enforced, and the act was repealed in 1547 with other criminal legislation from the reign of Henry VIII. An Elizabethan act of 1563 reestablished witchcraft as a felony, requiring the

56. Richard Kieckhefer, *Magic in the Middle Ages* (Cambridge: Cambridge University Press, 1989), 153.

57. Christopher S. Mackay, introduction to *Malleus Maleficarum*, by Heinrich Institoris and Jakob Sprenger, ed. and trans. Christopher S. Mackay (Cambridge: Cambridge University Press, 2006), 1:1–4, 143.

58. Bailey, "Diabolic Magic," 377–80; Maxwell-Stuart, *Witchcraft in Europe*, 44.

59. Alan Charles Kors and Edward Peters, eds., *Witchcraft in Europe, 400–1700: A Documentary History* (Philadelphia: University of Pennsylvania Press, 2001), 261–62, 265.

60. Sharpe, *Witchcraft in Early Modern England*, 12. See page 11 for a history of research and bibliography on witchcraft in England. In its witch trials, England tended to focus on particular acts of maleficium rather than diabolism. This was partially due to the statute law system, which was pragmatic rather than inquisitorial like those systems based on Roman law (Larner, *Witchcraft and Religion*, 77). England saw very little initiative taken by clerics and lawyers in prosecution of witchcraft. Most trials stemmed from neighborly accusations (Thomas, *Religion and the Decline of Magic*, 458).

death penalty for using witchcraft to kill. All other uses, good or bad, were punishable with a year's imprisonment, including four occasions in the pillory, for the first offense and execution for the second. The 1604 Jacobean statute extended the death penalty to other aspects of witchcraft, but again, it was sporadically enforced. We notice, then, that witchcraft was made illegal and prosecuted in secular courts before English theologians constructed a comprehensive model of diabolical witchcraft. In fact, Reginald Scot's skeptical work in 1584 was the first major publication on witchcraft by an Englishman. English demonological writing did come, however, and Perkins became its most significant author.[61]

A Discourse of the Damned Art of Witchcraft is Perkins's polemic against witchcraft and sorcery. Published in 1608, the work began as sermons in the ordinary course of Perkins's preaching. The publisher, Thomas Pickering, notes in the dedicatory epistle that the treatise sought to acquaint the people of God "with the dealing of Satan in this kinde, that knowing the subtill devices, they may learne to avoid them."[62] The subtitle of the work, "*so far forth as it is revealed in the Scriptures and manifested by true experience*," is fitting, given its melding of biblical interpretation and what Perkins understands to be people's experience with the devil. Perkins indeed draws from the conventional wisdom of his day regarding this topic. That said, his overall discourse is framed by exegesis and often brings Scripture to bear.

Perkins opens his treatise with Exodus 22:18: "Thou shalt not suffer a Witch to live." This is a judicial law of Moses regarding the punishment of witchcraft. Perkins says he chose to expound this verse for two primary reasons. First, he considers witchcraft a common sin in his context, though varied in degree. Second, many among both the ignorant and educated believe there is no such thing as witches, that witchcraft is mere illusion.[63] Perkins intends to demonstrate otherwise. He writes, "For these and such like considerations, I have bin moved to undertake the Interpretation of this Judiciall Law, as a sufficient ground of the doctrine which shall be

---

61. Sharpe, *Witchcraft in Early Modern England*, 15–17. The first two antiwitchcraft laws did not reference its diabolic nature but forbade maleficium. The 1604 act took on the full doctrine of the demonic pact (Thomas, *Religion and the Decline of Magic*, 442).

62. Perkins, *Whole Works*, 3:n.p.

63. Contemporary evidence supports these two notions (Sharpe, *Witchcraft in Early Modern England*, 17, 32–35, 58).

delivered." He wants to consider what a witch is and what the punishment for being one should be. Because describing a witch is an abundantly difficult task, Perkins begins by discussing the nature of witchcraft "so farre forth as it is delivered in the bookes of the Old and New Testament, and may be gathered out of the true experience of learned and godly men."[64] He ends the work by applying the truths to his setting.

For the first movement in his argument, Perkins considers what witchcraft is by discerning the ground of all its practices and its variances. He defines witchcraft as "a wicked Art, serving for the working of wonders by the assistance of the devill so far forth as God shall in justice permit."[65] He then explains his definition phrase by phrase. Regarding its wickedness, he appeals to 1 Samuel 15:23. The author uses it as a synonym for a most horrible and grievous crime. True wonders, such as those surrounding the exodus, can only be worked by God. Those done with Satan's assistance are lies and deceits, mimicking God as they are performed according to nature. This can be done by illusion, as in the case of the witch of Endor making Saul think he saw Samuel in 1 Samuel 28. But they can also be real works. For example, the tragedies in Job's life were real but orchestrated by Satan according to nature.[66]

The ground of witchcraft is a covenant between the devil and the witch. Perkins appeals to Psalm 58:5, where the charmer makes association "cunningly," or with the devil. Deuteronomy 18:11 also warns of making a compact with wicked spirits. In the New Testament, one looks to the temptation of Jesus as an example of such a relationship between the devil and man. That Satan is willing to bind himself in such ways is to counterfeit the covenant of grace and draw people from it.[67]

---

64. Perkins, *Whole Works*, 3:607.

65. Perkins, *Whole Works*, 3:607. This definition includes all three elements that Sharpe argues were needed for witchcraft: divine permission, satanic power, and human agency (Sharpe, *Witchcraft in Early Modern England*, 17).

66. Perkins, *Whole Works*, 3:607–14. Aquinas and the scholastics put demonic power in the confines of creation. Demonic power was preternatural in that it could marvelously manipulate the world, but it was not truly supernatural (Bailey, "Diabolic Magic," 366). This understanding was dominant in England (Sharpe, *Witchcraft in Early Modern England*, 18).

67. Perkins, *Whole Works*, 3:614–16. The demonic pact was a central theme in English works on witchcraft. According to Sharpe, because there was no direct biblical basis for the pact, writers appealed to Satan's counterfeiting of God's covenant of grace (*Witchcraft in Early Modern England*, 18).

Perkins divides witchcraft into two types: divination and what Perkins calls "working witchcraft." When witches reveal the future by the assistance of the devil, it is divination. Satan grants this power as a counterfeit of God's prophets and apostles. Perkins is clear that Satan is not omniscient; rather, he knows the predictions of Scripture, the rules of nature, and the perspectives of different parties in any situation. In short, the future is either revealed to Satan, as in the case of Scripture and the witch of Endor, or he makes what amounts to an educated guess. The kinds of divination that use created means found in Scripture are the observation of birds (Deut 18:10), the examination of entrails (Ezek 21:21), astrology (Isa 47:13–14), dreams (Deut 13:3), and the casting of lots (Acts 1:26 is a positive example). Divination by forged means is necromancy. In this case, the devil appears in the likeness of a dead body. Divination is also possible by the immediate assistance of spirits, as with the woman at Philippi whom Paul encounters in Acts 16.[68] Perkins's extended discussion on necromancy in his interpretation of 1 Samuel 28 warrants a closer look.

At Saul's request, the witch of Endor raised up the devil, with whom she was covenanted, in the likeness of Samuel. Perkins argues, using context and collation, that the apparition was not Samuel brought back from the grave. First, God's Spirit had already been withdrawn from Saul. He confesses that God was not answering him by ordinary means. Therefore, it would be extremely odd for God to bless Saul's attempted circumvention. Further, this Samuel accepts Saul's adoration, something for which the true Samuel would have reproved Saul. Second, Revelation 14:13 teaches that those who die in the Lord immediately rest from their labors. Some may object that Ecclesiasticus 46:20 attributes the prophecy of Saul's death to Samuel after his death. Perkins responds that because this contradicts canonical Scripture, it is a flat untruth.

Others object by making the point that Scripture calls what appeared to Saul "Samuel." To this, Perkins responds with the doctrine of accommodation. He gives multiple examples where the Bible speaks of things as they seem to human beings rather than as they are in themselves. In this case, the apparition appeared to be Samuel. The prophecy's detail and truthfulness reveals little more than God using Satan in Saul's overthrow. Another

68. Perkins, *Whole Works*, 3:617–26, 628.

objection is that dead men often appear and walk the earth after they are buried. Perkins appeals to the analogy of faith, claiming that it is clear from Scripture that men die either righteous or wicked and go straight to heaven or hell. The two times God allowed the dead to be raised were the planting of the church and the restoring of it; Samuel falls into neither category. These exceptions explain the appearance of Moses and Elijah at the transfiguration, the miracles of Christ and the apostles, and the miracles associated with Elijah and Elisha. Finally, the appearance of Samuel was more than a mere a witch's trick, a fact made clear by the prophecy's truthfulness. Further, according to Perkins, that the witch called the devil forth in the likeness of Samuel proves the existence of covenants between Satan and witches.[69]

"Working witchcraft" or "Witch-craft in Operation" consists of enchantment and juggling. Enchantment is the working of wonders by charms; it is expressly forbidden by Deuteronomy 18:11. An example of an enchanting witch from Scripture is Balaam, hired by Balak to curse Israel in Numbers 22–23. Perkins defines juggling as "the deluding of the eye with some strange sleight done above the ordinary course of nature." This is what Paul refers to in Galatians 3:1 when he asks the Galatian believers who has "bewitched" them. This is what the Egyptian magicians do in their contest with Moses and Aaron.[70] In Perkins's conception, witchcraft consists of divinization and these more active forms.

At this point in his argument, Perkins transitions from laying the foundation for his interpretation of Exodus 22:18 to a discussion of what a witch is and the just punishment of witchcraft. His definition of a witch is "a Magician, who by either open or secret league, wittingly and willingly, consenteth to use the aid and assistance of the Devill, in the working of wonders." To the already enumerated list of witches, Perkins adds those of Persia from Daniel 2 and those the early church encountered in Acts. From these biblical examples, he concludes that there are both bad and good witches. Bad witches do harm, as in the case of Balaam's cursing. Good witches, such as Simon Magus, help people through their cures and works. The latter are most detestable because though they help

69. Perkins, *Whole Works*, 3:626–28.

70. Perkins, *Whole Works*, 3:629–30, 635–36.

the body, they kill the soul.[71] The just punishment for witchcraft in all its forms is death. This is the clear teaching of the verse and the rest of Scripture. The offense warrants death, not on account of the hurt caused to others but because of the intimacy with the devil. The witch may not live because they have bound themselves to the enemy of God and his church. In Perkins's context, this makes the witch also an enemy of the commonwealth.[72]

In his application of the text, Perkins claims the witches of his time are the same as those in the Old Testament.[73] He gives practical guidance on how to discern whether someone is a witch, condemning superstitious ways of trial.[74] He discusses how to protect oneself from witchcraft, citing the promise of God's protection of his elect. He then defends execution as proper punishment. Perkins draws from conventional wisdom and larger human experience throughout his treatise, and this is especially true of his application. However, as demonstrated, Perkins's polemic is framed by his interpretation of Exodus 22:18, and he defends his points with Scripture and its interpretation, striving to let the Bible expound itself.

Witchcraft was perceived as a very real threat in sixteenth-century England. This threat is why Perkins fought it with his strongest weapon: God's word. Elizabeth's reign marked the high point of witchcraft prosecution.[75] In Scotland, witch hunts manifested continental excesses. During this period, James VI became intensely interested in witchcraft trials and published *Daemonologia*, making witchcraft a very public concern throughout the British Isles. His *Newes from Scotland*, published in London in 1591, was basically propaganda directed at the English people,

---

71. Perkins, *Whole Works*, 3:636–38. The role of the "good witch" in English society included countermagic, which was prevalent, as an alternative to prosecution and suffering like Job. This practice was denounced along with the rest of witchcraft by English theologians (Sharpe, *Witchcraft in Early Modern England*, 53).

72. Perkins, *Whole Works*, 3:639. Sharpe cites Perkins to show that witches were seen as enemies of both God's laws and the king's laws (*Witchcraft in Early Modern England*, 14).

73. This was true among the first- and second-generation Reformers as well (Kors and Peters, *Witchcraft in Europe*, 266).

74. Deborah Willis's use of Perkins as an illustration of being "less humane" in the area of prosecution and punishment is unfounded (*Malevolent Nurture: Witch-Hunting and Maternal Power in Early Modern England* [Ithaca, NY: Cornell University Press, 1995], 111).

75. Alan Macfarlane, *Witchcraft in Tudor and Stuart England: A Regional and Comparative Study* (New York: Harper & Row, 1970), 18.

explaining Scotland's witch hunt in the winter of 1590–1591.[76] England possessed a heightened sensitivity to witchcraft during Perkins's writing career.

POLEMICS AGAINST ASTROLOGY

Another aspect of the dark arts and divination interested Perkins: astrology. Medieval scholasticism worked out a compromise with regard to astrology. The church fathers saw it as a remnant of pagan superstition, even a threat to free will. However, from the twelfth century, the European influx of Aristotelian and Arab sources encouraged widespread acceptance of astrology as a science. A compromise was struck: astrology is permissible because stars only affect the body, not the soul. The will is free to resist their influence, but because most people are governed by their passions, many predictions come true. However, many believed predicting with certainty specific human acts led to mingling with demons; therefore, such practices were deemed illicit. However, predicting events determined by heavenly bodies—such as rains and droughts—remained acceptable. So, for Aquinas, individual horoscopes were problematic but almanacs and annual predictions were not.[77]

The prevalence of astrology throughout English society substantiates Perkins's concern. Astrology became part of the intellectual framework promulgated in schools. The Aristotelian worldview understood the stars and the earth—in fact, the whole physical universe—as bound together. This understandably permeated all learned disciplines.[78] Even among the highest levels of Elizabethan society, astrology proved prominent. For example, the queen commissioned John Dee, a man associated with science and magic, to pick an astrologically propitious date for her coronation. She used his services multiple times during her reign, consulting him for things such as interpreting comets and warding off occult threats. Some data suggests that the queen perhaps even asked Dee for private lessons in astrology and science. Even Francis Bacon, the theorist of Elizabethan science and an apologist for the empirical approach to nature, wanted to

76. Larner, *Witchcraft and Religion*, 5, 69.

77. Laura Ackerman Smoller, *History, Prophecy, and the Stars: The Christian Astrology of Pierre d'Ailly, 1350–1420* (Princeton: Princeton University Press, 1994), 25–32.

78. Thomas, *Religion and the Decline of Magic*, 285.

reform astrology, not do away with it. He affirmed the medieval compromise. For Bacon, astrology applied to the world of nature and humanity collectively but not to the life and future of any individual.[79]

However, Elizabethan England assented to the vulgarization and commercialization of astrology—and in its popular forms, the particulars of the future were indeed relevant. For example, from 1545 to 1600, over six hundred different almanacs were published. Like Bibles, these were exempt from the limit of twelve hundred to fifteen hundred single-edition copies. In fact, in the seventeenth century, almanacs outsold the Bible.[80] Astrology was clearly big business. William Lilly published an almanac for forty years and during his career cast more than one thousand horoscopes annually. The upheaval of 1640–1670 brought even more attention to astrology. Lilly made predictions for Oliver Cromwell himself and was commissioned by the parliamentary army.[81]

Perkins participated in England's larger struggle between religion and astrology. The battle raged over explanations of causation. The sovereignty of God was determinative in the world—not the sun, moon, or stars. Foreknowledge existed in God's mind alone unless he chose to reveal the future in Scripture. Despite this, many people looked to almanacs rather than Scripture; they gave more credit to astrologers than preachers. Clergymen in general but especially the Puritans were patently suspicious of astrology. With Miles Coverdale, John Hooper, and Roger Hutchinson, attacks from Puritan ranks started early. For them, the issue was not intellectual deficiencies of astrology alone but its diabolical nature. This is clearly illustrated in Perkins's *Damned Art of Witchcraft*.[82]

Perkins's writings against astrology were among his earliest works. In both cases, the year they were written is revealed in the text itself. For example, his *A Resolution to the Countrey-man* uses a prognostication from 1585. *A Fruitfull Dialogue Concerning the End of the World* references next year as "dooms-day," which evinces a publication of 1587. There are also extremely rare autobiographical statements in these works hinting at why

79. Peter Whitfield, *Astrology: A History* (New York: H. N. Abrams, 2001), 167–69.
80. Thomas, *Religion and the Decline of Magic*, 294.
81. Whitfield, *Astrology*, 171–72; Thomas, *Religion and the Decline of Magic*, 303–22, 369.
82. Thomas, *Religion and the Decline of Magic*, 358–68.

Perkins took up the issue of astrology in his early polemics. In *A Resolution*, he says of prognostication, "I have long studied this Art, and was never quiet untill I had seene all the secrets of the same: but at the length, it pleased God to lay before mee the prophanenesse of it, nay, I dare boldly say, Idolotrie, although it be covered with faire and golden shewes." In *A Fruitfull Dialogue*, it can safely be assumed that the "Christian" speaks for Perkins himself. Here again, in regard to astrology, he says, "I have labored in these matters."[83] In his youth, Perkins was involved in astrology and is therefore able to go on the offensive against it with an impressive knowledge. Yet even at this beginning stage of his career, his arguments remain thoroughly biblical.

A RESOLUTION TO THE COUNTREY-MAN

Perkins uses Isaiah 47:12–14 and its dismissal of astrologers, stargazers, and prognosticators as biblical warrant for the overall thrust of *A Resolution to the Countrey-man*. In short, he argues, it is unlawful to buy or use yearly prognostications. He concerns himself first with the user. In this case, reading the stars is meant to help the farmer heap up his wealth, which is contrary to the Lord's Prayer's "give us this day our daily bread" and Jesus' words in Matthew 6:34 about not caring for tomorrow. Depending on prognostications reveals greed, inordinate care about the future, and a lack of trust in God's providence. Further, they encourage a neglect of providence altogether, focusing on the stars rather than God. Perkins cites Jeremiah 10:1–2 as proof that God's people should not be afraid of the signs of heaven; Isaiah 44:25, which says trying to see the future is foolishness; and Deuteronomy 18:9–14, which expressly forbids it.[84] Perkins's condemnation of astrology is biblical.

Perkins gives most of his attention to prognosticators themselves. Their inability to tell the future is clear from the use and purpose of the heavens. Here, Perkins appeals to Scripture. Psalm 19 claims the heavens

---

83. William Perkins, *Foure Great Lyers, Striuing Who Shall Win the Siluer Whetstone Also, a Resolution to the Countri-Man, Prouing Is Vtterly Vnlawfull to Buye or vse Our Yeerly Prognostications* (London: Robert Waldegraue, 1585), n.p.; Perkins, *Whole Works*, 3:653, 667, 467, 469, 472, 474, 477. Much of the material attributed to the "Christian" comes from *A Resolution*, some of it word for word. This serves as evidence that Perkins is "Christian" in the dialogue.

84. Perkins, *Foure Great Lyers*, n.p.; Perkins, *Whole Works*, 3:653–55.

point to God's glory. In Romans 1, Paul says creation gives evidence for God. Genesis 1 speaks of the heavenly bodies marking the passing of time. At times, there are heavenly signs of particular events, such as the darkness accompanying Christ's suffering. But these instances only appear in extraordinary works of God.

Therefore, the future cannot be determined by the stars. Objectors appeal to Genesis 1:14, where God says to let the heavenly lights "be for signs." Perkins uses collation to demonstrate that this cannot mean signs for prognosticating. Isaiah 47:13–14 explicitly condemns using the heavens for this purpose. Perkins also makes his point by looking at the context of Genesis. The order of creation excludes the heavenly lights from possibly indicating famine or plenty, wars or plagues, or any other particular estate of men. After all, the creation of vegetation preceded them—and man was not created until later. Moreover, prognosticators cannot possibly account for God's providential intervention without the use of means, as in the case of Noah's preservation in the ark, Israel's in the wilderness, and Daniel's in the lion's den. Perkins concludes that searching for secret or special knowledge about the future is not only unwarranted in Scripture but plainly forbidden by it.[85]

A FRUITFULL DIALOGUE

A Fruitfull Dialogue Concerning the End the World is a discussion between a Christian and a worldling about covetousness and the end of the world as foretold by astrologers. In the dedication, William Crashaw notes that it was originally published in a year of dearth, which provides important historical context for the attention Perkins gives to the sinful hoarding up of corn. Perkins viewed astrology as one of the tools of Satan to keep people under his dominion, one used with some success during Perkins's life in England. In his preface to the reader, Perkins reports that people's "mindes are greatly occupied with foolish dreames of the yeare next ensuing," the year the world was allegedly supposed to end.[86] The conversation begins with the worldling telling the Christian that he hopes to sell his wheat for a high price, for his stockpile of corn may rot because he is

85. Perkins, *Foure Great Lyers*, n.p.; Perkins, *Whole Works*, 3:655–57, 667.
86. Perkins, *Whole Works*, 3:464.

unwilling to sell it at the low market price. The dialogue starts with the topic of covetousness.

The Christian pointedly charges the worldling with hard-heartedness and being devoid of compassion for the poor. He reminds the worldling of the words in Amos 2 against those who abuse the poor. He even compares him to the rich man who neglected poor Lazarus in Luke 16, those for whom it is more difficult to enter the kingdom than for a camel to pass through the eye of a needle.[87] The root of all this is covetousness. The worldling comforts himself that the miserable state of the world will not last long, which transitions the dialogue to the impending end of the world, predicted by astrologers.

The Christian demonstrates that no man can know the timing of the end of the world. To do so, he appeals to Scripture. Daniel 12:9 states that it is hidden until the end of time. Jesus tells his disciples in Acts 1:7 that it was not for them to know. When the martyrs cry out for an answer in Revelation 6:9–11, they are not given a specific time. Perkins then lists several signs that are to appear before the coming of Christ that have yet to come. One of these is the fulfillment of the Great Commission, which Perkins understands as in the process of being accomplished. Another is the mass conversion of Jews spoken of in Romans 11, which is yet to be fulfilled. In the discussion of astrology in general, Perkins uses the same biblical argument as in *A Resolution*. When responding to a question about why God does not want the future revealed, he cites Matthew 14:41, showing the Lord's desire is that his people watch and pray. The Christian concedes there will indeed be calamity in 1588, but it will be judgment on disobedience and the testing of the church. But this promise in Scripture applies to every year.[88]

CONCLUSION

In order to battle the Church of Rome and the dark arts, Perkins used Scripture according to his stated method in the *The Arte of Prophecying*. His polemics grew largely out of the exposition of specific biblical passages. Superstition hindered reformation in sixteenth-century England. Perkins

87. Perkins, *Whole Works*, 3:465–66.

88. Perkins, *Whole Works*, 3:467–68, 470, 473–75.

justifiably understood Catholicism to be the greatest threat to an established Protestant church. To a lesser degree, the superstitions of witchcraft and astrology also impeded reformation. Against such powerful and prevalent foes, Perkins employed the exposition of Scripture. Given that Scripture is the very word of God, he could think of no more appropriate strategy.

7

CONCLUSION

William Perkins expounded Scripture throughout his works according to the method he presented in *The Arte of Prophecying*. His method was determined by the nature of the Scripture. If Scripture is inspired by God and has the Holy Spirit as its author, then the Spirit is the ultimate determiner of meaning. If Scripture is the word of God, it is therefore perspicuous, sufficient, and without error or contradiction. If Scripture is the word of God, it necessarily possesses the authority of God himself. Because Perkins affirmed all of this, he believed Scripture must be the final interpreter of itself. Perkins articulated a mechanism for Scripture to interpret itself, which consisted primarily of the analogy of faith, context, and collation.

While Donald McKim has definitively proven the influence of Ramism on Perkins's form of presentation and theological method, he goes too far in seeing Ramism as Perkins's method of biblical interpretation. This misstep perhaps stems from several possible sources. One is the tendency McKim has to see defining, dividing, and classifying from general to specific as exclusively a Ramist impulse in the interpretation of a given text. Another is sharply distinguishing between scholasticism and humanism, or Ramism more specifically.[1] A further tendency is viewing a Ramist chart at the beginning of a commentary as the totality of interpretation rather than a method of outlining secondary to Perkins's scriptural hermeneutic. To be fair, McKim does recognize the Scripture hermeneutic but understands Perkins only to employ the three non-Ramist tools of that hermeneutic when interpreting a "cryptic" passage, thus relegating it to secondary status.[2] The Ramist chart is better understood as part

1. For example, McKim states that "Scriptural interpretation and theological reflection were not ends in themselves for Ramist Puritans," as if the larger world of Reformed orthodoxy were unconcerned with praxis (*Ramism in William Perkins' Theology*, 129).

2. McKim, *Ramism in William Perkins' Theology*, 73, 86, 129.

of the consideration of context, showing the relationship of individual parts to each other and to the whole. In this sense, Ramism is a tool in the all-encompassing Scripture hermeneutic. McKim valuably and definitively demonstrates that Wilbur Howell was wrong in his claim that Perkins "must be regarded as a traditionalist in respect to most of his subject matter, and as a Ramist only in respct to method of presentation and to a few points of doctrine."[3] However, this book has proven that Howell's conclusion is accurate when applied to Perkins's biblical interpretation. Perkins presented his exegetical method in his preaching manual with no explicit mention of Ramism and consistently implemented it throughout his works.

When the meaning of a text was self-evident, then Scripture interpreted itself through immediate clarity. When Perkins came to what he called a cryptic or dark passage of Scripture, he was nonetheless compelled to arrive at its single, natural sense. To do so, he utilized his three hermeneutical tools. The analogy of faith and its robust, historical understanding of theology limited interpretive options, setting boundaries within which the interpreter must operate. Drawn from Scripture, the analogy of faith is not a man-made paradigm imposed on Scripture. Instead, Perkins believed it is authoritative only insofar as it faithfully reflects the clear teaching of the Bible. With boundaries set for right interpretation, the next step is to look closely at a passage's context, where the meaning of words and phrases is primarily determined. Here, Perkins encouraged facility in the original languages and education in figurative and rhetorical forms. A careful reading of the text in context, within the boundaries set by the analogy of faith, will finally be affirmed and nuanced according to other passages of Scripture. In short, Perkins used the analogy of faith, context, and collation to interpret Scripture with itself. The only consistent exception to this rule was his eschatology, which, as has been noted, neatly followed the apocalyptic interpretations common in his historical situation.

As I have showed, Perkins employed his method throughout his works, regardless of genre. Scholars who work with Perkins's corpus rarely highlight this key component, yet the reality is demonstrable. In Perkins's sermons, many of which became commentaries, he faithfully implemented his stated method of biblical interpretation. As an Elizabethan Puritan,

3. Howell, *Logic and Rhetoric*, 207.

Perkins devoted his public ministry to the reformation of church and society according to Protestant and Reformed principles. The primary weapon in his armory was preaching, which he defined as the proclamation and application of God's word to men and women. He was not interested in proclaiming merely his own opinions or the ideas of other men. For preaching to be preaching—for preaching to be effectual—it must faithfully expound the word of God. Therefore, Perkins in particular and the Puritans in general strove to preach and apply Scripture's own interpretation of itself.

Perkins believed Scripture spoke to every aspect of the Christian's life. This manifested itself not only in his stress on sermon application but also in his writings on practical divinity. Perkins applied Scripture to a host of practical themes, from dying well to everything public and private in between. Scripture could only effectively be applied to such issues if it was properly understood, so here Perkins employs his method of biblical interpretation. In his practical works for pastors, this remained important. For example, his era's most significant pastoral problem was assurance. Certainly, pastors wanted to avoid giving false counsel when eternity hung in the balance. But only the proper interpretation of Scripture could avoid this. Scripture had to be properly interpreted in order to be properly applied. Perkins devoted himself to this enterprise even in his practical writings.

Always zealous for theological education and doctrinal precision, Perkins deeply embedded his catechetical and soteriological works in Scripture. For Perkins, Scripture is the source and norm of theology. As the final arbiter of truth, it becomes extremely important to understand Scripture's meaning. With nowhere else to turn, Perkins looks to Scripture to interpret itself. This always grounds his theology, from his catechism to his discussions on the *ordo salutis*. The Cambridge controversies over predestination stemmed from considering interpretations of people over the interpretation of God, which could only be accessed through Scripture, interpreted according to the analogy of faith, context, and collation.

Perkins wielded Scripture against two prevalent forms of superstition in England: the Church of Rome and witchcraft. His polemics against these threats were based on his proper interpretation of Scripture. The Church of Rome served as a foil for Perkins in many of his works and sermons. In a polemic directed entirely at Rome, he goes through theology and practice point by point, showing from Scripture where the religion of the pope is wrong. Perkins also attacked witchcraft and astrology from Scripture. It would not work to utilize improper interpretation. After all, this was precisely what caused—or at least allowed—the superstition in the first place. Even in his polemics, Scripture saturates Perkins's work, interpreted according to the method proposed in *The Arte of Prophecying*.

Regardless of genre, the interpretation of Scripture is front and center in Perkins's works. His historical context determined his emphases, his doctrinal topics, and his opponents, but the fact that he was an Elizabethan Puritan did not make his method of biblical interpretation utterly unique. In fact, Perkins was a part of the Reformed tradition, which was part of Protestantism, which was part of the Western church, which was part of the catholic church stretching back through the patristic era to the New Testament. While we see development, we also see continuity in Perkins, especially in his hermeneutics and exegetical method. I have tried to demonstrate this, showing that there is continuity even in spiritual exegesis. But there is much work to be done. More attention needs to be given to patristic and medieval exegesis, more to the Protestant Reformers, particularly those without the renown of Luther and Calvin. More attention definitely needs to be given to the biblical interpretation of Reformed orthodoxy, of which Perkins was a part.

Looking at the exegesis of this period helps to correct the misrepresentation of Reformed orthodoxy as scholastic, rationalistic, cold, dead, and, in short, unbiblical. An examination of Perkins's exegesis has shown that while he was an internationally recognized scholastic theologian, he was also a pastor who cared for his people. The majority of his corpus consists of sermons and commentaries; another large portion is devoted to practical matters. Both of these categories are intensely focused on applying biblical truth to life. In fact, Perkins spent the majority of his time on pastoral matters. Even when he wrote academically or polemically, his work was more biblical and exegetically grounded than is often recognized. When theologians of the Reformed tradition cited Scripture in their theology, it was not mere prooftexting. These men were often pastors with exegetical and homiletical careers that undergirded their doctrinal formulation.

Therefore, giving attention to dogmatic works alone leads to a skewed picture of Protestant orthodoxy. Highlighting exegesis is a key to painting a more complete picture.

I hope that this work on Perkins's biblical interpretation will be considered in current discussions and open up inquiry into other kinds of questions. The fact that the Bible and its interpretation of itself is central to understanding Perkins must speak into the discussions of his relationship to Calvin and the Westminster Standards, to his position in the development of covenant theology, to his contribution to homiletical theory, to the character of his supralapsarian double predestination, to his counseling on the issue of assurance, and so on. But it also provides a larger paradigm within which others may ask other fruitful questions and provides historically appropriate criteria from which to evaluate his thought on individual theological issues. In short, understanding the driving force of Perkins's efforts has ramifications for all discussions of his thought, making room for further streams of inquiry.

More than merely speaking into the conversation about Perkins, this project on his biblical interpretation is important for Puritan studies as well. Perkins was the giant of Elizabethan Puritanism and played a founding role in the movement, which turned out to be significant in both Old and New England throughout the seventeenth century. He helped shape two of the movement's pillars: preaching and piety. These Puritan emphases drew their life from Scripture, which Perkins interpreted in an intentional way according to itself. This project is also noteworthy for the history of exegesis. Perkins systematized and popularized more than he contributed groundbreaking insights. Yet precisely because of this reality, his simple and reproducible method of interpretation made an impact on the English-speaking world. This effect can be observed late into the seventeenth century and beyond, principally in the traditions of dissent.

Most exciting is the prospect of exploring the history of Perkins's influence in the seventeenth century and beyond. Perkins was internationally known. He has earned such labels as the father of Puritanism and the greatest Elizabethan theologian. We have noted the enduring use of his catechism and seen the influence of *The Arte of Prophecying* on other preaching manuals. But what about his other numerous works? What was Perkins's real influence on the Church of England, nonconformity, and dissent? Related to these, one might ask why his works and reputation seem to have disappeared. If Perkins was so significant in his own day, why was he largely forgotten after the seventeenth century? Why did his numerous publications and collective works go out of print after the 1630s until the twentieth century? Why did it take until 2014 for a project to be devoted to a modern edition of his complete works? The influence and eventual eclipse of Perkins remains an interesting topic.

Perkins was a resourceful man of his times who devoted his multidimensional career as preacher, pastor, professor, theologian, polemicist, and popular author to the exposition of Scripture for the purpose of furthering the Reformation in England. For Perkins, the Bible was the word of God and the only effectual recourse for the Puritan cause. His method of biblical interpretation and application remained true to the Reformed tradition. In short, he believed Scripture interprets itself. His popular preaching manual and powerful preaching ministry reinforced this conviction. Without a doubt, Perkins has earned the attention of early modern historians, even more so with those exploring the history of exegesis.

BIBLIOGRAPHY

—

WILLIAM PERKINS SOURCES

Armilla Aurea, Id Est, Miranda Series Causarum et Salutis & Damnationis Iuxta Verbum Dei Eius Synopsin Continet Annexa Tabula. Cantabridgiae: Ex officina Iohannis Legatt, 1590.

Armilla Aurea Id Est, Theologiae Descriptio Mirandam Seriem Causarum & Salutis & Damnationis Juxta Verbum Dei Proponens: Eius Synopsim Continet Annexa Tabula. Editio Tertia Recognita & Aucta. Accesit Practica Th. Bezae pro Consolandis Afflictis Conscientiis. Cantabridgiae: Ex officina Johannis Legatt. Extant Londini apud Abrahamum Kitson, ad insigne Solis in Camiserio D. Pauli, 1592.

A Case of Conscience the Greatest That Euer Was; Hovv a Man May Know Whether He Be the Childe of God, or No. Resolued by the Word of God. Whereunto Is Added a Briefe Discourse, Taken out of Hier. Zanchius. London: Printed by Adam Islip for Iohn Legat, Cambridge, 1595.

A Case of Conscience the Greatest That Euer Was; How a Man May Knowe Whether He Be the Child of God or No. Resolued by the Worde of God. Whereunto Is Added a Briefe Discourse, Taken out of Hier. Zanchius. London: Thomas Orwin, for Thomas Man and Iohn Porter, 1592.

De Praedestinationis Modo et Ordine et de Amplitudine Gratiae Diuinae Christiana & Perspicua Disceptatio. Cantabridgiae: Ex officina Iohannis Legat, 1598.

A Declaration of the True Manner of Knowing Christ Crucified. Cambridge: Iohn Legate, printer to the Vniversitie of Cambridge, 1596.

A Direction for the Gouernment of the Tongue according to God's Word. London: Iohn Legat printer to the Vniuersitie of Cambridge. And are to be sold in Pauls churchyard at the signe of the Crowne by Simon Waterson, 1603.

A Direction for the Governement of the Tongue, according to Gods VVorde. Edinburgh: Robert Waldegraue, printer to the Kings Maiestie, 1593.

A Discourse of Conscience Wherein Is Set Downe the Nature, Properties, and Differences Thereof: As Also the Way to Get and Keepe Good Conscience. Cambridge: Iohn Legate, printer to the Vniversitie of Cambridge, 1596.

An Exposition of the Lords Prayer in the Vvay of Catechising Seruing for Ignorant People. Hereunto Are Adioined the Praiers of Paule, Taken out of His Epistles. London: Adam Islip for Iohn Legat, Cambridge, 1595.

An Exposition of the Lords Prayer in the Way of Catechising Seruing for Ignorant People. London: Robert Bourne and John Porter, 1592.

An Exposition of the Symbole or Creed of the Apostles according to the Tenour of the Scriptures, and the Consent of Orthodoxe Fathers of the Church. Cambridge: Iohn Legatt, printer to the Vniuersitie of Cambridge. And are to be solde by R. Bankworth at the signe of the Sunne in Pauls Church-yard in London, 1595.

The Foundation of Christian Religion, Gathered into Sixe Principles. And It Is to Be Learned of Ignorant People, That They May Be Fit to Heare Sermons with Profit, and to Receiue the Lords Supper with Comfort. London: Thomas Orwin for Iohn Porter, 1590.

Foure Great Lyers, Striuing Who Shall Win the Siluer Whetstone Also, a Resolution to the Countri-Man, Prouing Is Vtterly Vnlawfull to Buye or vse Our Yeerly Prognostications. London: Robert Waldegraue, 1585.

A Golden Chaine, or the Description of Theologie Containing the Order of the Causes of Saluation and Damnation, according to Gods Woord. A View of the Order Wherof, Is to Be Seene in the Table Annexed. Written in Latine by William Perkins, and Translated by an Other. Hereunto Is Adioyned the Order Which M. Theodore Beza Vsed in Comforting Troubled Consciences. London: Edward Alde, and are to be sold by Edward White at the little north doore of S. Paules Church at the signe of the Gunne, 1591.

A Graine of Musterd-Seed, Or, The Least Measure of Grace That Is or Can Be Effectuall to Saluation. London: Thomas Creed, for Raphe Iackson and Hugh Burwell, 1597.

How to Liue, and That Well in All Estates and Times, Specially When Helps and Comforts Faile. Cambridge: Iohn Legat, printer to the Vniuersitie of Cambridge, and are to be sold at the Crowne in Pauls Churchyard by Simon Waterson, 1601.

Prophetica. Cambridge: Johannis Legatt, 1592.

A Reformed Catholike, Or, A Declaration Shewing How Neere We May Come to the Present Church of Rome in Sundrie Points of Religion. London: J. Legat, 1597.

A Salve for a Sicke Man, Or, A Treatise Containing the Nature, Differences, and Kindes of Death as Also the Right Manner of Dying Well. And It May Serue for Spirituall Instruction to 1. Mariners When They Goe to Sea. 2. Souldiers When They Goe to Battell. 3. Women When They Trauell of Child. Cambridge: Iohn Legate, printer to the Vniversitie of Cambridge, 1595.

Specimen Digesti, Sive Harmoniae Bibliorum Veteris et Novi Testamneti. Cantabridgiae: Ex officiis J. Legat, 1598.

A Treatise of Gods Free Grace, and Mans Free Will. Cambridge: Iohn Legat, printer to the Vniuersitie of Cambridge. And are to be sold at the signe of the Crowne in Pauls churchybard by Simon Waterson, 1601.

A Treatise of the Vocations, Or, Callings of Men, with the Sorts and Kinds of Them, and the Right vse Thereof. London: Iohn Legat, printer to the Vniuersitie of Cambridge, 1603.

A Treatise Tending Vnto a Declaration Whether a Man Be in the Estate of Damnation or in the Estate of Grace and If He Be in the First, How He May in Time Come out of It: If in the Second, How He Maie Discerne It, and Perseuere in the Same to the End. London: R. Robinson, for T. Gubbin, and I. Porter, 1590.

A Treatise Tending Vnto a Declaration, Whether a Man Be in the Estate of Damnation, or in the Estate of Grace and If He Be in the First, How He May in Time Come out of It: If in the Second, How He May Discerne It, and Perseuer in the Same to the End. Reuiewed and Corrected by the Author. London: The Widdow Orwin, for Iohn Porter, and Iohn Legate, Cambridge, 1595.

The True Gaine More in Worth Then All the Goods in the World. Cambridge: Iohn Legat, printer to the Vniuersitie of Cambridge, 1601.

Two Treatises· I. Of the Nature and Practise of Repentance. II. Of the Combat of the Flesh and Spirit. Cambridge: Iohn Legate printer to the Vniversitie of Cambridge. And are to be sold by Abraham Kitson at the signe of the Sunne in Paules Church-yard in London, 1593.

Two Treatises. I. Of the Nature and Practise of Repentance. II. Of the Combat of the Flesh and Spirit. Cambridge: Iohn Legate, Printer to the Vniuersitie of Cambridge, 1600.

A Warning against the Idolatrie of the Last Times And an Instruction Touching Religious, or Diuine Worship. Cambridge: Printed by Iohn Legat, printer to the Vniuersitie of Cambridge. And are to be sold at the signe of the Crowne in Pauls Churchyard by Simon Waterson, 1601.

The Whole Works of That Famous and Worthy Minister of Christ in the Universitie of Cambridge, M. William Perkins. 3 vols. London: John Legatt, 1631.

The Works of William Perkins. Edited by Ian Breward. Courtenay Library of Reformation Classics 3. Appleford, UK: Sutton Courtenay, 1970.

The Works of William Perkins. Edited by Joel R. Beeke and Derek W. H. Thomas. 10 vols. Grand Rapids: Reformation Heritage Books, 2014–.

PRIMARY SOURCES

Bentham, Thomas. *A Notable and Comfortable Exposition, Vpon the Fourth of Mathevv; Concerning the Tentations of Christ Preached in S.Peters Church, in Oxenford; By Thomas Bentham, Fellovv Ov Magdalin Colledge and Afterwards Vyshop of Liechfeeld and Coventrie*. London: Robert Waldegraue, dwelling in Foster-Lane, ouer against Goldsmiths Hall, 1583.

Bernard, Richard. *The Faithfull Shepheard, or the Shepheards Faithfulnesse: Wherein Is for the Matter Largely, but for the Maner, in Few Words, Set Forth the Excellencie and Necessitie of the Ministerie; a Ministers Properties and Dutie; His Entrance into This Function and Charge; How to Begin Fitly to Instruct His People; Catechising and Preaching; and a Good Plaine Order and Method Therein*. London: Arnold Hatfield for John Bill, 1607.

Bird, Samuel. *The Lectures of Samuel Bird of Ipswidge upon the 11. Chapter of the Epistle Vnto the Hebrewes, and Vpon the 38 Psalme*. Cambridge: Iohn Legate, Printer to the Vniversitie of Cambridge, 1580.

Burton, William. *Ten Sermons Vpon the First, Second, Third and Fourth Verses of the Sixt of Matthew Containing Diuerse Necessary and Profitable Treatises , Viz. a Preseruative against the Poyson of Vaine-Glory in the 1 & 2, the Reward of Sincerity in the 3, the Vncasing of the Hypocrite in the 4, 5 and 6, the Reward of Hypocrisie in the 7 and 8, an Admonition to Left-Handed Christians in the 9 and 10 : Whereunto Is Annexed Another Treatise Called The Anatomie of Belial, Set Foorth in Ten Sermons Vpon the 12, 13, 14, 15 Verses of the 6 Chapter of the Prouerbs of Salomon*. London: Richard Field for Thomas Man, 1602.

———. *The Marrow of Ecclesiastical History Contained in the Lives of One Hundred Forty Eight Fathers, Schoolmen, First Reformers and Modern Divines Which Have Flourished in the Church since Christ's Time to This Present Age: Faithfully Collected and Orderly Disposed according to the Centuries Wherein They Lived, Together with the Lively Effigies of Most of the Eminentest of Them Cut in Copper*. London: Robert White for William Roybould, 1654.

Fuller, Thomas. *Abel Redevivus, Or, The Dead yet Speaking the Lives and Deaths of the Moderne Divines*. London: Tho. Brudenell, 1651.

———. *The Holy State*. Cambridge: Roger Daniel for John Williams, 1642.

Gifford, George. *Sermons Vpon the Whole Booke of the Reuelation. Set Forth by George Gyffard, Preacher of the Word at Mauldin in Essex*. London: T. Orwin for Thomas Man and Toby Cooke, 1596.

Hemmingsen, Niels. *The Preacher, or Methode of Preachinge*. Translated by John Horsfall. London: Thomas Marsh, 1574.

Hyperius, Andreas. *The Practise of Preaching, Otherwise Called the Pathway to the Pulpet Conteyning an Excellent Method How to Frame Diuine Sermons, & to Interpret the Holy Scriptures according to the*

Capacitie of the Vulgar People. Translated by John Ludham. London: Thomas East, 1577.

Junius, Franciscus. *Apocalypsis: A Briefe and Learned Commentarie Vpon the Reuelation of Saint Iohn the Apostle and Euangelist, Applyed Vnto the History of the Catholicke and Christian Church. Written in Latine by M. Francis Iunius Doctor of Diuinitie, and Professor in the Vniuersitie of Heidelberge: And Translated into English for the Benefit of Those That Vnderstand Not the Latine*. London: Richard Field for Robert Dexter, dwelling in Paules Church yard, at the signe of the brasen serpent, 1592.

Knox, John. *A Notable and Comfortable Exposition of M. Iohn Knoxes, Vpon the Fourth of Mathew, Concerning the Tentations of Christ: First Had in the Publique Church, and Then Afterwards Written for the Comfort of Certaine Priuate Friends, but Now Published in Print for the Benefite of All That Feare God*. London: Robert Waldegraue, for Thomas Man, dwelling in Pater-noster-row, at the signe of the Talbot, 1583.

Merrill, Thomas F. *William Perkins, 1558–1602: English Puritanist*. Nieukoop, Netherlands: B. De Graaf, 1966.

Musculus, Wolfgang. *Commonplaces of Christian Religion*. Translated by John Man. London: Henry Bynneman, 1578.

Napier, John. *A Plaine Discouery of the Whole Reuelation of Saint Iohn Set Downe in Two Treatises: The One Searching and Prouing the True Interpretation Thereof: The Other Applying the Same Paraphrastically and Historically to the Text. Set Foorth by Iohn Napeir L. of Marchistoun Younger. Whereunto Are Annexed Certaine Oracles of Sibylla, Agreeing with the Reuelation and Other Places of Scripture*. Edinburgh: Robert Waldegraue, printer to the Kings Majestie, 1593.

Prime, John. *An Exposition, and Observations upon Saint Paul to the Galathians Togither with Incident Quaestions Debated, and Motiues Remoued*. Oxford: Printed by Ioseph Barnes and are to be sold by T. Cooke in Pauls Church-yard at the signe of the Tygers head, 1587.

Turnbull, Richard. *An Exposition Vpon the Canonical Epistle of S. Iames, Diuided into 28 Sermons or Lectures Made and Written by Richard*

Turnbul ... ; Whereunto Is Annexed the Exposition of the Same Authour Vpon the Canonicall Epistle of Sainte Iude, with Foure Sermons Made Vpon the Fiftenth Psalme. London: Iohn Windet, dwelling by Paules VVharfe, at the signe of the Crosse Keyes, 1592.

Tyndale, William. *An Exposicion Vppon the v. Vi. Vii. Chapters of Mathew Which Thre Chaptres Are the Keye and the Dore of the Scripture, and the Restoringe Agayne of Moses Lawe Corrupte by the Scrybes and Pharises: And the Exposicion Is the Restoringe Agayne of Christes Lawe Corrupte by the Papistes: Item before the Booke, Thou Hast a Prologe Very Necessarie, Contaynynge the Whole Somme of the Couenaunt Made Betwene God and vs, Vppon Which We Be Baptised to Kepe It: And after Thou Hast a Table That Leadeth the by the Notes in the Mergentes, Vnto All That Is Intreated of in the Booke*. Antwerp: J. Grapheus, 1533.

Whitaker, William. *A Disputation on Holy Scripture: Against the Papists, Especially Bellarmine and Stapleton*. Translated by William Fitzgerald. Cambridge: Cambridge University Press, 1849.

Whitgift, John. *The Defense of the Aunswere to the Admonition against the Replie of T.C.* London: Henry Binneman, for Humfrey Toye, 1574.

Wilkins, John. *Ecclesiastes, Or, A Discourse Concerning the Gift of Preaching as It Fals under the Rules of Art Shewing the Most Proper Rules and Directions, for Method, Invention, Books, Expression, Whereby a Minister May Be Furnished with Such Abilities as May Make Him a Workman That Needs Not to Be Ashamed : Very Seasonable for These Times, Wherein the Harvest Is Great, and the Skilfull Labourers but Few*. London: M. F. for Samuel Gellibrand, 1646.

Willet, Andrew. A Catholicon, *That Is, A Generall Preservative or Remedie against the Pseudocatholike Religion Gathered out of the Catholike Epistle of S. Jude, Briefly Expounded, and Aptly, according to the Time, Applied to More Then Halfe an Hundreth of Popish Errours, and as Many Corruptions of Manners. With a Preface Seruing as a Preparatiue to the Catholicon, and a Dyet Prescribed after*. Cambridge: Iohn Legat, Printer to the Vniversitie of Cambridge. And are to be sold at the signe of the Crowne in Paules Churchyard, London, by Simon Waterson, 1602.

SECONDARY SOURCES

BOOKS

Amos, N. Scott. *Bucer, Ephesians and Biblical Humanism: The Exegete as Theologian*. Studies in Early Modern Religious Tradition, Culture and Society 7. Cham, Switzerland: Springer, 2015.

Aquinas, Thomas. *Nature and Grace: Selections from the Summa Theologica of Thomas Aquinas*. Edited and translated by A. M. Fairweather. Library of Christian Classics. Philadelphia: Westminster, 1954.

Archer, Ian W., and F. Douglas Price, eds. *English Historical Documents, 1558–1603*. London: Routledge, 2011.

Asselt, Willem J. van. *Introduction to Reformed Scholasticism*. Reformed Historical-Theological Studies. Grand Rapids: Reformation Heritage Books, 2011.

Aveling, J. C. H. *The Handle and the Axe: The Catholic Recusants in England from Reformation to Emancipation*. London: Blond and Briggs, 1976.

Backus, Irena. *Reformation Readings of the Apocalypse: Geneva, Zurich, and Wittenberg*. Oxford: Oxford University Press, 2000.

Ball, Bryan W. *A Great Expectation: Eschatological Thought in English Protestantism to 1660*. Studies in the History of Christian Thought. Leiden: Brill, 1975.

Ballor, Jordan J. *Covenant, Causality, and Law: A Study in the Theology of Wolfgang Musculus*. Refo500 Academic Studies 3. Göttingen: Vandenhoeck & Ruprecht, 2012.

Barth, Karl. *Church Dogmatics*. Edinburgh: T&T Clark, 1961.

Baukham, Richard. *Tudor Apocalypse: Sixteenth-Century Apocalypticism, Millenarianism and the English Reformation, from John Bale to John Foxe and Thomas Brightman*. Appleford, UK: Sutton Courtenay, 1978.

Beeke, Joel R. *Assurance of Faith: Calvin, English Puritanism, and the Dutch Second Reformation*. New York: Peter Lang, 1991.

———. *Puritan Evangelism: A Biblical Approach*. Grand Rapids: Reformation Heritage Books, 1999.

Beeke, Joel R., and Mark Jones. *A Puritan Theology: Doctrine for Life*. Grand Rapids: Reformation Heritage Books, 2012.

Beeke, Joel R., and Randall J. Pederson. *Meet the Puritans: With a Guide to Modern Reprints*. Grand Rapids: Reformation Heritage Books, 2006.

Beeke, Joel R., and J. Stephen Yuille. *William Perkins*. Bitesize Biographies. Welwyn Garden City, UK: EP Books, 2015.

Bell, M. Charles. *Calvin and Scottish Theology: The Doctrine of Assurance*. Edinburgh: Handsel, 1985.

Bernard, G. W. *The King's Reformation: Henry VIII and the Remaking of the English Church*. New Haven, CT: Yale University Press, 2005.

Berry, Helen, and Elizabeth A. Foyster, eds. *The Family in Early Modern England*. Cambridge: Cambridge University Press, 2007.

Bickel, R. Bruce. *Light and Heat: The Puritan View of the Pulpit; And, the Focus of the Gospel in Puritan Preaching*. Morgan, PA: Soli Deo Gloria, 1999.

Blench, J. W. *Preaching in England in the Late Fifteenth and Sixteenth Centuries: A Study of English Sermons 1450–C. 1600*. New York: Barnes & Noble, 1964.

Bossy, John. *The English Catholic Community, 1570–1850*. New York: Oxford University Press, 1976.

Bozeman, Theodore Dwight. *The Precisianist Strain: Disciplinary Religion and Antinomian Backlash in Puritanism to 1638*. Chapel Hill: University of North Carolina Press, 2004.

———. *To Live Ancient Lives: The Primitivist Dimension in Puritanism*. Chapel Hill: University of North Carolina Press, 1988.

Brachlow, Stephen. *The Communion of Saints: Radical Puritan and Separatist Ecclesiology, 1570–1625*. Oxford: Oxford University Press, 1988.

Braun, Harold E., and Edward Vallance, eds. *Contexts of Conscience in Early Modern Europe, 1500–1700*. Basingstoke, UK: Palgrave Macmillan, 2004.

———, eds. *The Renaissance Conscience*. Chichester, UK: Wiley-Blackwell, 2011.

Brook, Benjamin. *The Lives of the Puritans: Containing a Biographical Account of Those Divines Who Distinguished Themselves in the Cause of Religious Liberty, from the Reformation under Queen Elizabeth, to the Act of Uniformity in 1662*. 3 vols. Pittsburgh: Soli Deo Gloria, 1994.

Bucer, Martin. *Common Places of Martin Bucer*. Edited and translated by David F. Wright. Courtenay Library of Reformation Classics 4. Appleford, UK: Sutton Courtenay, 1972.

Calvin, John. *The Epistles of Paul the Apostle to the Galatians, Ephesians, Philippians and Colossians*. Translated by T. H. L. Parker. Calvin's Commentaries 11. Grand Rapids: Eerdmans, 1965.

———. *The Epistles of Paul the Apostle to the Romans and to the Thessalonians*. Translated by Ross Mackenzie. Calvin's Commentaries 8. Grand Rapids: Eerdmans, 1960.

———. *A Harmony of the Gospels, Matthew, Mark and Luke*. Edited by David W. Torrance and Thomas F. Torrance. Translated by A. W. Morrison. Calvin's Commentaries 1. Grand Rapids: Eerdmans, 1972.

Campbell, Kenneth L. *The Intellectual Struggle of the English Papists in the Seventeenth Century: The Catholic Dilemma*. Lewiston, NY: E. Mellen, 1986.

Capill, Murray A. *Preaching with Spiritual Vigour: Including Lessons from the Life and Practice of Richard Baxter*. Fearn, UK: Mentor, 2003.

Cochrane, Arthur C., ed. *Reformed Confessions of the 16th Century*. Philadelphia: Westminster, 1966.

Coffey, John. *Politics, Religion and the British Revolutions: The Mind of Samuel Rutherford*. Cambridge: Cambridge University Press, 1997.

Collins, David J., ed. *The Cambridge History of Magic and Witchcraft in the West: From Antiquity to the Present*. New York: Cambridge University Press, 2015.

Collinson, Patrick. *Archbishop Grindal, 1519–1583: The Struggle for a Reformed Church*. Berkeley: University of California Press, 1979.

———. *The Elizabethan Puritan Movement*. London: Cape, 1967.

———. *The Religion of Protestants: The Church in English Society, 1559–1625*. New York: Oxford University Press, 1982.

———. *Richard Bancroft and Elizabethan Anti-Puritanism*. Cambridge: Cambridge University Press, 2013.

Collinson, Patrick, Brett Usher, and John Craig, eds. *Conferences and Combination Lectures in the Elizabethan Church: Dedham and Bury St Edmunds, 1582–1590*. Church of England Record Society 10. London: Boydell, 2003.

Cressy, David. *Birth, Marriage, and Death: Ritual, Religion, and Life-Cycle in Tudor and Stuart England*. Oxford: Oxford University Press, 1997.

Davies, Horton. *Like Angels from a Cloud: The English Metaphysical Preachers, 1588–1645*. San Marino, CA: Huntington Library, 1986.

———. *Worship and Theology in England: From Cranmer to Hooker, 1534–1603*. Princeton: Princeton University Press, 1970.

Dent, C. M. *Protestant Reformers in Elizabethan Oxford*. Oxford Theological Monographs. Oxford: Oxford University Press, 1983.

Di Gangi, Mariano. *Great Themes in Puritan Preaching*. Guelph, Canada: Joshua Press, 2007.

Dickens, A. G. *The English Reformation*. 2nd ed. University Park: Pennsylvania State University Press, 2005.

Doran, Susan. *Queen Elizabeth I*. New York: New York University Press, 2003.

Doran, Susan, and Christopher Durston. *Princes, Pastors, and People: The Church and Religion in England, 1500–1700*. London: Routledge, 2003.

Duffy, Eamon. *Saints, Sacrilege and Sedition: Religion and Conflict in the Tudor Reformations*. London: Bloomsbury, 2012.

Emerson, Everett H. *John Cotton*. New York: Twayne, 1965.

Farmer, Craig S. *The Gospel of John in the Sixteenth Century: The Johannine Exegesis of Wolfgang Musculus*. Oxford Studies in Historical Theology. New York: Oxford University Press, 1997.

Ferrell, Lori Anne, and Peter E. McCullough, eds. *The English Sermon Revised: Religion, Literature and History 1600–1750*. Manchester: Manchester University Press, 2000.

Frandsen, Henrik. *Hemmingius in the Same World as Perkinsius and Arminius: Niels Hemmingsen 1513–2013*. Praestoe, Denmark: Grafik Werk Praestoe, 2013.

Frost, R. N. *Richard Sibbes: God's Spreading Goodness*. Vancouver: Cor Deo, 2012.

George, Charles H., and Katherine George. *The Protestant Mind of the English Reformation, 1570–1640*. Princeton: Princeton University Press, 1961.

Gordis, Lisa M. *Opening Scripture: Bible Reading and Interpretive Authority in Puritan New England*. Chicago: University of Chicago Press, 2003.

Greaves, Richard L. *Society and Religion in Elizabethan England*. Minneapolis: University of Minnesota Press, 1981.

Green, Ian. *The Christian's ABC: Catechisms and Catechizing in England c.1530–1740*. New York: Oxford University Press, 1996.

Gribben, Crawford. *The Puritan Millennium: Literature and Theology, 1550–1682*. Rev. ed. Studies in Christian History and Thought. Milton Keynes, UK: Paternoster, 2008.

Griffiths, Paul. *Lost Londons: Change, Crime, and Control in the Capital City, 1550–1660*. Cambridge: Cambridge University Press, 2008.

Guy, John. *Tudor England*. Oxford: Oxford University Press, 1988.

Haigh, Christopher. *English Reformations: Religion, Politics, and Society under the Tudors*. Oxford: Oxford University Press, 1993.

———. *The Plain Man's Pathways to Heaven: Kinds of Christianity in Post-Reformation England*. Oxford: Oxford University Press, 2007.

Haller, William. *The Rise of Puritanism: Or, The Way to the New Jerusalem as Set Forth in Pulpit and Press from Thomas Cartwright to John Lilburne and John Milton, 1570–1643*. New York: Columbia University Press, 1957.

Hammer, Paul E. J. *Elizabeth's Wars: War, Government, and Society in Tudor England, 1544–1604*. New York: Palgrave Macmillan, 2003.

Harmsen, Theodor. *"Drink from This Fountain": Jacques Lefèvre d'Étaples, Inspired Humanist and Dedicated Editor*. Amsterdam: Bibliotheca Philosophica Hermetica, 2004.

Hart, D. G. *Calvinism: A History*. New Haven, CT: Yale University Press, 2013.

Helm, Paul. *Calvin and the Calvinists*. Edinburgh: Banner of Truth Trust, 1982.

Herr, Alan Fager. *The Elizabethan Sermon: A Survey and a Bibliography*. New York: Octagon Books, 1969.

Hill, Christopher. *Society and Puritanism in Pre-Revolutionary England*. London: Secker & Warburg, 1964.

Hindle, Steve. *The State and Social Change in Tudor and Stuart England, C. 1550–1640*. Basingstoke, UK: Palgrave Macmillan, 2002.

Howell, Wilbur Samuel. *Logic and Rhetoric in England, 1500–1700*. New York: Russell & Russell, 1961.

Hoyle, David. *Reformation and Religious Identity in Cambridge, 1590–1644*. Woodbridge, UK: Boydell, 2007.

Hsia, R. Po-chia. *The World of Catholic Renewal, 1540–1770*. 2nd ed. Cambridge: Cambridge University Press, 2005.

Hunt, Arnold. *The Art of Hearing: English Preachers and Their Audiences, 1590–1640*. Cambridge Studies in Early Modern British History. Cambridge: Cambridge University Press, 2010.

Jonsen, Albert R., and Stephen Toulmin. *The Abuse of Casuistry: A History of Moral Reasoning*. Berkeley: University of California Press, 1988.

Jue, Jeffrey K. *Heaven upon Earth: Joseph Mede (1586–1638) and the Legacy of Millenarianism*. International Archives of the History of Ideas. Dordrecht, Netherlands: Springer, 2006.

Keenan, James F., and Thomas A. Shannon, eds. *The Context of Casuistry*. Washington, DC: Georgetown University Press, 1995.

Kelly, Kevin T. *Conscience: Dictator or Guide? A Study in Seventeenth-Century English Protestant Moral Theology*. London: G. Chapman, 1967.

Kendall, R. T. *Calvin and English Calvinism to 1649*. New ed. Studies in Christian History and Thought. Eugene, OR: Wipf & Stock, 1997.

Kieckhefer, Richard. *Magic in the Middle Ages*. Cambridge: Cambridge University Press, 1989.

Knappen, M. M. *Tudor Puritanism: A Chapter in the History of Idealism*. Chicago: University of Chicago Press, 1939.

Knight, Janice. *Orthodoxies in Massachusetts: Rereading American Puritanism*. Cambridge, MA: Harvard University Press, 1994.

Kors, Alan Charles, and Edward Peters, eds. *Witchcraft in Europe, 400–1700: A Documentary History*. Philadelphia: University of Pennsylvania Press, 2001.

Krey, Philip D. W., and Lesley Smith, eds. *Nicholas of Lyra: The Senses of Scripture*. Studies in the History of Christian Thought 90. Leiden: Brill, 2000.

Lake, Peter. *Moderate Puritans and the Elizabethan Church*. Cambridge: Cambridge University Press, 1982.

Larner, Christina. *Witchcraft and Religion: The Politics of Popular Belief*. Edited by Alan Macfarlane. New York: Blackwell, 1984.

Leites, Edmund, ed. *Conscience and Casuistry in Early Modern Europe*. Cambridge: Cambridge University Press, 1988.

Letham, Robert. *The Westminster Assembly: Reading Its Theology in Historical Context*. Phillipsburg, NJ: P&R, 2009.

Lewis, Peter. *The Genius of Puritanism*. Grand Rapids: Reformation Heritage Books, 2008.

Lillback, Peter A. *The Binding of God: Calvin's Role in the Development of Covenant Theology*. Grand Rapids: Baker Academic, 2001.

Lloyd-Jones, D. M. *The Puritans: Their Origins and Successors*. Edinburgh: Banner of Truth Trust, 1987.

Loades, David Michael. *Elizabeth I*. London: Hambledon, 2003.

Lubac, Henri de. *Exégèse mediaevale: Les quatre sens de l'Ecriture*. 4 vols. Paris: Aubier, 1959–1964.

MacCulloch, Diarmaid. *The Later Reformation in England, 1547–1603*. New York: Palgrave, 2001.

Macfarlane, Alan. *Witchcraft in Tudor and Stuart England: A Regional and Comparative Study*. New York: Harper & Row, 1970.

Mahoney, John. *The Making of Moral Theology: A Study of the Roman Catholic Tradition*. Oxford: Clarendon, 1987.

Marshall, Peter. *Reformation England, 1480–1642*. London: Arnold, 2003.

Maxwell-Stuart, P. G. *Witchcraft in Europe and the New World, 1400–1800*. New York: Palgrave, 2001.

McCullough, Peter E., Hugh Adlington, and Emma Rhatigan, eds. *The Oxford Handbook of the Early Modern Sermon*. Oxford: Oxford University Press, 2011.

McIntosh, Marjorie K. *Poor Relief in England, 1350–1600*. Cambridge: Cambridge University Press, 2012.

McKim, Donald K., ed. *Dictionary of Major Biblical Interpreters*. 2nd ed. Downers Grove, IL: IVP Academic, 2007.

———. *Ramism in William Perkins' Theology*. American University Studies. Series VII, Theology and Religion 15. New York: Peter Lang, 1987.

Merrill, Thomas F. *William Perkins, 1558–1602: English Puritanist*. Nieukoop, Netherlands: B. De Graaf, 1966.

Miller, Perry. *Errand into the Wilderness*. Cambridge, MA: Harvard University Press, 1956.

———. *The New England Mind: From Colony to Province*. Cambridge, MA: Harvard University Press, 1953.

———. *The New England Mind: The Seventeenth Century*. New York: Macmillan, 1939.

Moore, Jonathan D. *English Hypothetical Universalism: John Preston and the Softening of Reformed Theology*. Grand Rapids: Eerdmans, 2007.

Morgan, Irvonwy. *The Godly Preachers of the Elizabethan Church*. London: Epworth, 1965.

Morgan, John. *Godly Learning: Puritan Attitudes towards Reason, Learning, and Education, 1560–1640*. Cambridge: Cambridge University Press, 1986.

Morison, Samuel. *The Intellectual Life of Colonial New England*. 2nd ed. New York: New York University Press, 1956.

Morrill, John, Paul Slack, and Daniel Woolf, eds. *Public Duty and Private Conscience in Seventeenth-Century England: Essays Presented to G. E. Aylmer*. Oxford: Clarendon, 1993.

Mosse, George L. *The Holy Pretence: A Study in Christianity and Reason of State from William Perkins to John Winthrop*. Oxford: Blackwell, 1957.

Muller, Richard A. *After Calvin: Studies in the Development of a Theological Tradition*. Oxford Studies in Historical Theology. New York: Oxford University Press, 2003.

———. *Calvin and the Reformed Tradition: On the Work of Christ and the Order of Salvation*. Grand Rapids: Baker Academic, 2012.

———. *Christ and the Decree: Christology and Predestination in Reformed Theology from Calvin to Perkins*. Grand Rapids: Baker Academic, 2008.

———. *Dictionary of Latin and Greek Theological Terms: Drawn Principally from Protestant Scholastic Theology*. Grand Rapids: Baker Academic, 1985.

———. *Post-Reformation Reformed Dogmatics: The Rise and Development of Reformed Orthodoxy, Ca. 1520 to Ca. 1725*. 2nd ed. 4 vols. Grand Rapids: Baker Academic, 2003.

———. *The Unaccommodated Calvin: Studies in the Foundation of a Theological Tradition*. Oxford Studies in Historical Theology. New York: Oxford University Press, 2000.

New, John F. H. *Anglican and Puritan: The Basis of Their Opposition, 1558–1640*. London: Adam & Charles Black, 1964.

Oberman, Heiko A. *Forerunners of the Reformation: The Shape of Late Medieval Thought*. Cambridge: James Clarke, 2002.

O'Keefe, John J., and Russell R. Reno. *Sanctified Vision: An Introduction to Early Christian Interpretation of the Bible*. Baltimore: Johns Hopkins University Press, 2005.

Old, Hughes Oliphant. *The Age of the Reformation*. Vol. 4, *The Reading and Preaching of the Scriptures in the Worship of the Christian Church*. Grand Rapids: Eerdmans, 2002.

Ong, Walter J. *Ramus, Method, and the Decay of Dialogue: From the Art of Discourse to the Art of Reason*. Cambridge, MA: Harvard University Press, 1958.

Overton, Mark. *Agricultural Revolution in England: The Transformation of the Agrarian Economy, 1500–1850*. Cambridge: Cambridge University Press, 1996.

Packer, J. I. *An Anglican to Remember: William Perkins; Puritan Popularizer*. London: St Antholin's Lectureship Charity, 1996.

Palliser, D. M. *The Age of Elizabeth: England under the Later Tudors, 1547–1603*. 2nd ed. London: Longman, 1992.

Parker, T. H. L. *Calvin's New Testament Commentaries*. 2nd ed. Louisville, KY: Westminster John Knox, 1993.

———. *Calvin's Preaching*. 1st American ed. Louisville, KY: Westminster John Knox, 1992.

Patterson, W. B. *William Perkins and the Making of a Protestant England*. Oxford: Oxford University Press, 2014.

Pettit, Norman. *The Heart Prepared; Grace and Conversion in Puritan Spiritual Life*. New Haven, CT: Yale University Press, 1966.

Porter, H. C. *Reformation and Reaction in Tudor Cambridge*. Cambridge: Cambridge University Press, 1958.

Preus, James S. *From Shadow to Promise: Old Testament Interpretation from Augustine to the Young Luther*. Cambridge, MA: Harvard University Press, 1969.

Pritchard, Arnold. *Catholic Loyalism in Elizabethan England*. Chapel Hill: University of North Carolina Press, 1979.

Puckett, David L. *John Calvin's Exegesis of the Old Testament*. Louisville, KY: Westminster John Knox, 1995.

Questier, Michael C. *Catholicism and Community in Early Modern England: Politics, Aristocratic Patronage and Religion, C. 1550–1640*. Cambridge Studies in Early Modern British History. Cambridge: Cambridge University Press, 2006.

Rogers, Jack Bartlett, and Donald K. McKim. *The Authority and Interpretation of the Bible: An Historical Approach*. San Francisco: Harper & Row, 1979.

Rogers, Richard, and Samuel Ward. *Two Elizabethan Puritan Diaries*. Edited by M. M. Knappen. Gloucester, MA: P. Smith, 1966.

Rohr, John von. *The Covenant of Grace in Puritan Thought*. Atlanta: Scholars Press, 1986.

Roszak, Piotr, and Jögen Vijgen, eds. *Reading Sacred Scripture with Thomas Aquinas: Hermeneutical Tools, Theological Questions and New Perspectives*. Textes et Études Du Moyen Âge 80. Turnhout: Brepols, 2015.

Ryken, Leland. *Worldly Saints: The Puritans as They Really Were*. Grand Rapids: Zondervan, 1986.

Ryrie, Alec. *The Gospel and Henry VIII: Evangelicals in the Early English Reformation*. Cambridge: Cambridge University Press, 2003.

Scarisbrick, J. J. *The Reformation and the English People*. Oxford: Blackwell, 1984.

Schaefer, Paul R. *The Spiritual Brotherhood: Cambridge Puritans and the Nature of Christian Piety*. Reformed Historical-Theological Studies. Grand Rapids: Reformation Heritage Books, 2011.

Seaver, Paul S. *The Puritan Lectureships; the Politics of Religious Dissent, 1560–1662*. Stanford, CA: Stanford University Press, 1970.

Shagan, Ethan H. *Popular Politics and the English Reformation*. Cambridge: Cambridge University Press, 2003.

Sharpe, J. A. *Early Modern England: A Social History, 1550–1760*. 2nd ed. London: Arnold, 1997.

———. *Witchcraft in Early Modern England*. New York: Longman, 2001.

Slack, Paul. *Poverty and Policy in Tudor and Stuart England*. London: Longman, 1988.

Smalley, Beryl. *The Study of the Bible in the Middle Ages*. 2nd ed. Oxford: Blackwell, 1952.

Smoller, Laura Ackerman. *History, Prophecy, and the Stars: The Christian Astrology of Pierre d'Ailly, 1350–1420*. Princeton: Princeton University Press, 1994.

Song, Young Jae Timothy. *Theology and Piety in the Reformed Federal Thought of William Perkins and John Preston*. Lewiston, NY: Edwin Mellen, 1998.

Spicq, Ceslas. *Esquisse d'une histoirde l'exégèse latine au moyen âge*. Paris: J. Vrin, 1944.

Spinks, Bryan D. *Two Faces of Elizabethan Anglican Theology: Sacraments and Salvation in the Thought of William Perkins and Richard Hooker*. Lanham, MD: Scarecrow, 1999.

Steinmetz, David C. *Calvin in Context*. New York: Oxford University Press, 1995.

Stephens, W. P. *The Theology of Huldrych Zwingli*. Oxford: Oxford University Press, 1986.

———. *Zwingli: An Introduction to His Thought*. Oxford: Clarendon, 1992.

Stevenson, Kenneth. *The Lord's Prayer: A Text in Tradition*. Minneapolis: Fortress, 2004.

Stoeffler, F. Ernest. *The Rise of Evangelical Pietism*. Leiden: Brill, 1965.

Stout, Harry S. *The New England Soul: Preaching and Religious Culture in Colonial New England*. New York: Oxford University Press, 1986.

Strauss, Gerald. *Luther's House of Learning: Indoctrination of the Young in the German Reformation*. Baltimore: Johns Hopkins University Press, 1978.

Taylor, Larissa. *Preachers and People in the Reformations and Early Modern Period*. Leiden: Brill, 2001.

Thirsk, Joan. *Economic Policy and Projects: The Development of a Consumer Society in Early Modern England*. Oxford: Clarendon, 1978.

Thomas, Keith. *Religion and the Decline of Magic*. New York: Scribner, 1971.

Todd, Margo. *Christian Humanism and the Puritan Social Order*. Cambridge: Cambridge University Press, 1987.

Toon, Peter. *Puritans, the Millennium and the Future of Israel: Puritan Eschatology 1600 to 1600*. London: James Clarke, 1970.

Torrance, Thomas F. *The School of Faith: The Catechisms of the Reformed Church*. New York: Harper, 1959.

Trueman, Carl R. *Luther's Legacy: Salvation and English Reformers, 1525–1556*. Oxford: Clarendon, 1994.

Tyacke, Nicholas. *Anti-Calvinists: The Rise of English Arminianism, C. 1590–1640*. New York: Clarendon, 1987.

Wallace, Dewey D. *Puritans and Predestination: Grace in English Protestant Theology, 1525–1695*. Chapel Hill: University of North Carolina Press, 1982.

Walsham, Alexandra. *Catholic Reformation in Protestant Britain*. Aldershot, UK: Ashgate, 2014.

Walzer, Michael. *The Revolution of the Saints: A Study in the Origins of Radical Politics*. Cambridge, MA: Harvard University Press, 1965.

Webster, Tom. *Godly Clergy in Early Stuart England: The Caroline Puritan Movement, C. 1620–1643*. Cambridge: Cambridge University Press, 1997.

White, Peter. *Predestination, Policy and Polemic: Conflict and Consensus in the English Church from the Reformation to the Civil War*. Cambridge: Cambridge University Press, 1992.

Whitfield, Peter. *Astrology: A History*. New York: H. N. Abrams, 2001.

Willis, Deborah. *Malevolent Nurture: Witch-Hunting and Maternal Power in Early Modern England*. Ithaca, NY: Cornell University Press, 1995.

Wilson, John Frederick. *Pulpit in Parliament: Puritanism during the English Civil Wars, 1640–1648*. Princeton: Princeton University Press, 1969.

Wooding, Lucy E. C. *Rethinking Catholicism in Reformation England*. New York: Oxford University Press, 2000.

Woolsey, Andrew A. *Unity and Continuity in Covenantal Thought: A Study in the Reformed Tradition to the Westminster Assembly*. Reformed Historical-Theological Studies. Grand Rapids: Reformation Heritage Books, 2012.

Wright, Shawn D. *Our Sovereign Refuge: The Pastoral Theology of Theodore Beza*. Eugene, OR: Paternoster, 2004.

———. *Theodore Beza: The Man and the Myth*. Fearn, UK: Christian Focus, 2015.

Wrightson, Keith. *Earthly Necessities: Economic Lives in Early Modern Britain*. New Haven, CT: Yale University Press, 2000.

Yuille, J. Stephen. *Living Blessedly Forever*. Grand Rapids: Reformation Heritage Books, 2012.

Zachman, Randall C. *The Assurance of Faith: Conscience in the Theology of Martin Luther and John Calvin*. Minneapolis: Fortress, 1993.

Zwingli, Ulrich. *Commentary on True and False Religion*. Edited by Samuel Macauley Jackson and Clarence Nevin Heller. Durham, UK: Labryrinth, 1981.

ARTICLES

Amussen, S. D. "Gender, Family and the Social Order, 1560–1726." In *Order and Disorder in Early Modern England*, edited by Anthony Fletcher and Joan Stevenson, 196–217. Cambridge: Cambridge University Press, 1985.

Archer, Ian W. "Commerce and Consumption." In *The Elizabethan World*, edited by Susan Doran and Norman Jones, 411–26. London: Routledge, 2011.

Augustine, John H. "Authority and Interpretation in Perkins' Commentary on Galatians." In *A Commentary on Galatians*, by William Perkins, edited by Gerald T. Sheppard, xiv–xlvii. Pilgrim Classic Commentaries. New York: Pilgrim, 1989.

Backus, Irena. "Church, Communion and Community in Bucer's Commentary on the Gospel of John." In *Martin Bucer: Reforming Church and Community*, edited by David F. Wright, 61–71. Cambridge: Cambridge University Press, 1994.

Bailey, Michael D. "Diabolic Magic." In *The Cambridge History of Magic and Witchcraft in the West: From Antiquity to the Present*, edited by David J. Collins, 361–92. New York: Cambridge University Press, 2015.

Beeke, Joel R. "William Perkins and His Greatest Case of Conscience: 'How a Man May Know Whether He Be the Child of God, or No.'" *CTJ* 41, no. 2 (2006): 255–77.

———. "William Perkins on Predestination, Preaching, and Conversion." In *The Practical Calvinist: An Introduction to the Presbyterian and Reformed Heritage*, edited by Peter A. Lillback, 183–213. Fearn, UK: Christian Focus, 2002.

Beeke, Joel R., and J. Stephen Yuille. "Biographical Preface." In vol. 1 of *The Works of William Perkins*, by William Perkins, ix–xxxii. Grand Rapids: Reformation Heritage Books, 2014.

Bierma, Lyle D. "Federal Theology in the 16th Century: Two Traditions?" *WTJ* 45, no. 2 (1983): 304–21.

———. "The Role of Covenant Theology in Early Reformed Orthodoxy." *SCJ* 21, no. 3 (1990): 453–62.

Breward, Ian. "The Significance of William Perkins." *Journal of Religious History* 4, no. 2 (1966): 113–28.

———. "William Perkins and the Ideal of the Ministry in the Elizabethan Church." *Reformed Theological Review* 24 (1965): 73–84.

———. "William Perkins and the Origins of Puritan Casuistry." In *Faith and a Good Conscience: Papers Read at the Puritan and Reformed Studies Conference, 18th and 19th December, 1962*, 5–17. Clonmel, UK: Clonmel Evangelical Bookroom, 1992.

———. "William Perkins and the Origins of Reformed Casuistry." *Evangelical Quarterly* 40 (1968): 3–20.

Büsser, Fritz. "Zwingli the Exegete: A Contribution to the 450th Anniversary of the Death of Erasmus." In *Probing the Reformed Tradition: Historical Studies in Honor of Edward A. Dowey, Jr.*, edited by Elsie Anne McKee and Brian G. Armstrong, translated by Bruce McCormack, 175–96. Louisville, KY: Westminster John Knox, 1989.

Carlson, Eric Josef. "The Boring of the Ear: Shaping the Pastoral Vision of Preaching in England, 1540–1640." In *Preachers and People in the Reformations and the Early Modern Period*, edited by Larissa Taylor, 249–96. A New History of the Sermon 2. Leiden: Brill, 2001.

Clary, Ian Hugh. "Hot Protestants: A Taxonomy of English Puritanism." *Puritan Reformed Journal* 2 (2010): 41–66.

Collins, David J. "Learned Magic. In *The Cambridge History of Magic and Witchcraft in the West: From Antiquity to the Present*, edited by David J. Collins, 333–48. New York: Cambridge University Press, 2015.

Collinson, Patrick. "Lectures by Combination: Structures and Characteristics of Church Life in 17th-Century England." In *Godly People: Essays on English Protestantism and Puritanism*, 467–98. History Series. London: Hambledon, 1983.

Craig, John. "Sermon Reception." In *The Oxford Handbook of the Early Modern Sermon*, edited by Peter E. McCullough, Hugh Adlington, and Emma Rhatigan, 178–97. Oxford: Oxford University Press, 2011.

Cummings, Brian. "Protestant Allegory." In *The Cambridge Companion to Allegory*, edited by Rita Copeland and Peter T. Struck, 177–90. Cambridge: Cambridge University Press, 2010.

Davidson, Edward H. "'God's Well-Trodden Foot-Paths': Puritan Preaching and Sermon Form." *Texas Studies in Literature and Language* 25, no. 4 (1983): 503–27.

Emerson, Everett H. "Calvin and Covenant Theology." *CH* 25, no. 2 (1956): 136–44.

Farmer, Craig S. "Wolfgang Musculus and the Allegory of Malchus's Ear." *WTJ* 56, no. 2 (1994): 285–301.

———. "Wolfgang Musculus's Commentary on John: Tradition and Innovation in the Story of the Woman Taken in Adultery." In *Biblical Interpretation in the Era of the Reformation: Essays Presented to David C. Steinmetz in Honor of His Sixtieth Birthday*, edited by Richard A. Muller and John L. Thompson, 216–40. Grand Rapids: Eerdmans, 1996.

Ford, James Thomas. "Preaching in the Reformed Tradition." In *Preachers and People in the Reformations and the Early Modern Period*, edited by Larissa Taylor, 65–88. A New History of the Sermon 2. Leiden: Brill, 2001.

Gane, Erwin R. "The Exegetical Methods of Some Sixteenth-Century Anglican Preachers: Latimer, Jewel, Hooker, and Andrewes." *AUSS* 17, no. 1 (1979): 23–38, 169–88.

———. "The Exegetical Methods of Some Sixteenth-Century Puritan Preachers: Hooper, Cartwright, and Perkins, Pt 1." *AUSS* 19, no. 1 (1981): 21–36, 99–114.

———. "The Exegetical Methods of Some Sixteenth-Century Roman Catholic Preachers in England: Fisher, Peryn, Bonner, and Watson." *AUSS* 23, no. 3 (1985): 161–80, 259–75.

Godfrey, W. Robert. "Reformed Thought on the Extent of the Atonement to 1618." *WTJ* 37, no. 2 (1975): 133–71.

Greaves, Richard L. "The Origins and Early Development of English Covenant Thought." *The Historian* 31, no. 1 (1968): 21–35.

Green, Ian. "Preaching in the Parishes." In *The Oxford Handbook of the Early Modern Sermon*, edited by Peter E. McCullough, Hugh Adlington, and Emma Rhatigan, 137–54. Oxford: Oxford University Press, 2011.

Griffiths, Paul. "Tudor Troubles: Problems of Youth in Elizabethan England." In *The Elizabethan World*, edited by Susan Doran and Norman Jones, 316–34. London: Routledge, 2011.

Habegger, Alfred. "Preparing the Soul for Christ: The Contrasting Sermon Forms of John Cotton and Thomas Hooker." *American Literature* 41, no. 3 (1969): 342–54.

Hagen, Kenneth G. "'De Exegetica Methodo': Niels Hemmingsen's *De Methodis* (1555)." In *The Bible in the Sixteenth Century*, ed. David C. Steinmetz, 181–96. Duke Monographs in Medieval and Renaissance Studies 11. Durham, NC: Duke University Press, 1990.

Haigh, Christopher. "The Church of England, the Catholics and the People." In *The Impact of the English Reformation, 1500–1640*, edited by Peter Marshall, 235–56. London: Arnold, 1997.

———. "The Continuity of Catholicism in the English Reformation." In *The English Reformation Revised*, edited by Christopher Haigh, 176–208. Cambridge: Cambridge University Press, 1987.

———. "The Taming of Reformation: Preachers, Pastors and Parishioners in Elizabethan and Early Stuart England." *History* 85 (October 2000): 572–88.

Hall, Basil. "Calvin against the Calvinists." In *John Calvin*, edited by G. E. Duffield, 19–37. Courtenay Studies in Reformation Theology 1. Appleford, UK: Sutton Courtenay, 1966.

———. "Puritanism: The Problem of Definition." In *Studies in Church History* 2, edited by G. J. Cuming, 283–96. London: Nelson, 1965.

Hambrick-Stowe, Charles E.-"Practical Divinity and Spirituality." In *The Cambridge Companion to Puritanism*, edited by John Coffey and Paul Chang-Ha Lim, 191–205. Cambridge: Cambridge University Press, 2008.

Hazlett, W. Ian P. "Calvin's Latin Preface to His Proposed French Edition of Chrysostom's Homilies: Translation and Commentary." In *Humanism and Reform: The Church in Europe, England, and Scotland, 1400–1643; Essays in Honour of James K. Cameron*, edited by James Kirk, 129–50. Studies in Church History 8. Oxford: Blackwell, 1991.

Hindle, Steve. "Poverty and the Poor Laws." In *The Elizabethan World*, edited by Susan Doran and Norman Jones, 301–15. London: Routledge, 2011.

Hobbs, R. Gerald. "How Firm a Foundation: Martin Bucer's Historical Exegesis of the Psalms." *CH* 53, no. 4 (1984): 477–91.

Hoekema, Anthony A. "The Covenant of Grace in Calvin's Teaching." *CTJ* 2, no. 2 (1967): 133–61.

Hoyle, R. W. "Rural Economies under Stress: 'A World So Altered.'" In *The Elizabethan World*, edited by Susan Doran and Norman Jones, 439–57. London: Routledge, 2011.

Jue, Jeffrey. "Puritan Millenarianism in Old and New England." In *The Cambridge Companion to Puritanism*, edited by John Coffey and Paul Chang-Ha Lim, 259–76. Cambridge: Cambridge University Press, 2008.

Kaufman, Peter Iver. "'Prophesying Again.'" *CH* 68, no. 2 (June 1999): 337–58.

———. "The Protestant Opposition to Elizabethan Religious Reform." In *A Companion to Tudor Britain*, 271–88. Oxford: Blackwell, 2004.

Keenan, James F. "Jesuit Casuistry or Jesuit Spirituality? The Roots of Seventeenth-Century British Practical Divinity." In *The Jesuits: Cultures, Sciences, and the Arts, 1540–1773*, edited by John W. O'Malley, Gauvin A. Bailey, Steven J. Harris, and T. Frank Kennedy, 627–40. Toronto: University of Toronto Press, 1999.

———. "Was William Perkins' *Whole Treatise of Cases of Conscience* Casuistry? Hermeneutics and British Practical Divinity." In *Contexts of Conscience in Early Modern Europe, 1500–1700*, edited by Harold E. Braun and Edward Vallance, 17–31. Basingstoke, UK: Palgrave Macmillan, 2004.

———. "William Perkins (1558–1602) and the Birth of British Casuistry." In *The Context of Casuistry*, edited by James F. Keenan and Thomas A. Shannon, 105–30. Moral Traditions & Moral Arguments. Washington, DC: Georgetown University Press, 1995.

Kendall, R. T. "John Cotton—First English Calvinist?" In *The Puritan Experiment in the New World*, 38–50. London: Westminster Conference, 1976.

———. "Living the Christian Life in the Teaching of William Perkins and His Followers." In *Living the Christian Life*, 45–60. London: Westminster Conference, 1974.

———. "The Puritan Modification of Calvin's Theology." In *John Calvin, His Influence in the Western World*, edited by W. Stanford Reid, 199–214. Grand Rapids: Zondervan, 1982.

Kesselring, K. J. "Rebellion and Disorder." In *The Elizabethan World*, edited by Susan Doran and Norman Jones,372–86 . London: Routledge, 2011.

Kneidel, Greg. "*Ars Praedicendi*: Theories and Practice." In *The Oxford Handbook of the Early Modern Sermon*, edited by Peter E. McCullough, Hugh Adlington, and Emma Rhatigan, 3–20. Oxford: Oxford University Press, 2011.

Lake, Peter. "The Historiography of Puritanism." In *The Cambridge Companion to Puritanism*, edited by John Coffey and Paul Chang-Ha Lim, 346–72. Cambridge: Cambridge University Press, 2008.

Lea, Thomas D. "The Hermeneutics of the Puritans." *Journal of the Evangelical Theological Society* 39, no. 2 (June 1996): 271–84.

Letham, Robert. "Faith and Assurance in Early Calvinism: A Model of Continuity and Diversity." In *Later Calvinism: International Perspectives*, edited by W. Fred Graham, 355–84. Sixteenth Century Essays & Studies 22. Kirksville, MO: Sixteenth Century Journal Publishers, 1994.

———. "The Foedus Operum: Some Factors Accounting for Its Development." *SCJ* 14, no. 4 (1983): 457–67.

Long, Jonathan. "William Perkins: 'Apostle of Practical Divinity.'" *Churchman* 103, no. 1 (1989): 53–59.

Mackay, Christopher S. Introduction to vol. 1 of *Malleus Maleficarum*, by Heinrich Institoris and Jakob Sprenger, edited and translated by Christopher S. Mackay, 1–58. Cambridge: Cambridge University Press, 2006.

Manetsch, Scott M. "(Re)constructing the Pastoral Office: Wolfgang Musculus's Commentaries on 1 & 2 Corinthians." In *On the Writing of New Testament Commentaries: Festschrift for Grant R. Osborne on the Occasion of His 70th Birthday*, edited by Stanley E. Porter and Eckhard J. Schnabel, 253–66. Texts and Editions for New Testament Study 8. Leiden: Brill, 2013.

McClendon, Muriel C., and Joseph P. Ward. "Urban Economies." In *The Elizabethan World*, edited by Susan Doran and Norman Jones, 427–38. London: Routledge, 2011.

McGiffert, Michael. "Grace and Works: The Rise and Division of Covenant Divinity in Elizabethan Puritanism." *Harvard Theological Review* 75, no. 4 (1982): 463–502.

———. "The Perkinsian Moment of Federal Theology." *CTJ* 29, no. 1 (1994): 117–48.

McKim, Donald K. "William Perkins and the Christian Life: The Place of the Moral Law and Sanctification in Perkins' Theology." *Evangelical Quarterly* 59, no. 2 (April 1987): 125–37.

———. "William Perkins' Use of Ramism as an Exegetical Tool." In *A Commentary on Hebrews 11 (1609 Edition)*, by William Perkins, edited by John H. Augustine, 32–45. Pilgrim Classic Commentaries. New York: Pilgrim, 1991.

Merrill, Eugene H. "Rashi, Nicholas de Lyra, and Christian Exegesis." *WTJ* 38 (September 1975): 66–79.

Møller, Jens G. "The Beginnings of Puritan Covenant Theology." *Journal of Ecclesiastical History* 14, no. 1 (1963): 46–67.

Morrissey, Mary. "Scripture, Style and Persuasion in Seventeenth-Century English Theories of Preaching." *Journal of Ecclesiastical History* 53, no. 4 (2002): 686–706.

Muller, Richard A. "Biblical Interpretation in the Era of the Reformation: The View from the Middle Ages." In *Biblical Interpretation in the Era of the Reformation: Essays Presented to David C. Steinmetz in Honor of His Sixtieth Birthday*, edited by Richard A. Muller and John L. Thompson, 3–22. Grand Rapids: Eerdmans, 1996.

———. "Covenant and Conscience in English Reformed Theology: Three Variations on a 17th Century Theme." *WTJ* 42, no. 2 (1980): 308–34.

———. "The Hermeneutic of Promise and Fulfillment in Calvin's Exegesis of the Old Testament Prophecies of the Kingdom." In *The Bible in the Sixteenth Century*, ed. David C. Steinmetz, 68–82. Duke Monographs in Medieval and Renaissance Studies 11. Durham, NC: Duke University Press, 1990.

———. "Perkins' A Golden Chaine: Predestinarian System or Schematized Ordo Salutis?" *SCJ* 9 (1978): 68–81.

———. "William Perkins and the Protestant Exegetical Tradition: Interpretation, Style and Method." In *A Commentary on Hebrews 11 (1609 Edition)*, by William Perkins, edited by John H. Augustine, 71–94. Pilgrim Classic Commentaries. New York: Pilgrim, 1991.

Nicole, Roger R. "John Calvin's View of the Extent of the Atonement." *WTJ* 47, no. 2 (1985): 197–225.

O'Banion, Patrick J. "Jerome Zanchi, the Application of Theology, and the Rise of the English Practical Divinity Tradition." *Renaissance and Reformation / Renaissance et Réforme* 29, no. 2/3 (2005): 97–120.

Packer, J. I. "The Puritan Conscience." In *Faith and a Good Conscience: Papers Read at the Puritan and Reformed Studies Conference, 18th and 19th December, 1962*, 18–31. Clonmel, UK: Clonmel Evangelical Bookroom, 1992.

Parish, Helen. "Magic and Priestcraft." In *The Cambridge History of Magic and Witchcraft in the West: From Antiquity to the Present*, edited by David J. Collins, 393–427. New York: Cambridge University Press, 2015.

Pipa, Joseph A. "Puritan Preaching." In *The Practical Calvinist: An Introduction to the Presbyterian and Reformed Heritage*, edited by Peter A. Lillback, 163–82. Fearn, UK: Mentor, 2002.

Prügl, Thomas. "Thomas Aquinas as Interpreter of Scripture." In *The Theology of Thomas Aquinas*, edited by Rik van Nieuwenhove and Joseph Wawrykow, 386–415. Notre Dame, IN: University of Notre Dame Press, 2005.

Rider, Catherine. "Common Magic." In *The Cambridge History of Magic and Witchcraft in the West: From Antiquity to the Present*, edited by David J. Collins, 303–21. New York: Cambridge University Press, 2015.

Rigney, James. "Sermons to Print." In *The Oxford Handbook of the Early Modern Sermon*, edited by Peter E. McCullough, Hugh Adlington, and Emma Rhatigan, 198–212. Oxford: Oxford University Press, 2011.

Rohr, John von. "Covenant and Assurance in Early English Puritanism." *CH* 34, no. 2 (1965): 195–203.

Roussel, Bernard. "Bucer Exégète." In vol. 1 of *Martin Bucer and Sixteenth Century Europe: Actes Du Colloque de Strasbourg (28–31 Août 1991)*, edited by Christian Krieger and Marc Lienhard, 39–54. Studies in Medieval and Reformation Thought. Leiden: Brill, 1993.

Sharpe, Jim. "Social Strain and Social Dislocation, 1585–1603." In *The Reign of Elizabeth I: Court and Culture in the Last Decade*, edited by John Guy, 192–211. Cambridge: Cambridge University Press, 1995.

Shaw, Mark R. "Drama in the Meeting House: The Concept of Conversion in the Theology of William Perkins." *WTJ* 45 (1983): 41–72.

———. "William Perkins and the New Pelagians: Another Look at the Cambridge Predestination Controversy of the 1590s." *WTJ* 58, no. 2 (1996): 267–301.

Shugar, Debora. "Isaiah 63 and the Literal Senses of Scripture." In *The Oxford Handbook of the Bible in Early Modern England, C. 1530–1700*, ed. Kevin Killeen, Helen Smith, and Rachel Willie, 149–63. Oxford: Oxford University Press, 2015.

Smalley, Paul. Preface to vol. 2 of *The Works of William Perkins*, edited by Paul M. Smalley. Grand Rapids: Reformation Heritage Books, 2015.

Sommer, Mattias Skat. "Niels Hemmingsen and the Construction of a Seventeenth-Century Protestant Memory." *Journal of Early Modern Christianity* 4 (2016): 135–60.

Steinmetz, David C. "John Calvin as an Interpreter of the Bible." In *Calvin and the Bible*, edited by Donald K. McKim, 282–91. Cambridge: Cambridge University Press, 2006.

Stump, Eleonore. "Biblical Commentary and Philosophy." In *The Cambridge Companion to Aquinas*, edited by Norman Kretzmann and Eleonore Stump, 252–68. Cambridge: Cambridge University Press, 1993.

Sytsma, David S. "Thomas Aquinas and Reformed Biblical Interpretation: The Contribution of William Whitaker." In *Aquinas among the Protestants*, edited by David VanDrunen and Manfred Svensson, 49–74. Hoboken, NJ: Wiley-Blackwell, 2018.

Thompsett, Fredrica Harris. "Godly Instruction in Reformation England: The Challenge of Religious Education in the Tudor Commonwealth." In *A Faithful Church: Issues in the History of Catechesis*, edited by John H. Westerhoff and O. C. Edwards, 174–99. Wilton, CT: Morehouse-Barlow, 1981.

Toulouse, Teresa. "'The Art of Prophesying': John Cotton and the Rhetoric of Election." *Early American Literature* 19, no. 3 (1985): 279–99.

Trinterud, Leonard J. "The Origins of Puritanism." *CH* 20, no. 1 (1951): 37–57.

Trueman, Carl R. "Preachers and Medieval and Renaissance Commentary." In *The Oxford Handbook of the Early Modern Sermon*, edited by Peter E. McCullough, Hugh Adlington, and Emma Rhatigan, 54–71. Oxford: Oxford University Press, 2011.

———. "The Reception of Calvin: Historical Considerations." *Church History and Religious Culture* 91, nos. 1–2 (2011): 19–27.

Tudor, Philippa. "Religious Instruction for Children and Adolescents in the Early English Reformation." *Journal of Ecclesiastical History* 35, no. 3 (July 1984): 391–413.

Waddell, Brodie. "Economic Immorality and Social Reformation in English Popular Preaching, 1585–1625." *Cultural and Social History* 5, no. 2 (2008): 165–82.

Walsham, Alexandra. "Holy Families: The Spiritualization of the Early Modern Household Revisited." In *Religion and Household*, edited by John Doran, Alexandra Walsham, and Charlotte Methuen, 122–60. Studies in Church History 50. Woodbridge, UK: Boydell, 2014.

Winship, Michael P. "Weak Christians, Backsliders, and Carnal Gospelers: Assurance of Salvation and the Pastoral Origins of Puritan Practical Divinity in the 1580s." *CH* 70, no. 3 (September 2001): 462–81.

Young, Frances. "Alexandrian and Antiochene Exegesis." In *The Ancient Period*, vol. 1 of *A History of Biblical Interpretation*, edited by Alan J. Hauser and Duane F. Watson, 334–54. Grand Rapids: Eerdmans, 2003.

Zwingli, Huldrych. "Of the Clarity and Certainty of the Word of God." In *Zwingli and Bullinger*, edited and translated by Geoffrey W. Bromiley, 59–95. Library of Christian Classics. Philadelphia: Westminster, 1953.

DISSERTATIONS AND THESES

Barbee, David M. "A Reformed Catholike: William Perkins' Use of the Church Fathers." PhD diss., University of Pennsylvania, 2013.

Bernstein, Eugenie Hershon. "A Reevaluation of the Plain Genre of Homiletics in Its Evolution as a Theory of Persuasion from Ramus to John Wilkins." PhD diss., University of California, 1975.

Chalker, William H. "Calvin and Some Seventeenth Century English Calvinists: A Comparison of Their Thought through an Examination of Their Doctrines of the Knowledge of God, Faith, and Assurance." PhD diss., Duke University, 1973.

Cushing, Douglas D. "The Inspiration of Scripture in the Theologies of William Perkins and John Calvin." MA thesis, Trinity Evangelical Divinity School, 1993.

Durbin, Lynne Diane. "Education by Catechism: Development of the Sixteenth Century English Catechism." PhD diss., Northwestern University, 1987.

Greve, Lionel. "Freedom and Discipline in the Theology of John Calvin, William Perkins, and John Wesley: An Examination of the Origin and Nature of Pietism." PhD diss., Hartford Seminary Foundation, 1975.

Hutchinson, Margarita Patricia. "Social and Religious Change: The Case of the English Catechism, 1560–1640." PhD diss., Stanford University, 1984.

Jensen, Peter F. "The Life of Faith in the Teaching of Elizabethan Protestants." PhD diss., University of Oxford, 1979.

Kiecker, James George. "The Hermeneutical Principles and Exegetical Methods of Nicholas of Lyra, O.F.M., Ca. 1270–1349." PhD diss., Marquette University, 1978.

Knapp, Henry M. "Understanding the Mind of God: John Owen and Seventeenth-Century Exegetical Methodology." PhD diss., Calvin Theological Seminary, 2002.

Lightfoot, R. David. "William Perkins' View of Sanctification." ThM thesis, Dallas Theological Seminary, 1984.

Lunt, Anders Robert. "The Reinvention of Preaching: A Study of Sixteenth and Seventeenth Century English Preaching Theories." PhD diss., University of Maryland College Park, 1998.

Markham, Coleman Cain. "William Perkins' Understanding of the Function of Conscience." PhD diss., Vanderbilt University, 1967.

Meyer, Edward Cecil. "The First Protestant Handbook on Preaching: An Analysis of the *De formandis concionibus sacris seu de iterpretationescripturarum populair libri II* of Andreas Hyperius in Relation to Medieval Homiletical Manuals." PhD diss., Boston University, 1967.

Munson, Charles Robert. "William Perkins: Theologian of Transition." PhD diss., Case Western Reserve University, 1971.

Park, Tae-Hyeun. "The Sacred Rhetoric of the Holy Spirit: A Study of Puritan Preaching in a Pneumatological Perspective." PhD diss., Theologische Universiteit Apeldoorn, 2005.

Pipa, Joseph A. "William Perkins and the Development of Puritan Preaching." PhD diss., Westminster Theological Seminary, 1985.

Priebe, V. L. "The Covenant Theology of William Perkins." PhD diss., Drew University, 1967.

Scott, Graham Allan David. "La première Homilétique Protestante: Le 'De formandis concionibus sacris seu de interpretatione scriptuarum populari libri II,' 1553 et 1562, d'André Gérard Hyperius

(1511–1564), introduction, traduction, et notes." PhD diss., Protestant Faculty of the University of Strasbourg II, 1971.

Shaw, Mark R. "The Marrow of Practical Divinity: A Study in the Theology of William Perkins." ThD diss., Westminster Theological Seminary, 1981.

Sommerville, C. J. "Conversion, Sacrament and Assurance in the Puritan Covenant of Grace to 1650." MA thesis, University of Kansas, 1963.

Tufft, John R. "William Perkins, 1558–1602, His Thought and Activity." PhD diss., University of Edinburgh, 1951.

Weisiger, Cary Nelson, III. "The Doctrine of the Holy Spirit in the Preaching of Richard Sibbes." PhD diss., Fuller Theological Seminary, 1984.

Williams, James Eugene. "An Evaluation of William Perkins' Doctrine of Predestination in the Light of John Calvin's Writings." ThM thesis, Dallas Theological Seminary, 1986.

SUBJECT INDEX

SCRIPTURE INDEX

Old Testament

New Testament

Matthew

Mark

Luke

John

Acts

STUDIES IN HISTORICAL & SYSTEMATIC THEOLOGY

Studies in Historical and Systematic Theology is a peer-reviewed series of contemporary monographs exploring key figures, themes, and issues in historical and systematic theology from an evangelical perspective.

—

Learn more at LexhamPress.com/SHST

HISTORICAL & SYSTEMATIC THEOLOGY